P9-CLU-167

345.51
G875c

Phillips Library
Bethany College
Bethany, W. Va. 26032

DISCARD
BETHANY
COLLEGE
LIBRARY

The Chinese Communist Treatment of Counterrevolutionaries: 1924-1949

Studies in East Asian Law
Harvard University

The Chinese Communist Treatment of Counterrevolutionaries: 1924-1949

by Patricia E. Griffin

Princeton University Press
Princeton, New Jersey

The Harvard Law School, in cooperation with
Harvard's East Asian Research Center, the Harvard-
Yenching Institute, and scholars from other
institutions, has initiated a program of training and
research designed to further scholarly understanding of
the legal systems of China, Japan, Korea, and
adjacent areas. A series of publications has been
established in conjunction with this program.
A list of the *Studies in East Asian Law* appears at the
back of this book.

Copyright © 1976 by Princeton University Press

All Rights Reserved

Library of Congress Cataloging in Publication data will
be found on the last printed page of this book

Publication of this book has been aided by
The Andrew W. Mellon Foundation

This book has been composed in Linotype Granjon

Printed in the United States of America
by Princeton University Press, Princeton, New Jersey

Preface

No research project of this magnitude can be completed without considerable aid and assistance. W. Allyn Rickett, who served as dissertation supervisor, deserves special acknowledgment for his continuing faith in the project and his untiring efforts in revising and improving it. Derk Bodde, Alvin Rubinstein, Victor Li, and Chung Sik-lee also offered valuable suggestions. In the publication stage Jerome Cohen was particularly encouraging and helpful. During the research period, Nancy Cheng at the University of Pennsylvania library and Richard Sorich at Columbia provided valuable bibliographical assistance. Wilma Liang Sturman and T. S. Chia furnished translation aid. For her editorial assistance and many retypings, my mother, Mrs. V. A. Peck, deserves special thanks.

Finally, a tremendous share of the credit for the finished product belongs to my husband, Jim, for his continuous encouragement and support, both financial and moral.

345.51
Y875c

Note on Sources

Since this study is based primarily on Chinese materials, it is useful to provide the reader information concerning the nature and origin of the data. In the analysis of the Kiangsi Soviet (Chapters II and III), the bulk of the data is taken from the twenty-one reels of microfilm in the *Shih-sou tzu-liao-shih kung-fei tzu-liao* (hereafter referred to as the *Shih-sou Collection*). These documents were gathered by the late president of the Republic of China, General Ch'en Ch'eng during his campaign against the Communists in the 1930's and are available in the United States through the Hoover Institute, Stanford University.

This collection contains regulations, directives, and reports from both the Party and the government, including some from the judicial departments. A few issues of two legal publications, *Szu-fa hui-k'an* (Justice Magazine) and *Ts'ai-p'an hui-k'an* (Judgment Magazine), are also included. Of the many newspapers in the collection, the most useful for our purposes was *Hung-se Chung-hua* (Red China), which was the official organ of the Provisional Central Government of the Chinese Soviet Republic. Published from December 11, 1931 to October 20, 1934, the paper had a circulation of 40,000. This newspaper provides descriptions of the written decisions of various judicial departments and replies by the Supreme Court as well as detailed descriptions of mass trials. Another valuable source was the weekly newspaper, *Tou-cheng* (Struggle), which was published by the Chinese Communist Party Central Bureau. A secondary but still valuable collection of documents is the *Ch'ih-fei fan-tung wen-chien hui-pien* (A Collection of Red Bandit Reactionary Documents).

The data for the Yenan period (1935-1944), which are presented in Chapter IV, are probably the most comprehensive in the study since collections of the major statutes are available for the two main border regions, Shensi-Kansu-Ninghsia and Shansi-Chahar-Hopei. The *Chieh-fang jih-pao* (Libera-tion Daily), the most important CCP newspaper, published in the capital of Yenan also provided valuable information. The newspaper, which was published from 1937 to 1946, provides excellent accounts of judicial reports and of mass trials; how-ever, in contrast to the Kiangsi newspapers, only sensational cases rather than normal court proceedings are reported. The absence of court decisions and written statements may signify either a decreased functioning of the judicial organs or, more likely, the decreased reporting of such mundane events in view of the relative importance of war stories.

The *T'ai-hang ch'ü szu-fa kung-tso kai-k'uang* (hereafter referred to as the *T'ai-hang Report*) was the primary data source for Chapter vi on "Prison Management." It is a report on judicial work in T'ai-hang Ch'ü from 1937 to 1945, which was published by the T'ai-hang Administrative Office in May 1946. In accordance with normal Communist practice, no names or information are given concerning the individual authors. T'ai-hang Ch'ü, part of the Shansi-Hopei-Honan military region, was located in the T'ai-hang mountains, which were considered a strategic area overlooking the North China Plain. Historically, the mountainous area had provided a base for launching attacks against Peking and was the scene of heavy fighting as the Communist forces under Ho Lung fought the Nationalists in January 1938 and the Japanese in 1943. In view of this environment, the T'ai-hang Report takes on added importance as the final recommendations of local Communist leaders based on years of experience with handling counterrevolutionaries during extremely critical situations. The lenient tone of the report reflects its timing—a period after the end of the war but prior to the severe class struggle of the civil war period.

Table of Contents

List of Tables and Figure

The Chinese Communist Treatment of
Counterrevolutionaries: 1924-1949

CHAPTER I. Introduction

THE AIM of this study is to present a clear impression of how and why the Chinese Communist legal system functioned as it did with respect to counterrevolutionaries from 1924 to 1949. This topic is of vital importance both because of the politically sensitive nature of the subject matter and because of the time period examined. During the 1924 to 1949 period, China's current leadership was experimenting with local governments, at first in the Kiangsi Soviet, then in the border regions of the northwest, especially around the capital of Yenan and later in enclaves over all of the country. In China as in other societies, governmental methods depend, *inter alia*, on the philosophy of the people who devise them and the environment in which they take place. Modern behavioral scientists[1] have stressed the importance of political culture in shaping the political attitudes of both leaders and followers. However, it should be recalled that the Chinese leadership group emerged during a period of transition when the political culture of the past was under assault. Through trial and error, the Communists deliberately sought to create their own political culture, distinctive from that of the past. Important members of the pre-1949 leadership group, especially Mao Tse-tung and Chou En-lai, have institutionalized many pre-1949 problem-solving techniques, thereby passing them on to subsequent generations. Consequently, a detailed study of the 1924 to 1949 period, in which these techniques evolved, leads to a clearer understanding of the governmental methods and leadership styles of modern China.

In the area of law, pre-1949 data are especially indicative of subsequent practices. From 1949 to 1953 the Chinese Com-

[1] See particularly Lucian W. Pye, *The Spirit of Chinese Politics* and Richard H. Solomon, *Mao's Revolution and the Chinese Political Culture.*

3

munists simply continued their pre-Liberation legal policies, for most criminal cases were handled outside the regular legal system by the police, by ad hoc "people's tribunals" or by the masses at mass trials. In 1953 the Communists began what could be called in Western terms their "golden age"[2] of law by adopting a constitution and a series of laws that provided a framework for a more systematic and orderly legal approach. However, in the People's Republic of China the trend toward regularization of law has not been a smooth one paralleling either economic development or the example of the USSR. The history of Chinese Communist legal development is broken by periods of reversion to ad hoc procedures, such as occurred in 1957. Oscillations between guerrillaism and regularization were noted as early as the Kiangsi Soviet period, and an examination of the events from 1924 to 1949 may help to define the conditions under which each is likely to occur. Accounts of the wall posters, mass rallies, and mass trials of the recent Cultural Revolution are reminiscent of stories from the 1924 to 1949 period. Are there also similarities in the social and political conditions of the two periods that might, at least partially, explain the revival of past tactics?

This book concentrates on the treatment of counterrevolutionaries for several reasons. First, political crimes received major news coverage, making available more extensive documentation and data than for non-political crimes. Second, counterrevolutionary law has implications for broader questions of interest to lawyers, political scientists, and sociologists. For example, how a government defines and punishes its political enemies is a good indicator of the function of law in that society. Specifically, the legal approach to counterrevolutionary activity reflects to what extent law functions solely as a tool of the government or also as a protector of the rights of the individual. A revolutionary period such as existed in China from 1924 to 1949 is of particular interest since a revolutionary

[2] Jerome Cohen, *The Criminal Process in the People's Republic of China 1949-1963: An Introduction* (Cambridge, Mass.: Harvard University Press, 1968), p. 11.

situation often tends to place the interests of the individual in conflict with the exigencies of the state, thereby providing an appropriate sample period in which to observe a regime's philosophy of law. While the treatment of counterrevolutionaries during a revolutionary period is not an accurate indicator of how the aggregate legal system functions, it does measure the limit to which the state will use law to enhance its power at the expense of other interests.

Despite its importance, until recently the 1924 to 1949 period had generally been overlooked in the literature. This is particularly true for the study of law, which had centered on describing the law of traditional China[3] and the law of the People's Republic of China.[4] This study aims at increasing our knowledge of the transitional period, 1924 to 1949.

Questions of Interest

The descriptive material presented in the bulk of this study raises some interesting questions of a more general nature that will be considered as they arise in the analysis. One of the primary areas of inquiry will be the relationship between the legal system and the environment. Throughout this work the term "environment" is used in its wider connotation, which includes political, economic, military, and social conditions as well as geographic ones. Thus, the environment is the total milieu in which the legal system operates. Changes in the definition of counterrevolutionary activity, in the severity of the penalty, and in the legal process will be noted to determine the extent to which shifts in policy coincided with changes in

[3] The most comprehensive work on the subject is Derk Bodde and Clarence Morris, *Law in Imperial China*. See also T'ung-tsu Ch'ü, *Law and Society in Traditional China*; Kung-chuan Hsiao, *Rural China: Imperial Control in the Nineteenth Century*; and Sybile Van der Sprenkle, *Legal Institutions in Manchu China*.

[4] See Cohen, *op.cit.*, and Shao-chuan Leng, *Justice in Communist China*. Some of the major articles on the subject are reprinted in Jerome Cohen (ed.), *Contemporary Chinese Law*.

the environment. The degree to which the environment limited the policy options open to the Communists also will be discussed. For example, consider whether the environment of the 1924 to 1949 period precluded a centralized legal system, given the internal political instability and the communication and transportation network of the period.

Another possible explanation for inter-temporal shifts in legal policy is the role of ideology. The treatment of counter-revolutionaries by the Communists may offer insights as to their view of the function of law in society. Legal systems vary in the degree to which they protect the rights of the minority from encroachment by the majority or by the state. This trade-off may be ascertained by inquiring what provisions in the legal system protected the rights of individuals and to what extent they were upheld consistently. Differences between the theoretical formulation of laws and their practical application also may reveal the leader's philosophy of law. The Communists viewed flexibility as a positive attribute necessary to respond to a changing revolutionary situation, and purposely built it into their legal system through imprecise legal codes, frequently changing laws, and flexible interpretation of laws. This raises the interesting dilemma of how much flexibility can be allowed in a legal system before anarchy is reached. If laws become too broad and vague, do they become meaningless?

Even after the constraints imposed by the environment and ideology are considered, a wide area of policy choice still exists, particularly with respect to the implementation of specific policies to achieve broad objectives. The growing experience and sophistication of the Communist leaders may have caused some modification of their policies over time. Casual empiricism would suggest that experience could be an important explanatory variable in predicting policy choices, since the leaders began in 1924 with very little practical knowledge of how a legal system should function in a revolutionary situation. By 1949, they could be termed relatively mature as the intervening period had provided an abundance of varied revolutionary situations. Were improvements in legal techniques observed over the period or did their Marxian ideology and philosophy of law stifle innovative legal policies? In addition, the 1924 to 1949 data may be useful in gauging the mental attitude of the Communist leaders. Did they appear to learn by doing and to modify their techniques readily in response to past experience or did they continue dogmatically to apply past policies? In sum, the evidence accumulated from the 1924 to 1949 period may suggest a number of explanations for subsequent legal developments in China.

Limitations

The description of the legal treatment of counterrevolutionaries is circumscribed by the quantity and quality of the data. The only English-language source describing the legal system during the pre-Liberation period is Chapter 1 of Shao-chuan Leng's book, *Justice in Communist China*. This short (26 pages) account furnished a framework from which to build and was an invaluable bibliographic aid. No study in English deals solely with the counterrevolutionary aspect of the subject.

The Chinese materials are plentiful but often badly reproduced and inadequately indexed.[5] The scanning necessitated by this lack of a satisfactory index substantially increased both the work load and the chance of omitting potentially valuable materials. For example, the primary data source for the Kiangsi period, the twenty-one reels of microfilm in the *Shih-sou Collection*,[6] is a collection of miscellaneous documents gathered

[5] For a bibliographical review of the *Shih-sou Collection*, which unfortunately does not cover "law" as one of its subjects, see Tien-wei Wu, "The Kiangsi Soviet Period," *The Journal of Asian Studies*, February 1970, pp. 395-412. A list of major documents on law in the *Shih-sou Collection* has been compiled. However, since titles were taken from the table of contents alone, this list does not include potentially useful sources such as sub-sections of reports and newspaper articles. See Tao-tai Hsia, "Chinese Legal Publications: An Appraisal," in Jerome Cohen (ed.), *Contemporary Chinese Law*, Appendix III, pp. 80-83.

[6] *Shih-sou tzu-liao-shih kung-fei tzu-liao* (Stanford, California: Hoover Institute, 1960).

by the late vice-president of the Republic of China, General Ch'en Ch'eng, during his campaign against the Communists in the 1930's. It is not a complete record of events of the period and accounts must often be pieced together from various sources, thus producing an imprecise and fragmentary description. The data for the Yenan and Civil War periods are probably more comprehensive since collections of the major statutes are available.

Aside from the author's subjectivity, bias may arise from either of two causes—incompleteness of the data or the Communist origin of most of the data. Since the sources were not complete collections of all the documents of the periods, the question of their representativeness must be raised. Unfortunately, the non-statistical nature of the data prevents checking for bias by showing the frequency distribution of the described events.

Potentially more important than the sample size and data gaps is the bias resulting from the Communist origin of the data, which may give an idealized account that reflects aspirations rather than accomplishments. Heavy reliance is placed upon Communist newspaper accounts for both the Kiangsi and Yenan periods. In Communist societies, newspapers serve primarily a political socialization function and thus contain a great deal of what we call propaganda. Newspapers tend to reflect accurately how the leaders wanted the system to function, but not necessarily how it actually did operate. Because of the need to inform the populace, accounts of laws, punishments, and trials are probably reliable; however, Communist newspapers are not very dependable sources for ascertaining mistakes in the application of the laws. Consequently, the implementation of the laws is deduced primarily from internal government and Party documents. Since these documents were intended solely for Party cadre, errors and failures were admitted candidly in the hope of correction. Nevertheless, the descriptions in the "Law in Practice" sections of the subsequent chapters remain the most sketchy and tentative parts of the study.

Usually, biased reporting can be detected through comparisons with independent eyewitness accounts; however, for the Kiangsi period such accounts are unavailable. During the Yenan period, some observers (primarily Chinese students, journalists, or Western journalists) paid brief visits to the liberated areas. Unfortunately, most of them had neither the interest nor the opportunity to observe judicial procedures.[7]

Outline of the Study

To emphasize temporal changes, the data base is presented chronologically. The chronological approach aids in correlating changes in the law with changes in the environment and in government policy. Chapter II concerns the beginning of the Kiangsi Soviet (1924-1933) and is subdivided into an examination of the sprouting of a legal approach in the peasant movements (1924-1927) and the formation of a legal system with the establishment of a Soviet government in Kiangsi (1927-1933). The crisis policies necessitated by the KMT Encirclement Campaigns (1933-1934) are examined in Chapter III. Chapter IV covers the Communist policies in the border regions during the united front period (1935-1944). Following the war with Japan, open civil war again erupted and lasted until the victory of the Communists in 1949. The legal policies of the Communists during the civil war period (1945-1949) are the subject of Chapter V. Each time period is discussed topically in terms of the environment, legal organization, definition of counterrevolutionary activity, laws and punishments, and laws in practice.

Of special interest is the treatment of counterrevolutionaries in prisons, which is presented in Chapter VI. Prison conditions and policies are the logical extension of our study of the legal system, since the criminal has become a ward of the state. The primary focus of this chapter is the evolution of prison policies

[7] Kenneth E. Shewmaker, *Americans and Chinese Communists, 1927-45: A Persuading Encounter* (Ithaca: Cornell University, 1971).

toward an increasing emphasis on reform. Early techniques of reform such as labor and thought reform are described.

In the concluding chapter, the descriptive material is analyzed with respect to more general questions including the role of law in society and the role of the environment in the choice of a legal system. The primary characteristics, inherent problems, and future implications of the Chinese Communist legal approach toward counterrevolutionaries are discussed. Since the basic documents on the subject are available only in Chinese, an appendix containing the author's translations is included. Furthermore, to aid future research, an extensive bibliography of both English and Chinese sources is included, as well as a glossary that could serve to unify the terminology for the period.

CHAPTER II. Beginning of the Kiangsi
Soviet, 1924-1933

Introduction

THE EVOLUTION of the policies of the Chinese
Communists toward counterrevolutionaries from
1924 to 1933 is primarily a saga of trial-and-error
experimentation with methods of controlling opposition. Policies of this period should be viewed as possible
alternatives and not as a firm doctrine of the Communist
Party. The experimental nature of CCP policies is particularly
evident from the discussion of the 1924 to 1927 period. During
this time, the Chinese Communists' ideas of the treatment of
counterrevolutionaries first sprouted during the peasant movements in Hunan and Kwangtung provinces. Concerned primarily with arousing the apathetic peasants, the Communists
experimented with temporary solutions to impending problems, with little attention to establishing long-term procedures.

During the second time period considered in this chapter—
1927 to 1933—the ad hoc nature of the legal system continued,
but Party debates increasingly also considered the longer-run
implications of various means of achieving a policy goal. With
the establishment of the Chinese Soviet Republic in 1931, an
attempt was initiated to regularize and organize procedures for
dealing with counterrevolutionaries.

A number of interesting questions will arise as the descriptive material is presented in this chapter. First, from the material in the section on environmental conditions, it becomes
apparent that the legal system did not function in a vacuum.
The extent to which the environment circumscribed the policy
options open to the Communists helps to explain many of
their techniques. Other questions emerge from the analysis
of the organizational structure adopted by the Communists.
Was the legal system designed to allow flexibility or centralized
control over local cadre? How did the organization change

from one period to the next, and were these shifts in organization correlated with environmental changes? To the student of jurisprudence, perhaps the most critical questions emanate from the sections on the definition of counterrevolutionary activity and on the laws and punishments. Were counterrevolutionary crimes defined narrowly to protect individual rights or categorized broadly to allow judicial discretion? For a given type of counterrevolutionary activity, were all guilty individuals punished equally? If they were punished differently, what factors seemed to be the primary determinants of the severity of punishment? Finally, as nearly as the incomplete data will allow, we consider how the legal policies worked in practice. Was there strict control by the main Party organs, or local autonomy? From 1927 to 1933 was the situation in Communist-controlled areas nearer to total anarchy than to the rule of law? Did the Communist leaders seem to appreciate the utility of a legal system in organizing a government?

Sprouting, 1924-1927

The period 1924-1927 was one of disunity for China, with the nation informally divided into numerous areas, each governed by its own warlord. Fighting between warlord troops destroyed crops and created ripe conditions for banditry. Supporting these armies necessitated higher taxes. At the same time, rapid population growth, coupled with unseasonably bad weather, led to declining per-capita incomes. The resulting sense of frustration and hopelessness among the people created unlimited potential for domestic revolution.

In response to this situation, the Kuomintang (KMT)[1] established a Peasant Bureau (*Nung-min-pu*) on January 31, 1924. It was mainly through this and other KMT organs that the Chinese Communist Party first worked to carry out its peasant program. In 1924, a Peasant Movement Institute was established to train revolutionary leaders, and during the

[1] The political party of Sun Yat-sen and later of Chiang Kai-shek, alternatively referred to as the Nationalists.

years 1924-1927 some 1,700 students were trained by a predominately Communist staff, which included such well-known Communist leaders as P'eng P'ai and Mao Tse-tung.[2]

On the local level, the KMT organizations established peasant associations that met with varying success in their attempts to organize the peasants and to control the countryside. Since the Peasant Self-Defense Armies were usually too small to protect themselves, the peasant associations were forced to depend upon the unreliable support of bandit groups, secret societies, warlord troops, or government troops (prior to the KMT-CCP split in 1927) for protection. Lacking an independent army, many peasant associations in Kwangtung reportedly had their headquarters burned by the gentry's *min-t'uan*.

An exception in Kwangtung was the Hai-lu-feng Soviet formed under the leadership of P'eng P'ai in November 1927. It was committed to the policies of "confiscation of land," "improvement of workers' life," and "extermination of local bullies and bad gentry." In the course of the uprisings the Communists allowed the peasants to maltreat and execute counterrevolutionaries at will.[3] According to one source some 1,822 landlords were executed within a few months.[4] Under the Hai-lu-feng Soviet government a judicial committee of nine men was established to handle litigation and to try counterrevolutionaries. Each *ch'ü* government had a judicial committee of five and each *hsiang* had a judge.[5] The masses were aroused at anti-counterrevolutionary meetings, where

[2] Roy Hofheinz, "The Peasant Movement and Rural Revolution: Chinese Communists in the Countryside (1923-1927)" (unpublished Ph.D. dissertation, Harvard University, 1966), p. 82.

[3] Shinkichi Eto, "Hao-lu-feng—The First Chinese Soviet Government" (Part 2), *The China Quarterly*, January-March 1962, p. 166.

[4] Shao-chuan Leng, *Justice in Communist China* (Dobbs Ferry, New York: Oceana Publications, 1967), p. 3.

[5] Each province was divided into *hsien* (county), *ch'ü* (district), and *hsiang* (township) levels. A *hsien* might contain 12-15 *ch'ü*; a *ch'ü*, 12 *hsiang*; and a *hsiang*, several villages. For the sake of clarity these terms will be untranslated.

landlords were killed on the spot before the cheering crowds.

According to Mao, the peasant associations met with more success in Hunan province, often becoming the sole authority in the countryside. The peasant associations attempted to exterminate banditry, maintain peace and order, and settle disputes among the peasants. One source mentioned three methods for dealing with counterrevolutionaries during this period. One technique was to parade the counterrevolutionaries through the streets in high hats. Meetings at which criminals were forced to confess and to donate money or grain to the poor in order to prove their repentance was another penal technique. A third method was to send them to the capital of the *hsien* or of the province for trial by special tribunals (*t'e-pieh fa-t'ing*), which were established especially to try "local bullies, bad gentry, and unlawful landlords."[6] Decisions of these tribunals were final, with no appeal.

Mao Tse-tung gives a detailed picture of the peasant associations in Hunan, where almost half the peasants were organized. The peasant associations and other mass groups formed a "Joint Council" to assist the *hsien* magistrate in making decisions. It was the magistrate's responsibility to handle judicial cases, but after the formation of the peasant associations, most disputes were reportedly settled by the peasant associations instead of by the magistrate. Even trifles such as a quarrel between husband and wife were brought before the peasant association. According to Mao: "The association actually dictates all rural affairs, and quite literally, 'whatever it says, goes.'"[7]

Mao elaborates that the peasant associations imposed fines for offenses such as embezzlement, "outrages against the peasants," gambling, and possession of opium pipes. In addition

[6] Yang Ch'i, "A Preliminary Discussion of the Development of the People's Criminal Law during the New Democratic Stage," *Fa-hsüeh* (Jurisprudence), Shanghai, No. 3, 1957, p. 40.

[7] Mao Tse-tung, "Report on an Investigation of the Peasant Movement in Hunan, March 1927," translated in *Selected Works of Mao Tse-tung* (Peking: Foreign Languages Press, 1965), Vol. 1, p. 25.

to being fined, landlords were also forced to contribute for poor relief, co-operatives, peasant credit societies, and other causes.

When someone committed an offense against a peasant association, the peasants collected a crowd and swarmed into the offender's house. If the offense was minor, the offender was usually let off after writing a pledge to "cease and desist" defaming the peasant association. In the case of a local tyrant or particularly evil gentry, a big crowd was rallied to demonstrate. There was one such case at Machiaho, Hsiangtan County, where 15,000 peasants demonstrated at the houses of six gentry. The affair lasted four days and 130 of the gentry's pigs were slaughtered and consumed.[8]

As in the case of counterrevolutionaries, it was very common to crown the landlords with tall paper hats labeled "Local tyrant so-and-so" or "So-and-so, the evil gentry," and to parade them through the streets on the end of a rope. Sometimes brass gongs were beaten and flags waved to attract large crowds.

Imprisonment and banishment were other punishments given to landlords. Banishment was reserved for those who had already fled the Soviet territory, thus escaping other forms of punishment. For the worst local tyrants and evil gentry, the punishment was execution. In some cases the masses conducted the execution, while in other instances the government authorities executed the victim "at the insistence of the peasants." When these two methods were applied, no mention is made of trials or other judicial proceedings prior to the execution. However, sometimes the decisions were reportedly left to the "special tribunal for trying local tyrants and evil gentry."[9]

Such circumstances created a wave of terror in Hunan. Refuting the charge of peasant excesses, Mao said: "Who is bad and who is not bad; who should be punished most severely and who should be punished lightly: the peasants judge this most clearly; only seldom do they hand out undeserved ver-

[8] *Ibid.*, p. 37.　　　　[9] *Ibid.*, p. 38.

dicts . . . every village should be in a state of terror for a brief period; otherwise, counter-revolutionary activities in the villages cannot be suppressed and the gentry's power cannot be overthrown. To correct wrongs one must go to the other extreme, without which they cannot be righted."[10]

Other leaders admitted mistakes had been made. The Russian advisor Borodin said: "All the mistakes lie in the fact that the movements of peasants and workers were overly drastic. Our comrades were very ignorant and could not direct the peasant movements. It was local rascals and the secret society, *Ko Lao Hui*, not we, who directed the peasants of Hunan."[11]

Ch'ü Ch'iu-pai explained that many officers of the Revolutionary Army were small landowners. Since the peasant movement violated the land and property rights of these small landowners, even the army officers turned against the peasant associations.[12]

A report on the Kwangtung movement was critical of the mistake of "extreme leftwing infantilism." It stated that the gentry were attacked regardless of the objective circumstances (the power of local gentry forces). People were sometimes seized and immediately shot, resulting in the peasant associations being called bandits.[13]

The picture that emerges from this period is one of terror, often chaotic and uncontrolled. The policy of repression (usually meaning death) and confiscation for those classified as counterrevolutionaries first sprouted during this period. The Communists justified these repressive actions on the grounds that they were necessary in order to arouse the masses. However, as a consequence they alienated such groups as landlords, gentry, capitalists, soldiers, and some terrified masses that had

[10] *Ibid.*, p. 28.

[11] Warren Kuo, *Analytical History of the Chinese Communist Party* (Taipei: Institute of International Relations, Republic of China, 1966), Vol. 1, p. 237.

[12] *Ibid.*

[13] *Kuang-tung nung-min yün-tung pao-kao* (A Report of the Kwangtung Peasant Movement), published October 1926. Microfilm.

superior political and military power. Furthermore, after arousing the peasants, the Communists faced the dilemma of controlling their actions. The indiscriminate killings and lootings reported in Hai-lu-feng and Hunan suggest that the CCP leaders lacked the organizational techniques and leadership experience necessary to control and channel mob action.

However, even in this early stage of experimentation, some techniques proved worthy of continuation. Execution by the masses, parades, and tall paper hats proved to be effective means of arousing people. The Communists quickly grasped the importance of the traditional Chinese concept of "loss of face," and from 1924 on humiliation became one of their basic penal methods. Lacking governmental control in most localities during 1924 to 1927, the Communists were forced to depend on special tribunals or mass action for trial and punishment of criminals. This deferrence to ad hoc action continued even into periods of greater government control and organization.

Formation, 1927-1933

Environment (1927-1933)

The year 1927 marked the turning point from political cooperation to open civil war. On April 18, 1927 Chiang Kai-shek set up his own government in Nanking in defiance of the left wing of the KMT at Wuhan. The CCP tried to continue cooperation with Wuhan, but in July it was expelled by the left KMT also. Under a policy of "White Terror," the Kuomintang executed many Communists and drove the CCP underground in the cities. No longer able to work within the KMT, the Communists developed an independent military power. Based upon the Comintern's estimate of a rising revolutionary wave in China, the new CCP leadership under Ch'ü Ch'iu-pai launched a series of insurrections beginning with the August 1st uprising at Nanchang. Mao Tse-tung led the "Autumn Harvest Uprising" in Hunan, which was quickly suppressed, as were other Communist putsches at Swatow in September and Canton in December 1927. In view of these disastrous failures, Ch'ü Ch'iu-pai was removed from leadership; however, the new leadership under Li Li-san continued a policy of armed uprising, this time in Changsha. In the meantime, Mao and Chu Teh had joined forces in the Ching-kang mountains on the Hunan-Kiangsi border in May 1928. They were joined there by other Communist leaders and their troops as well as by local bandit groups of impoverished peasants. With a secure territorial base, control of an army, and tax control over the local peasant population, the Mao-Chu group was able to develop a power base independent both of the CCP headquarters in Shanghai and of the Comintern in Moscow.

In the areas under their control, the Communists carried out a violent rural revolution. The Nationalist Government made the following estimate of damage inflicted by the Communists in Kiangsi in the years 1927-1931:

    186,000 persons massacred
    2,100,000 fugitives taking refuge in non-Soviet areas
    100,000 houses burned
    $630,000,000 personal property destroyed or confiscated[14]

By 1930 guerrillas were reported in 124 counties and were estimated to number 62,736, of whom 38,962 were armed.[15] On November 7, 1931 the First All-China Congress of the Soviets convened at Juichin and established the Chinese Soviet Republic with Mao Tse-tung as chairman, bringing centralized leadership to the scattered Soviet governments. To combat the growing Communist force, the Nationalists launched a series of extermination campaigns in 1931.

Meanwhile, the Nationalists had continued their Northern Expedition to unify the country, occupying Peking in June 1928. By the end of the year the unity of China was nominally

[14] Chin-jen Chen, "Book Review on T'ang Leang-li's *Suppressing Communist Banditry in China*," *The Chinese Social and Political Science Review*, XIX, No. 1 (April 1935), p. 141.

[15] Kuo, *op.cit.*, II, p. 16.

complete and the National Government received international recognition. However, warlordism died slowly: by 1930 Chiang Kai-shek became embroiled in a desperate struggle with Feng Yü-hsiang, Yen Hsi-shan, and Wang Ching-wei in the north. The central government was almost superficial anyway, since much of the countryside was still controlled by the former landlord-warlord rulers. Taking advantage of the lack of firm centralized control, the Japanese accelerated their aggression by establishing the puppet state of Manchukuo in March of 1932.

Organization[16] *(1927-1933)*

In the absence of centralized governmental structure, judicial organization was necessarily rather rudimentary until the establishment of the Chinese Soviet Republic. In 1931 as part of the apparatus of the new central government, a cabinet-type body called the Council of People's Commissars was established under the Central Executive Committee of the National Soviet Congress (figure 2.1). One of these commissars headed the People's Commissariat of Justice and another headed the State Political Security Bureau. The Supreme Court was administered directly by the Central Executive Committee.

At the provincial, *hsien, ch'ü,* and municipal levels, judicial departments were organized under the executive committee (i.e., governing body) of each respective area. In addition to

---

[16] Information on judicial organization has been pieced together from the following sources: Leng, *op.cit.*, pp. 3-5; Ilpyong Kim, "Communist Politics in China: A Study of the Development of Organization Concepts, Behavior and Techniques of the Chinese Soviet Movement During the Kiangsi Period" (unpublished Ph.D. dissertation, Columbia, 1968); "Central Executive Committee's Instruction No. 6 of 1931"; "Organic Law of the Local Soviets of 1933"; "Organic Law of the Central Soviet of 1934"; and the "Organic Program of the State Political Security Bureau of the Chinese Soviet Republic of 1931." These are found in *Ch'ih-fei fan-tung wen-chien hui-pien* (A Collection of Red Bandit Reactionary Documents), Vol. 5, pp. 1608-1612; Vol. 3, pp. 725-793, 682-691; Vol. 5, pp. 1616-1621, respectively.

this horizontal chain of command, the judicial departments also were subordinate to the People's Commissariat of Justice in matters regarding administration and to the Supreme Court in problems pertaining to investigations and trials. Each judicial department consisted of a director, vice director, several judges, circuit judges, procurators, a secretary, and a clerk. The judicial departments temporarily handled cases until the civil, criminal, and circuit courts could be set up. In addition, a judicial committee was established to discuss the decisions of the judicial departments.

Local political control of the judicial organs was encouraged by subordinating the judicial departments to the executive committee of each level and by using judicial committees to discuss and review the work of the judicial departments. In contrast, the Political Security Bureau (i.e., police department) was an independent, centralized system with a vertical chain of command. While executive committees could make suggestions to the branch bureaus or to special agents at their level, final orders came from the next higher organ within the Political Security Bureau system. Only the Council of People's Commissars could overturn these orders.[17]

In general, the responsibility for arresting, questioning, and investigating counterrevolutionaries belonged to the Political Security Bureau, while the responsibility for sentencing and implementing punishment belonged to the judicial organs. Under this division of labor, the Political Security Bureau investigated suspects and made arrests. Then the Political Security Bureau held a preliminary investigation (*yü-shen*) to determine whether or not a crime had been committed. If the suspect was found innocent, the director signed a release. If he was found guilty, the Political Security Bureau would act as the prosecutor in bringing charges to the judicial organs (courts or judicial departments). In the judicial department, the procurator took charge of the case, conducting another

[17] "Organic Program of the State Political Security Bureau of the Chinese Soviet Republic of 1931," Article 6, *op.cit.*, p. 1618.

preliminary investigation (*yü-shen*)[18] and prosecuting the case in court.

Since the case was thoroughly investigated by both the Political Security Bureau and the Procuracy prior to trial, the guilt of the suspect was usually clearly established before the case reached the trial stage. Consequently, the function of the judge was to answer any remaining questions through his and the assessors'[19] interrogation of the suspect and then to decide on the penalty after conferring with the director of the judicial department and members of the judicial committee. In the decision-making process, the Political Security Bureau effectively determined guilt or innocence while the procurator and the judge acted as checks. The primary decision made by the judge concerned the sentence. This decision was affected by such variables as seriousness of crime, background of the criminal, extenuating circumstances, degree of repentance, and the political situation.

In cases involving the death penalty, the accused could petition the central judicial organs within fourteen days. Judicial organs at the *hsien* level and below could give death sentences only with permission from the provincial judicial organs or under special conditions.[20] In practice, however, it was reported that judicial departments even at the *ch'ü* level frequently

---

[18] The same term is used in referring to both the preliminary investigation conducted by the Political Security Bureau and by the Procuracy. The exact procedures of the preliminary investigation by the Procuracy are unclear, even in the post-1949 period. It certainly entails a re-investigation of the facts and may also include a preliminary hearing to determine if there is sufficient evidence to warrant a trial. This second procedure is similar to one employed in several Continental countries; however, it is uncertain whether the Chinese require it in all cases.

[19] The use of lay judges, who were elected by mass organizations, military units, or trade unions, was borrowed from the Soviet Union and first introduced in China in the Kiangsi Soviet. While the system of assessors functioned to ease the manpower shortage and to furnish non-professional opinions concerning cases, its primary function was to educate the common people concerning the law and judicial procedures.

[20] "Instruction No. 6," Article 2, *op.cit.*, p. 1610.

FIGURE 2.1

ORGANIZATIONAL CHART

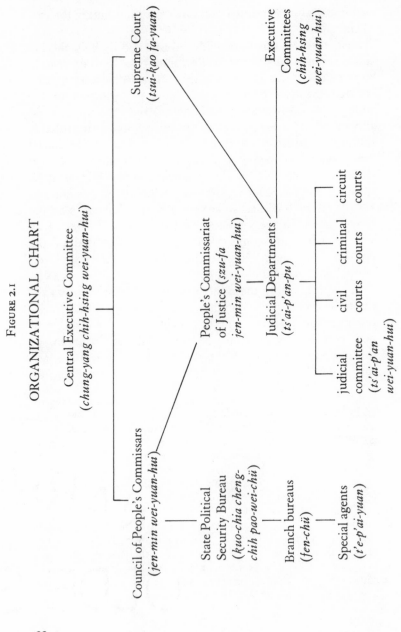

Central Executive Committee
(*chung-yang chih-hsing wei-yuan-hui*)

Supreme Court
(*tsui-kao fa-yuan*)

Executive Committees
(*chih-hsing wei-yuan-hui*)

Council of People's Commissars
(*jen-min wei-yuan-hui*)

People's Commissariat of Justice (*szu-fa jen-min wei-yuan-hui*)

Judicial Departments
(*ts'ai-p'an-pu*)

State Political Security Bureau
(*kuo-chia cheng-chih pao-wei-chü*)

Branch bureaus
(*fen-chü*)

Special agents
(*t'e-p'ai-yuan*)

judicial committee
(*ts'ai-p'an wei-yuan-hui*)

civil courts

criminal courts

circuit courts

executed criminals without authorization from higher levels.[21]

The division of labor between the judicial and Political Security Bureau organs was not always clearly maintained. Under normal conditions, the Political Security Bureau's involvement with a case ended with the completion of the preliminary investigation; however, a special provision extended the Political Security Bureau's function to include sentencing and implementing punishments. In theory, this right was limited, for it applied only during periods of civil war and periods of expansion of the Soviet movement and only to a certain kind (within the scope set by the Council of People's Commissars)[22] of counterrevolutionary criminal.[23] Despite these limitations, the data examined indicate that the Political Security Bureau actually replaced the judiciary as the primary organ in dealing with counterrevolutionaries in many places.[24] This was particularly true at the provincial and *hsien* levels, where the post of director of the judicial department was only a part-time job. In many instances, judicial departments existed only on paper, with their functions performed by the Political Security Bureau organs instead.[25]

During the early stages of an uprising, another organ, the Committee for the Suppression of Counterrevolutionaries (*su-fan-hui*) was to perform part of the functions later taken over by the Political Security Bureau and judicial organs. These committees were chosen by the people to serve under the lead-

[21] "The People's Commissariat of Justice Directive No. 14 Concerning the Work of Judicial Organs," dated June 1, 1933 and signed by Chang Kuo-t'ao and Liang Po-t'ai, p. 9. In the *Shih-sou Collection*, No. 008.548, 3449, 0759, reel 6.

[22] A clear demarcation of the counterrevolutionaries included in this category was not found by the author, but they were obviously those accused of the most serious crimes.

[23] "Organic Program of the State Political Security Bureau of the Chinese Soviet Republic of 1931," Article 10, *op.cit.*, p. 1620.

[24] Kiangsi Provincial Soviet Government, "Summary Report of Six Months' Work, May through October, of the Kiangsi Provincial Soviet Government," November 2, 1932. In the *Shih-sou Collection*, No. 008.61026, 3119, 0269, reel 10.

[25] *Ibid.*

ership of the Workers' and Peasants' Revolutionary Commit-tee[26] to organize the masses in arresting and accusing known counterrevolutionaries. How long such Suppression Commit-tees continued in existence depended on the time an area had been occupied by the Communists and on the strength of the Soviet regime. The State Political Security Bureau was to de-velop a governing relationship with the Committee until it gradually evolved into a subordinate organ of the Political Security Bureau.[27] Evidently these Committees became a source of local power, difficult even for the powerful Political Security Bureau to control, as the local Committees for the Suppression of Counterrevolutionaries were accused of be-coming "super dictatorships," which seldom obeyed Party instructions.[28]

In addition to the normal channels, many special provisions were made to allow for various contingencies. For example, if an organ of the State Political Security Bureau was located in an area, the local Soviet governments were not permitted to arrest or to try people independently without authorization from the Political Security Bureau organs.[29] However, since Political Security Bureau offices had not yet been established in all areas, provisions were made for this contingency. If the revolutionary government of an area had been established more than six months but a Political Security Bureau had not been opened, the *hsien* or *ch'ü* level governments were re-quired to obtain approval from the State Political Security Bureau at the provincial level before making an arrest. How-ever, under special circumstances, the *hsien* and *ch'ü* govern-

[26] Revolutionary Committees were provisional governing organs es-tablished to prepare for the election and establishment of a Soviet government.

[27] "Organic Program of the State Political Security Bureau of the Chinese Soviet Republic of 1931," Article 2, *op.cit.*, pp. 1616-1617.

[28] Central Bureau of Kiangsi Soviet, "Draft Decisions Concerning the Work of Eradicating Counterrevolutionaries in the Soviet Areas," Jan-uary 7, 1932. In the *Shih-sou Collection*, No. 008.237, 4475 c.2, 0292, reel 14.

[29] "Instruction No. 6," Article 3, *op.cit.*, p. 1610.

ments and their Committees for the Suppression of Counterrevolutionaries could make arrests independently, provided they had sufficient evidence. The four special circumstances mentioned illustrate the environments limiting effect upon the legal system. Independent action was authorized in the following circumstances: (1) when counterrevolutionaries were in the process of organizing a riot; (2) when the white-controlled areas separated the *hsien* or *ch'ü* government from the provincial Soviet; (3) when the red-controlled and white-controlled areas adjoined, making escape easy; and (4) when the enemy was attacking.[30]

In the event that the Soviet government of an area had been established less than six months, the Committee for the Suppression of Counterrevolutionaries had the right to arrest and to interrogate counterrevolutionaries with the agreement of the *hsien* or *ch'ü* level executive committee. The Committee was required to transfer the suspect to judicial organs for trial and to send the case records to the provincial judicial organs for final sentencing.[31] However, "if the crime of the gentry, landlord, rich peasant, and capitalist was very evident and if the local workers and peasant masses demanded it," the local authorities were allowed to implement the execution immediately without the permission of the provincial government.[32]

Finally, special provisions for an uprising's early stages, when the revolutionary regime had not yet established formal organs of government, allowed even the local revolutionary masses to arrest and punish the gentry, landlords, and all counterrevolutionaries. However, as soon as the revolutionary government was established, most offenders were to be handled by the judicial organs according to the procedures of Article 5.[33]

The principle underlying these special provisions appears to be that the shorter the period of Communist control over an area, the greater the additional powers granted. Under special

[30] *Ibid.*, Article 4, pp. 1610-1611.   [31] *Ibid.*, Article 5, p. 1611.
[32] *Ibid.*   [33] *Ibid.*, Article 6.

conditions, local governments or their Committees for the Suppression of Counterrevolutionaries were allowed to execute people independently if the government was newly established (i.e., less than six months). However, in areas where the government had been established for longer than six months, even under special circumstances the local government's power was restricted to arrest, and did not extend to trial and punishment. The greatest discretion was granted to those areas so newly occupied that no formal government had yet been established. When the Red Army initially entered an area, it was concerned solely with arousing the people to overthrow the traditional power structure. The problems of the orderly management of government became relevant only after an area had been occupied a sufficient time to establish firm governmental control.

Who Were the Counterrevolutionaries? (1927-1933)

The term "counterrevolutionary" was applied to many different individuals and groups during this period without an explicit elaboration of specific offenses committed. Basically, counterrevolutionaries seem to fall into three categories. First, there were the class enemies whose main offense was their socio-economic class background. The next category consisted of political enemies—those groups politically opposed to the Communist leadership. These disputes were mainly ideological and even might involve dissident factions within the Communist Party. The final category, which can be termed militant enemies, was composed of people who committed some overt action against the Communist regime.

From the very beginning, the imperialists, gentry, and landlords were considered class enemies. After the split with the KMT in 1927, the bourgeoisie was added to the list. The Political Resolution of the Sixth National Congress of the CCP in September 1928 said: "The national bourgeoisie of China betrayed the revolution and joined the counterrevolutionary camp of the imperialists, gentry, and landlords. They were once (before the spring of 1927) a force that could weaken the imperialists and undermine the warlord system, but they have now come to strengthen and unify the imperialist and warlord system."[34]

Because of their experience and traditional position of respect, some class enemies had been able to become important members of the Communist Party, other Communist organizations, and even the Soviet government. These were referred to as class deviates (i-chi fen-tzu). Most class deviates were landlords and rich peasants, but workers and peasants who had been bought off as the "running dogs" of the landlords and rich peasants could also be classified as class deviates. All class deviates were not to be treated alike. Those landlords, capitalists, and rich peasants who pretended to be workers in order to join the Party were to be eliminated. However, if the class deviates had not tried to hide their identity and had sought to aid the Communists, they were to be judged on their past political actions rather than on class background. The mistake of supposing that those who came from the enemy classes would *not* throw off their own class interest but would *always* struggle against the aims of Communism was criticized. Actual performance in the class struggle was considered a more reliable indicator than mere class background.[35] Thus, while certain classes, en masse, were condemned, punitive action was usually suggested only against those who showed themselves opposed to the class struggle led by the Communists.

Unable to work within the Kuomintang after 1927, the Communists identified the KMT as their main political enemy. The KMT, under Chiang Kai-shek's leadership, was accused of sending special agents and spies into the Soviet territory to infiltrate the Soviet and Party organizations and to sabotage their policies. The Reorganizationists within the KMT, origi-

[34] Translated in Conrad Brandt, Benjamin Schwartz, and John Fairbank, *A Documentary History of Chinese Communism* (New York: Atheneum Press, 1966), p. 131.

[35] "Eliminate Class Deviates and Unreliable Elements from the Party Organization," *Tou-cheng* (Struggle), April 28, 1934, pp. 13-15. In the *Shih-sou Collection*, No. 008.2105, 7720, v. 5, 1133, reel 18.

nally led by Wang Ching-wei, were also considered counter-revolutionary and called "counterfeit revolutionaries." It was charged that they "yelled reform with a knife in one hand and bullets in the other while continuing to slaughter revolutionaries."[36]

Other parties, who favored reform over revolution, were also branded as counterrevolutionaries. The Social Democratic Party (*she-hui min-chu-tang*) was alleged to have allied with the KMT in attacks on the Soviets. Despite their slogans of "labor and capital compromise" and "reduce rent by 25%," they were considered supporters of the bourgeoisie.

The Third Party (*ti-san-tang*), led by Tan Ping-shan and Teng Yen-ta, was another such group. They advocated local self-government and organizing the peasants, but were against the violent methods of the CCP. While they favored public ownership of land, the CCP charged that as long as the state was under the control of the landlord and gentry class, the Third Party's programs would be only empty promises.

Within the Communist Party, the Ch'en Tu-hsiu and a Trotskyite group formed a faction called the Liquidationists. They were condemned as rightist-opportunist and expelled from the Party for wanting to take a moderate approach and to join in the KMT-sponsored national assembly. Thus political groups favoring reform rather than revolution also were identified as threats to the Communists because they were competing with the CCP for the support of the workers, peasants, intelligentsia, and political activists.

Militant enemies were actually engaged in fighting or other overt actions against the Communist regime, such as spying, espionage, sabotage, assassination, or bombing. Primary among the militant enemies was the Anti-Bolshevik (A-B) League. This was a right-wing group of the KMT formed by Tuan Hsi-p'eng in 1927. Supposedly organized and funded by the KMT, the A-B League members operated as spies within

---

[36] *Ch'ih-fei wen-chien hui-pien* (A Collection of Red Bandit Documents), Vol. 7, p. 123. In the *Shih-sou Collection*, No. 008.2129, 4074, 0255, reel 20.

Communist organizations, collecting strategic information and sending it up through clandestine channels. They also organized dissatisfied Communists to perform disruptive functions within the Soviet area.[37] Captured KMT documents revealed that five high-level CCP members, some of them Red Army commanders, had connections with the A-B League. Mao decided to initiate an investigation to uncover the entire organization. In late November 1930, Mao ordered the mass arrests of more than 4,000 officers and men of the 20th Army in Huang-p'o who were suspected to be A-B members. In a separate action, all but two members of the Kiangsi Province Action Committee were also arrested on the charge of being members of the A-B League.

The mass arrests led to the Fu-t'ien Incident. Uncertainty surrounded this event, but it probably occurred on December 8, 1930, when Liu Ti, a battalion political commissar of the 20th Army, rose in revolt at Tung-ku and led his unit of a few hundred men to attack Fu-t'ien, a Communist stronghold. The rebels set free a group of high-ranking Communist members of the Action Committee, such as Tuan Liang-pi, Li Po-fang, and Chin Wan-pang, who had been arrested by Mao. The civilian population became upset by the mass arrests, charges of subversive activity, and the Fu-t'ien Incident. This was particularly true in the areas surrounding Tung-ku and Fu-t'ien, where the people grew hostile toward the Red Army.[38]

Between May and July of 1931 the Red Army arrested many more alleged members of the A-B League. Harsh measures were allowed in dealing with the A-B League. Torture was encouraged during both the questioning and the trial to insure confession of all relevant details about the League. Trial committees (*shen-p'an wei-yuan-hui*) were established on the brigade level to try suspected members. Four thousand counterrevolutionary elements were captured and given mass public

[37] Wang Chien-min, *Chung-kuo kung-ch'ang-tang shih-kao* (History of the Chinese Communist Party), (Taipei: Arthur, 1965), Vol. ii, pp. 538-539.

[38] Ronald Suleski, "The Fu-t'ien Incident, December, 1930," *Michigan Papers in Chinese Studies*, No. 4, 1969, p. 11.

trials at Po-sha. A revolutionary tribunal, with Mao as its chairman, tried the counterrevolutionaries at an open-air mass rally. Each rebel leader was brought before the rally to be charged with his crimes. Each rebel was given the opportunity to speak in his own defense before being questioned by the audience. The spectators reportedly became emotionally involved in the proceedings, shouting insults at the rebels and demanding "death!"

At the week-long trial, five men were convicted of being rebel leaders and received death sentences. However, for propaganda purposes their sentences were not carried out immediately; they were first sent, under guard, to tour the Soviet areas. In the small villages and towns the rebels were forced to stand on platforms while speakers described the trial at Po-sha for the villagers.[39]

Terror was not the only method used against the A-B League. In order to isolate the leaders of the League and to obtain additional information concerning their activities, some members were offered the opportunity to surrender voluntarily, confess, and reform themselves into new men (*tzu-shou, tzu-hsin*). Supposedly only those "innocent people who were deceived, paid, or coerced" into joining the League were allowed to *tzu-shou, tzu-hsin*. To obtain maximum benefit in return for leniency, the following conditions were suggested:

1. They must reveal the work and organization of the A-B League.

2. Perform anti-A-B League work.

3. Take part in New Men Groups (*tzu-hsin t'uan*) formed by the Soviet government and accept punishment of hard labor and political re-education. The period of supervision (*chien-shih*) was from 1 to 3 years, depending on the seriousness of the crime.

4. Repeaters would be severely punished.[40]

[39] Agnes Smedley, *China's Red Army Marches* (New York: 1934), pp. 261-279.
[40] *Fan-tung wen-chien hui-pien* (A Collection of Reactionary Docu-

The relevant criterion seems to have been their willingness to reveal information about the A-B League. For example, Ts'ao Li-i, Li Jen-chieh, Tseng Han-shan, and Lo Jih-hsin were released after revealing information about the League, while another, no more influential member, was given the death penalty for his refusal to tell about its organization.[41]

Probably, the charges against the A-B League were partially a facade for a policy conflict between the General Front Committee dominated by Mao and the Kiangsi Provincial Action Committee.[42] The Action Committee opposed equal land redistribution, instead favoring redistribution according to labor power (a policy that favored the rich peasants) and not expropriating the rich peasant. Despite their own favoring of rich peasants, the Action Committee accused Mao of favoring them because he welcomed into the Party those rich peasants who were willing to cooperate with the CCP. Militarily, the Action Committee favored swift and decisive attacks on the enemy territory, while Mao preferred maneuvering the enemy deep into Communist areas so as to defeat them by guerrilla tactics. As Tso-liang Hsiao asserts, the Action Committee was just following the Li Li-san line, which had fallen in ill repute.[43] On a personal level, Mao was even accused of using the Fu-t'ien Incident as an excuse to eliminate his political opponents and of trying to become a "Party Emperor."

After extensive research on the Incident, Suleski concludes that accusing Communists of being members of the A-B League was a plot used by Mao to obtain supreme leadership of the Party. He feels the alleged A-B members were obviously

---

ments) Vol. 1, No. 3. In the *Shih-sou Collection*, No. 008.2129, 7120, v. 1, reel 19.

[41] *Ibid.*

[42] The General Front Committee was a Party branch in the Red Army while the Kiangsi Provincial Action Committee was a regional Party branch with close connections with the Central Committee under Li Li-san.

[43] Tso-liang Hsiao, *Power Relations within the Chinese Communist Movement, 1930-34* (Seattle: University of Washington Press, 1961), p. 99.

dedicated Communists since they refused to seek safety after release from prison, choosing instead to stay and set up a rival Soviet government.[44]

The Central Bureau of the CCP, while siding with Mao in the Party dispute, admitted that exaggeration of the size of the A-B League was a mistake. The Central Bureau charged that everyone who made a slight mistake was considered a member of the League and any suspicious person was seized at random. The Bureau admitted that testimony extracted by torture often was taken at face value, with no investigation of the facts, resulting in punishment of many innocent people.[45] Chou Hsing, the Political Security Bureau chief admitted: "In Kiangsi, anybody who did not sympathize with us was regarded as counterrevolutionary. His property was confiscated, and if he was anti-Soviet he was deprived of rights, even though he might take no positive action against us."[46] This type of action created a situation of terror that turned many people against the Communists and gave the A-B League an opportunity to charge that the Red Army did not fight the White Army but just attacked the Soviet committees and the rich peasants.[47]

Law and Punishments (1927-1933)

Prior to the enactment of the "Statute Governing Punishment of Counterrevolutionaries" in 1934, directives, primarily from the Central Executive Committee, served as loose standards for dealing with counterrevolutionaries. In counterrevolutionary cases, the idea of equality of punishment was labeled petit bourgeois.[48] It was explained that treating everyone who

[44] Suleski, op.cit., pp. 14-16.

[45] Central Bureau, "Draft Decision Concerning the Work of Eradicating Counterrevolutionaries in the Soviet Areas," loc.cit.

[46] Edgar Snow, Random Notes on Red China 1936-45 (Cambridge: Harvard University Press, 1957), p. 43.

[47] "Circular Note #2 of Central Bureau—Resolution on the Fu-t'ien Incident," January 16, 1931. In the Shih-sou Collection, No. 008.2107, 5044, reel 14.

[48] Lo Mai (alias for Li Wei-han), "The Method of Smashing the

committed a certain crime similarly would result in a false equality, since such a procedure ignored differences in background, motivation, and circumstances. Thus punishments were not to be applied mechanically without regard for the particulars of the situation.

One method of differentiation was based on the identity of the suspect. For example, a Communist Party member could not be tried until he had explained his case to the Party organization. If the Party decided the member was guilty of breaking the law, he would be stripped of his Party membership before being tried by the masses.[49]

As outlined in the Central Executive Committee's Instruction No. 6 of December 1931, differentiated treatment was to depend on the individual's class background and his degree of involvement in the crime. In other words, all the counterrevolutionary elements from the landlord-gentry, rich peasant, and capitalist backgrounds were to be punished severely (including death penalty). Severe punishments were also prescribed for the principal instigator of a crime, irrespective of class background. On the other hand, criminals from the ranks of workers, peasants, and toiling masses as well as accomplices (*fu-ho*) were to be treated with leniency (e.g., either released or incarcerated, but given a chance to reform and become new men [*tzu-hsin*] while in prison).[50]

A similar provision in Article 11 of the "Organic Program of the State Political Security Bureau" elaborated that the way to handle those ordinary workers, Red Army soldiers, hired peasants, poor peasants, middle peasants, and independent laborers who were not hardened counterrevolutionary leaders, but who were coerced and deceived by counterrevolutionaries or who were secondary offenders, ranged from open advice, warning, detention, and dismissal from military membership to arrest and disfranchisement. As for the punishment of

---

Thought Struggle on Equality," *Tou-cheng* (Struggle), No. 61, May 26, 1934. In the *Shih-sou Collection* No. 008.2105, 7720, v. 6, 1134, reel 18.
[49] *Ibid.*
[50] "Instruction No. 6," Article 7, *op.cit.*, pp. 1611-1612.

counterrevolutionaries who were class deviates *(i-chi chieh-chi)*, the directive set forth punishments of death, imprisonment, hard labor *(k'u-kung)*, and exile from Soviet territory.[51]

While a person's class status would affect his punishment, it was not a sufficient condition for classifying him as a counter-revoluntionary. Rather, a person's actual behavior was to be considered. For example, the following policy toward the gentry and landlords differentiated the reactionary from the non-reactionary on the basis of conduct:

"The basic significance of the land revolution is to overthrow completely the economic bases of the gentry and landlord classes; but, if the gentry and landlords and their dependents do not have obvious reactionary, bad behavior, we still let them sacrifice their class interest and faithfully surrender to the proletariat. Under the governing of the workers and peasants, they can exist according to the laws.

"If a gentry is not a reactionary leader, we let him reform himself and become a new man *(tzu-hsin)*. Besides immediately confiscating the gentry's grains, oxen, pigs, etc., to give to the poor, we order him to hand in a fine to supply the workers' and peasants' revolution in order to show the sincerity of his repentance and surrender. . . . Also he has to write a statement of repentance.

"If he does not hand in the fine before the deadline and does not contact us, then he will be considered a firm reactionary. Then besides burning all his houses, digging up and destroying his family tombs, we also will make a pronouncement asking all people to arrest this gentry. His family will be punished by death."[52]

This policy was somewhat harsher than another order during this period that brands burning and slaughtering as "reveng-

---

[51] "Organic Program of the State Political Security Bureau of the Chinese Soviet Republic of 1931," Article 11, *op.cit.*, p. 1620.

[52] "Directive of the Chinese Workers' and Peasants' Red Army Third Army Corps' Political Department on Punishing Gentry and Landlords," dated 1932. In the *Shih-sou Collection*, No. 008.638, 0067, 0152, reel 10.

ism." This circular explained that burning was unnecessary since the houses would soon belong to the workers and peasants. The Central Committee ordered that only if there was a practical necessity of inciting the masses could a few houses belonging to reactionary gentry and landlords be burned.[53] The sources of these directives may explain this discrepancy in policy. The more stringent orders came from a specific army group that might have been conducting a temporary terror campaign in response to local conditions, while the second policy originated from the Central Committee of the CCP and was intended as a statement of general applicability.

The distinction of "reactionary" was also useful in the cities, where only reactionary merchants and capitalists who were opposed by the masses or who conspired to destroy the revolution were arrested and their property confiscated.[54] Other gentry, landlords, and reactionary merchants were forced to pay a fine that was called a "donation" when requisitioned from the middle merchants on a progressive rate with the rich paying proportionately more.[55] Small merchants were not asked to donate.

Reduced punishments were also stipulated for anyone who voluntarily surrendered and confessed before discovery (*tzu-shou*) or reformed and became new men (*tzu-hsin*). Workers and peasants who voluntarily surrendered and confessed after having been deceived and forced to join the counterrevolutionaries were to be spared punishment. People who reformed *after* being discovered and accused also were to be punished lightly or released. Class deviates who voluntarily surrendered and confessed were to be separated into leaders and followers and observed (*shen-ch'a*) for a given probationary period.[56] Those of worker or peasant background who complied with the requirements of *tzu-shou* and *tzu-hsin* were given the right

[53] "Red Bandit Central Committee Circular No. 10," dated October 30, 1931. In the *Shih-sou Collection*, No. 008.2129, 4074, 0255, reel 20.
[54] *Ibid.* [55] *Ibid.*
[56] "Organic Program of the State Political Security Bureau of the Chinese Soviet Republic of 1931," Article 11, *op.cit.*, p. 1620.

to join the armed forces in non-strategic capacities. However, the Central Committee in December 1932 warned that those who had joined the armed forces earlier but who were not reliable should be dismissed.[57]

In addition to the above-mentioned differences in punishment, others are apparent from court decisions of this period. Having performed valuable service for the revolution in the past and having been wounded or crippled seems to have merited a reduction of one-half to one and one-half years in a sentence.[58] Refusing to confess when confronted in court and trying to deny charges resulted in a six-month increase in punishment.[59]

A variety of punishments, ranging from death to fines, were employed in conjunction with the differentiated standards for dealing with counterrevolutionaries outlined above. Persons sentenced to death usually were shot, although in a few cases the traditional practice of mutilating the body by beheading was employed.[60] Prison sentences were limited to ten years; people sentenced to over ten years were given death. Hard labor (*ch'iang-p'o lao-tung* or *k'u-kung*)[61] appears to have been a frequently given punishment, for 1,108 people were sentenced to hard labor at the *hsien* and *ch'ü* level in Kiangsi Province

[57] Central Committee, "A Review Decision Concerning the Work of Eradicating the Counterrevolution," December 14, 1932. In the *Shih-sou Collection*, No. 008.237, 5071, c. 1, 0291.

[58] "The Soviet Court," *Hung-se Chung-hua* (Red China) March 2, 1932. In the *Shih-sou Collection*, No. 008.1052, 2125 v. 1, reel 16.

[59] "Decisions of the Central Executive Committee Concerning the Temporary Supreme Court's Handling of A-B Group, Reorganizationists, Military Prisoners and Other Important Prisoners," *Hung-se Chung-hua* (Red China), March 2, 1932. In the *Shih-sou Collection*, No. 008.1052, 2125 v. 1, reel 16.

[60] For an example of reactionary agents of Chiang Kai-shek who were beheaded, see "Announcement from the Headquarters of the First Army of the Workers' and Peasants' Red Army of China: Execute Huang Mei-chuang" dated June 1931 and signed by Chu Teh and Mao Tse-tung. In the *Shih-sou Collection*, No. 008.1052, 2125 v. 1, reel 16.

[61] These two terms appear to be synonymous during this period; both will be translated "hard labor."

during six months of 1932 (see Table 2.1). People were some-times sentenced to indefinite periods of hard labor (*chi-nien* or *ch'ang-chi k'u-kung*). This practice was criticized, and in 1933 the People's Commissariat of Justice directed that hard-labor sentences would be limited to one year.[62] However, news-paper accounts of cases reveal that the indefinite hard-labor sentences continued despite the directive. People sentenced to less than two years in prison or to hard labor were assigned to hard labor groups (*k'u-kung-tui*) that were sent to the front for transportation work. In 1932, it was estimated that in all the Soviet territory about 900 people were actually sent to the front.[63] Accounts of local *ch'ü* judicial departments being criticized for retaining these groups at the *ch'ü* level provide an explanation for the small numbers actually reaching the fighting area.[64]

Tables 2.1 and 2.2 show the only available statistics on punishments for this period. Apparently, the data overlap in both time and geographic region.[65] Since the completeness of

[62] "The People's Commissariat of Justice Directive No. 14," *op.cit.*, p. 21.

[63] "One Year's Work of the People's Commissariat of Justice," *Hung-se Chung-hua* (Red China), November 7, 1932. In the *Shih-sou Collection*, No. 008.1052, 2125 v. 2, reel 16.

[64] Kiangsi Provincial Soviet Government, "Summary Report of Six Months' Work, May through October, of the Kiangsi Provincial Soviet Government," *loc.cit.*

[65] Statistics for Table 2.1 were collected by the Kiangsi Provincial Government for those areas under its control. A Japanese intelligence officer in Shanghai estimated that 70 of the 81 *hsien* in Kiangsi Province were under Communist control in May 1932 (Reported in Ilpyong Kim, *op.cit.*, pp. 172-174). Statistics in Table 2.2 are supposedly for the entire area of the Chinese Soviet Republic, which included all the scattered areas under CCP control, including Kiangsi Province. The same Japanese source estimated that the CCP controlled 177 of the 631 *hsien* in the entire Soviet areas. Kim estimated that population in the Communist controlled areas never exceeded 30 million. Although the statistics in Table 2.2 cover the provincial level judicial departments as well as the *hsien* and *ch'ü* level covered in Table 2.1, the longer time period resulted in more cases being reported in Table 2.1. Because of

the data is uncertain, only a limited analysis is possible. For example, to use the total number of cases as an indicator of total criminal activity in the area would be misleading. However, to the extent that the recorded data are representative of the unrecorded cases, analysis of the frequency of a given punishment in comparison with other forms of punishment is probably meaningful.

TABLE 2.1[a]

Cases Handled by *Hsien* and *Ch'ü* Level Judicial Departments in Kiangsi Province May through October 1932[b]

Death	515
Imprisoned	233
Hard labor	1108
Fined	55
Total punished	1911
Released (*shih-fang*)	3769
Total cases	5680

[a] Statistics taken from Kiangsi Provincial Soviet Government, "Summary Report of Six Months' Work, May through October, of the Kiangsi Provincial Soviet Government," *loc.cit.*

[b] These statistics are not complete since the reports from four *hsien* were not included.

As forms of punishment, both sources indicate that hard labor was the most frequently used punishment, while fines were the most infrequent. Percentage-wise, hard labor accounted for 58 percent and 34 percent of the cases resulting in punishment in Tables 2.1 and 2.2, respectively. Fines accounted for 3 percent and 12 percent of the punishments, respectively.

According to Table 2.1, the second most frequently given punishment was death, although Table 2.2 indicates it was imprisonment.

the problems encountered in reporting statistics for the broader geographical area, the statistics in Table 2.2 may be less reliable than those in Table 2.1.

TABLE 2.2[a]

Cases Reported by Judicial Departments of All Levels to the People's Commissariat of Justice during July, August and September of 1932[b]

Death	271
Imprisoned	349
Hard labor	399
Fined	141
Total punished	1160
Innocent (*wu-tsui*)	481
Total cases	1641

[a] Statistics taken from "One Year's Work of the People's Commissariat of Justice," *loc.cit.*

[b] Only three months were covered, because the judicial system was not really established in most areas until June, and the November statistics had not yet been received. It was emphasized that even the report for three months was not complete since some judicial personnel were still not keeping accurate records.

The more frequent use of imprisonment in Table 2.2 (30 percent vs. 12 percent) appears to result directly from the less frequent use of hard labor (34 percent in Table 2.2 vs. 58 percent in Table 2.1) rather than from a substitution of imprisonment for death. The death penalty occurred with a similar frequency in both data samples (27 percent in Table 2.1 and 23 percent in Table 2.2). The substantial variance between the "released" category in Table 2.1 and the innocent category in Table 2.2 is explained by definitional differences.[66]

[66] The "released" category in Table 2.1 does not correspond to the "innocent" category in Table 2.2. A footnote explains that the "released" category contained three types of criminals. The largest portion were criminals arrested prior to the First National Soviet Congress who were investigated and released after the Congress. Others were arrested for investigation as they crossed the borders between Red and White controlled territory. Still others had reformed and were released. Therefore, many people were "released" for reasons other than innocence.

While the statistics in Tables 2.1 and 2.2 include all types of crime, it was recorded that 70 percent of the cases in Table 2.2 involved "political crimes."[67] Since the death punishment was given in only 23 percent of the punishments in Table 2.2, obviously not all counterrevolutionaries were sentenced to death. Furthermore, even the most frequent punishment—hard labor—accounts for only 34 percent of the punishments. The range of punishments indicated by these statistics and substantiated by the written decisions reported in *Hung-se Chung-hua* suggests that counterrevolutionary crimes were differentiated into various degrees of severity and that both major and minor counterrevolutionaries were brought before the courts.

In general, the early Communist directives reflected overriding concerns with seizing and maintaining power. From their position of weakness, the Communists needed to attract the peasants and yet to eliminate dangerous opponents. As the head of the State Political Security Bureau stated it, their policy needed to be, "Do not unnecessarily kill anyone, yet do not permit any counterrevolutionary activity in the Soviet area."[68] Reflecting this need, the primary determinant of policy toward counterrevolutionaries became the degree of danger to the Soviet government involved in each case. Those who were likely to continue their counterrevolutionary activities, such as principal criminals and "reactionary" elements, were treated harshly. Those who were willing to reform and to give intelligence reports were treated leniently if they did not appear to provide permanent opposition.

The Laws in Practice (1927-1933)

As expected, the application of the law differed substantially from that called for in theory. In October 1932, the People's

[67] "One Year's Work of the People's Commissariat of Justice," *loc.cit.*

[68] Teng Fa, "Concerning Recognizing and Struggling Against Negativism and Mistakes in Suppressing Counterrevolutionaries," *Ch'ing-nien shih-hua* (True Words of Youth), November 30, 1932. In the *Shih-sou Collection*, No. 008.2105, 3002, 1152, reel 18.

Commissariat of Justice called a joint meeting of all directors of *hsien* level judicial departments in Kiangsi and Fukien provinces to discuss past inadequacies in judicial administration.[69] Many of the problems mentioned at this meeting and in other reports resulted from the embryonic nature of the judicial organizations.

As mentioned previously, judicial departments were usually understaffed and sometimes actually nonexistent. Consequently, judicial functions were taken over by the Political Security Bureau organs or by the local Soviet governmental leaders. The staffing problem was intensified by the Soviet government's frequent transferral of specialized judicial cadre to other, non-judicial tasks.[70]

Where they did exist, judicial departments did not always function as envisioned. Judicial cadre did not record the court proceedings or keep detailed written judgments concerning cases, thus making it impossible for superiors to evaluate the accuracy of decisions. There was very little correspondence and supervision between levels of judicial administration. Reportedly, the *hsien* judicial department director often did not even know the names of the directors of the *ch'ü* judicial departments under him. In several cases, judicial cadre apparently either did not know or did not understand the law. For example, despite the prohibition of corporal punishment given in both the CEC's "Instruction No. 6" of December 1931 and the "People's Commissariat of Justice Directive No. 14" of June 1933, the traditional practice of using force to extract a confession continued in widespread use.[71]

Due to their inefficient organization, judicial departments often were slow in handling cases, with the result that many prisoners (over 100 in one center) were held in detention centers (*kan-shou-so*) for long periods (over six months)

[69] Kiangsi Provincial Soviet Government, "Summary Report of Six Months' Work, May through October, of the Kiangsi Provincial Soviet Government," *loc.cit.*

[70] "The People's Commissariat of Justice Directive No. 14," *op.cit.*, p. 8.

[71] *Ibid.*, p. 9.

waiting trial. Having to feed prisoners was viewed as a waste of money that was needed to buy more weapons;[72] therefore, a directive was issued requiring that cases should be decided within two weeks of the day they first came to the attention of the judicial organs.[73] In Hsing-kuo Hsien, a *ch'ü* judicial department director was criticized for holding a suspect for two months without trial. The frightened director immediately sentenced the suspect to death without trial, an act for which he was even more severely criticized.[74]

Another mistake mentioned was not following the mass line. In deciding cases, judicial department directors paid little attention to the opinions of the masses and devoted even less effort to educating them. Circuit courts were seldom organized and trials were not adequately publicized as to time and place. The decisions were publicly announced and the written decisions published in only a few places. In some areas, the trials were not even public but were held secretly in the home of the judicial director.[75]

Judicial workers were also accused of not having a "firm class consciousness." For example, cadre were criticized for sentencing a gentry who was a leader in the A-B League to only three years in prison while sentencing a 70-year-old poor peasant to death for casually saying that many people would support the White Army when it came. Another example of mistaken class line was the case of Liu Hu-fei, who directed the Red Army to loot the masses. He lost his military commission for only three years and his political rights for six months, while Hsü Wen-sung, a poor peasant, was imprisoned for two years just for carrying one letter for a prisoner.[76]

---

[72] "One Year's Work of the People's Commissariat of Justice," *loc.cit.*

[73] "The People's Commissariat of Justice Directive No. 14," *op.cit.*, p. 21.

[74] "A Bad Judicial Department Director," *Hung-te Chiang-hsi* (*Red Kiangsi*), #12, September 8, 1932. In the *Shih-sou Collection*, No. 008.1052, 2123-2, 0817, reel 1.

[75] "The People's Commissariat of Justice Directive No. 14," *op.cit.*, p. 7.

[76] *Ibid.*, pp. 5-6.

Judicial workers were also accused of being lax in their work of suppressing counterrevolutionaries. Some counterrevolutionaries were sentenced to only one or two years in prison and were merely called "bad," "rascals," or other less serious words in order to lessen the degree of their crimes. In Hsing-kuo Hsien, thirty percent of the cadre were considered too permissive in dealing with counterrevolutionaries.[77]

As a result of these mistakes in judicial work, plus the mass arrests of the A-B League, a situation of chaos and terror was created in the Soviet areas. Organs other than the judicial departments were arresting and executing people at will. Especially at the *ch'ü* level, people were arrested without sufficient evidence, tortured until they confessed, and then executed immediately without higher-level authorization. The objective of Communist supremacy and control over an area was clearly the overriding consideration.

Summary

Communist policy toward counterrevolutionaries first sprouted in 1924-1927 as the Communists, working through the KMT peasant associations, experimented with ad hoc measures to arouse the masses for a land revolution in Kiangsi and Hunan provinces. Their efforts were hindered by a broad definition of the enemy, resulting from an unrealistic appraisal of the power situation, and by an excessive use of terror, resulting from their inability to control the aroused peasants. Although the peasant associations were not usually successful in seizing power, the peasant movement of 1924-1927 did furnish the Communists valuable experience with techniques for controlling their political enemies.

During the period 1927-1933 the CCP was a party out of power. Torn by internal dissension and encircled by the KMT, the Communists were unable to agree upon or implement a

[77] Kiangsi Provincial Soviet Government, "Summary Report of Six Months' Work, May through October, of the Kiangsi Provincial Soviet Government," *loc.cit.*

unified legal policy. Counterrevolutionaries were defined on the basis of economic class, political party, or overt action. The term "counterrevolutionary" was even used as a camouflage for the leadership struggle within the CCP. While party affiliation, economic class, etc., were significant aspects in assigning penalties, the overriding consideration was the real or potential danger of the individual to the revolution.

Beginning in 1931, the campaign against counterrevolutionaries was to have been handled by the newly established judicial system. An organizational framework and systematic procedures were provided on paper, but their actual application was limited by the weakness of Communist governmental control over most areas. Numerous exceptions were enumerated to insure that the weakness of the formal organs of government would not hinder the suppression of counterrevolutionaries. Judicial power was temporarily allotted to the police, government, and mass groups, thereby creating a situation of cadre misapplication and disorder.

Nevertheless, even in this situation of terror, the trend, at least among the bureaucrats, was toward formalization and regularization. Detailed procedures for handling a variety of situations were suggested and counterrevolutionary offenses were differentiated into varying degrees of severity. Flagrant violations of procedures by judicial cadre were strongly condemned in the directives. In addition to being criticized, judicial workers were often fired and sometimes even tried and punished for their mistakes.[78] The People's Commissariat of Justice in its "Directive No. 14," of June 1933, was particularly fervent in pointing out mistakes and in suggesting new, systematic methods of judicial administration. The Communist leaders appeared to assume that once governmental control of an area was assured, formal laws and judicial machinery were both necessary and desirable.

[78] For examples see *Szu-fa hui-k'an* (Justice Magazine), No. 1, June 16, 1933. In the *Shih-sou Collection*, No. 008.54105, 1732, 0658, reel 6.

CHAPTER III. Crisis in the Kiangsi Soviet,
1933-1934

Introduction

DURING the 1924 to 1933 period, the Chinese
Communist Party evolved from a splinter group
of political activists into a governing body with
the ensuing problems of territorial control. A
direct correlation was noted between the degree of governmental control and the degree of flexibility sanctioned. As the
Communists satisfied their objective of territorial and finally
governmental takeover, they turned to more precise rules of
punishment. Conversely, the reversal of the trend toward
regularization is an understandable response to the initiation
of the Fifth Encirclement Campaign by the KMT in November 1933. Since 1933 is a pivotal year, it is included in both
Chapter II and Chapter III. The trend toward regularization
that began in 1931 seemed to culminate in 1933 with the
publication of the critical "Directive No. 14" and the circulation of the "Draft Statute of the Chinese Soviet Republic
Governing Punishment of Counterrevolutionaries." Concurrently, application of legal procedures was becoming more lax
as the military situation grew more critical. Because changes
in policy occur gradually and unevenly, no clear breaking
point appears, and 1933 is included in both discussions.

In this chapter, we will consider approximately the same
aspects as in Chapter II, i.e., environment, organization, laws,
and practical application. The definition of a counterrevolutionary did not change perceptively from the 1927 to 1933
period and consequently will not be re-examined. The primary
emphasis in Chapter III will be noting changes in these aspects
over time and speculating on causal relationships.

Environment (1933-1934)

From the fall of 1933 through 1934 the environment in the
Central Soviet area was characterized by increasing danger as

45

the KMT's Fifth Encirclement Campaign proved to be more threatening than previous assaults. The KMT, following the advice of German advisers, initiated a new tactic called the "policy of pillboxes." A strict economic blockade was set up against the Communist-held areas. Roads, forts, and pillboxes were built and slowly the military cordon was tightened around the Communists.

The effects of this new policy within the Soviet territory were quite significant. The economic blockade necessitated calls for increased production and crackdown on waste and corruption. To meet the needs of military defense, attempts were made to increase the size and armament of the Red Army, a development that only intensified the economic shortages in the private sector.

A series of campaigns were launched to deal with the situation. The Land Investigation Drive (*ch'a-t'ien yun-tung*) aimed at correcting the mistakes of the first stage of land redistribution by eliminating counterrevolutionaries and reactionary elements that had infiltrated the peasant and Soviet organizations. These people were to be reclassified and their land redistributed. Next, the Accusation Movement sought to eliminate inadequacies among the CCP members, such as laziness, corruption, and leniency toward landlords. There was also an Enlarging the Red Army Movement, a Production Movement, and a Collecting Supplies Movement. The more critical the situation became, the more desperate and excessive were the responses.

In an editorial in *Hung-se Chung-hua* on May 5, 1934 Chang Wen-t'ien explained the Communists' position: "The greater is the enemy pressure on the Soviet Area, and the more intensive is the war, the more active the alien class elements and counterrevolutionaries become. . . . The Red Terror is our only answer to the counterrevolutionary elements. In war zones and border areas in particular, we must take the most swift action against any counterrevolutionary activity."[1]

---

[1] Shao-chuan Leng, *Justice in Communist China* (Dobbs Ferry, New York: Oceana Publications, 1967), p. 10.

Organization (1933-1934)

The increasing KMT threat necessitated more expeditious procedures for dealing with counterrevolutionaries and other criminals. The previous system of requiring a superior's approval before carrying out a death sentence was called "obviously inappropriate during the class struggle."[2] It was explained that delays in obtaining approvals caused the masses to lose interest in counterrevolutionary cases.

Instead of requiring the superior's permission in all cases of capital punishment, only those cases in which the criminal appealed his sentence were reviewed at the higher level. Furthermore, the right of appeal was decreased from fourteen days to a maximum of seven days from the date of notification.[3] Also, a two-trial system was inaugurated; thereby, a case could be appealed only once unless the procurator protested the judgment.[4]

Another organizational change decentralized power by extending to the *ch'ü* level the right independently to arrest, try, sentence, and, in certain cases, even execute counterrevolutionaries. Laying the foundation for decentralization at the Land Investigation Conference in 1933, Mao pointed out that the directors of *ch'ü* level judicial departments did not have to know a lot of laws. If they could decide on the class standpoint, they could correctly punish the criminals.[5]

Power to deal with the counterrevolutionaries was reassigned in 1934 by the following articles from the "Judicial Procedures of the Chinese Soviet Republic":

"1. The special agents of the *ch'ü* Political Security Bureau, the *ch'ü* judicial department, the *ch'ü* Committee for the Sup-

[2] Lo Fu (alias for Chang Wen-t'ien), "Show Mercilessness Toward Our Class Enemies," *Tou-cheng* (Struggle), March 2, 1934. In the *Shih-sou Collection*, No. 008.2105, 7720, v. 4, 1133, reel 18.

[3] Central Executive Committee, "Judicial Procedures of the Chinese Soviet Republic," promulgated on April 8, 1934, Article 5, p. 58. In the *Shih-sou Collection*, No. 008.542, 4424 v. 2, 1146, reel 16.

[4] *Ibid.*, Article 6, p. 58.

[5] Lo Fu, *loc.cit.*

pression of Counterrevolutionaries (under the Revolutionary Committees in new Soviet areas), the people's police department, and the labor courts all have the right to arrest counterrevolutionaries and other criminals who ought to be arrested. In the past there was a regulation that the *ch'ü* level did not have the above right. This regulation is repealed. Moreover it is decided that in critical times, the *hsiang* Soviet, the municipal Soviet, the *hsiang* Revolutionary Committee, and the municipal Revolutionary Committee have the right to arrest counterrevolutionaries and other important criminals with the approval of the revolutionary masses.

"2. The *ch'ü* judicial organs and the *ch'ü* Committee for the Suppression of Counterrevolutionaries have the right to interrogate a suspect (*shen-hsün*) and to decide on all counterrevolutionary and other criminal cases in that locality. In the new areas, in areas under enemy attack, and in areas where counterrevolutionaries are especially active, and during the periods of mobilizing people for critical tasks (such as the Land Investigation Drive, Enlarging the Red Army, the Sudden Attack Movement, etc.), the *ch'ü* judicial organs and the *ch'ü* Committee for the Suppression of Counterrevolutionaries have the right after one trial to execute directly counterrevolutionaries, gentry, and landlord criminals with the support of the local revolutionary masses. After the execution they must report it to the next higher level.

"3. The judicial departments, Committees for the Suppression of Counterrevolutionaries, and the military judicial department of the provincial and *hsien* level all have the right to arrest, investigate, decide, and carry out the decision (including the death penalty) for all criminals."[6]

Note the dramatic impact the two changes simultaneously had on the system. Not only was power extended downward to the *ch'ü* level but also the review process was eliminated in many cases. Obviously, while the necessity of reporting an execution *after* the fact might deter capricious violations of the law, it did not function to protect the rights of the executed

---

[6] "Judicial Procedures," Articles 1-3, *op.cit.*, pp. 56-57.

individual in the same manner as a review *prior* to execution. The rationale justifying these changes was that during periods when the Communists were in particular danger (i.e., when areas had not been under Communist control for long, when the enemy was attacking, or when the government was conducting a campaign, etc.) more power should be given to the government to control political opposition. By using this justification, the Communist leaders still seemed to be implying that the stronger measures were inappropriate for normal conditions.

In addition to an extension of power to lower level judicial departments, the power of the Political Security Bureau was strengthened. The judicial organs were accused of taking a legalistic viewpoint that insisted on following judicial form rather than relying on mass opinion.

To circumvent this weakness of the judiciary, the Political Security Bureau system was to have utmost authority in dealing with counterrevolutionaries and was not to be responsible to any other organ. The Political Security Bureau organs could arrest, detain, try, and even execute counterrevolutionaries without the assistance or approval of the courts. This right was given in the following three articles from the Council of People's Commissar's Order No. 5 of February 9, 1934:

"1. In order severely to suppress enemy spies, Fascist elements in the border areas, and elements of the gentry and landlords who carry out plots and traitorous activities, the local Political Security Bureau in the border areas and the military Political Security Bureau in the battle areas have the right to handle directly cases involving these counterrevolutionaries without going through the courts. However, after handling a case, they must present a report to the State Political Security Bureau for recording and inquiry.

"2. In carrying out their work of arresting the leaders of the Big Sword Society and their members who are resolutely against the revolution and who come from landlord or rich peasant backgrounds in territories where the Big Sword Society's activities have not yet been eliminated, the State

Political Security Bureau and its local and military branches can handle these cases directly without going through the courts. However, after handling a case, they must make a report to the State Political Security Bureau for recording and inquiry.

"3. In important and critical counterrevolutionary cases, the State Political Security Bureau and its local and military branches have the right to handle the cases severely. After these cases are decided, if the local governments, their organs, or the military political commissars disagree, the dispute will be decided by the Council of People's Commissars."[7]

By these changes, discretion for executing criminals was delegated to lower-level cadre, with no method of double-checking until after the fact, and individuals of questionable training were given life-and-death power. Following the trend begun in the 1927-1932 period, judicial power was increasingly extended to extra-judicial organs, especially the Political Security Bureau. This extension of judicial functions was institutionalized in the "Judicial Procedures of the Chinese Soviet Republic," promulgated in 1934.

Laws and Punishments (1933-1934)

In December 1933 the People's Commissariat of Justice circulated a "Draft Statute of the Chinese Soviet Republic Governing Punishment of Counterrevolutionaries." After the suggestions of various groups and judicial organs were received, the statute was revised and promulgated by the Central Executive Committee on April 8, 1934. These two documents were very similar in most respects (see Appendices A and B). Both listed a number of crimes that were considered counterrevolutionary and punishable by death. These included such crimes as attempts to overthrow the government, sabotage, espionage, armed riot, assassination, responsibility in the reactionary regime, desertion with weapons, destroying weapons, or otherwise obstructing trade.

[7] Lo Fu, *loc.cit.*

Both documents had a provision that those who concealed or assisted in any of the activities mentioned in the statute should be punished the same as the main criminal (Article 25 and Article 30, respectively). Both also stated that those who plotted crimes but had not yet accomplished their aim and those who were accomplices might receive a reduced penalty (Article 26 and Article 32). The same was true for those who were coerced into committing a crime (Article 27 and Article 33).

Special provisions also stipulated lesser penalties for workers and peasants and persons sixteen and younger (Articles 28 and 29 in Appendix A and Articles 34 and 37 in Appendix B). However, in the enacted statute, this leniency was not applicable to workers and peasants who were "leaders or major offenders."

Both the draft and the statute included the principle of analogy, thus extending the law to cover criminal behavior not explicitly mentioned in the texts. Accordingly, undesignated crimes were to receive the same degree of punishment as similar crimes specifically listed (see Article 30 and Article 38, respectively). Thus, the concept of *nullum crimen sine lege, nulla poena sine lege*, which had no tradition in China, was likewise rejected by the Communists.

Provisions for additional punishment by confiscation of property and suspension of citizenship rights were contained in both documents (Article 31 and Article 39). The maximum period of imprisonment in both was limited to ten years (Article 32 and Article 40).

Although the two documents were basically similar, the statute contained a number of important changes. The statute was broadened to include prohibitions against committing any of the following acts with a counterrevolutionary purpose: using religion and superstition (Article 14); intentionally disobeying orders (Article 20); murdering the revolutionary masses; intentionally destroying or seizing the property of the masses (Article 21); and setting fire to houses or forests (Article 24).

Furthermore, two articles granting additional leniency were added to the statute. Article 35 stipulated that lighter punishment should be meted out to those who had made a contribution to the Soviet. Article 36 provided leniency for those who voluntarily surrendered and confessed before being discovered (*tzu-shou*) and for those who repented and reported all the facts after being discovered (*tzu-hsin*). As a rule, the minimum punishment given for less serious varieties of a crime was lighter in the statute than in the draft. This additional leniency may reflect the difficulties the Communists encountered in maintaining and protecting prison facilities in the face of increased KMT attacks. In addition, one should note that an increasing emphasis on leniency coincides with Mao's general ascendency in the Party.

Generally speaking, the statute represented a refinement in language and a more realistic appraisal of the changing revolutionary situation than the earlier draft. To gain the support of the masses, crimes that were injurious to the people or their property but only indirectly detrimental to the CCP were added to the list of counterrevolutionary offenses. In general, the Communists' first statute dealing with counterrevolutionaries reflected a continuation of policies set forth in the directives of 1932-1933. The main criterion for determining treatment of counterrevolutionaries was still the degree of potential danger to the Soviet regime involved in each case.

Laws in Practice (1933-1934)

Chang Wen-t'ien, the chairman of the Council of People's Commissars, explained CCP policy and criticized mistakes of application in two issues of *Hung-se Chung-hua* (Red China). Chang stressed that the policy of executing landlords and rich peasants who were counterrevolutionaries should be expanded to include some punishment for landlords and rich peasants who were not guilty of counterrevolutionary activities. To insure that more of the burden of supplying labor and money for the revolution would be shouldered by those two classes,

Chang suggested a policy of "exploiting the exploiters." Many landlords and peasants had not yet been assigned to labor groups (*lao-i tui*), and he called this a waste. Chang suggested registering the landlords and rich peasants in all the Soviet areas and assigning the landlords into permanent labor groups and the rich peasants into temporary labor groups. The dependents of landlords were to be exiled or forceably moved from war zones, while the dependents of the rich peasants generally were to be allowed to stay.[8]

In his second article,[9] Chang clarified and appeared to soften this policy. He said it was to be applied only in limited areas, such as those where military operations were in progress. In rear areas near to the fighting, labor groups were to be formed only when the military situation demanded it. In all other areas, Chang insisted that the formation of permanent labor groups was to consist only of registering the landlords' names for possible government or military service. Chang explained he did not intend for *all* the landlords, rich peasants, and gentry from *all* the Soviet areas to be detained, for this would create insurmountable logistical problems.[10]

Chang reports that some people were misinterpreting his original order and were arresting *all* landlords and rich peasants. After one reads Chang's article, it is easy to understand how errors could arise, for the limiting conditions for detention were not clearly stated in the first article.

Another provision called for the confiscation of the landlords' property. The property of the rich peasants, merchants, and capitalists was not to be confiscated; however, their "surplus" houses, animals, farm implements, and grains were to be taken without compensation. In addition, the rich peasants,

---

[8] Chang Wen-t'ien, "Only Hatred and No Forgiveness toward Our Class Enemies," *Hung-se Chung-hua* (Red China), May 25, 1934. In the *Shih-sou Collection*, No. 008.1052, 2125, v. 7, 1937, reel 17.

[9] Chang Wen-t'ien, "Is Critically Suppressing Counterrevolutionaries the Same as the Present Violent Disorder toward the Counterrevolution?" *Hung-se Chung-hua* (Red China), June 28, 1934. In the *Shih-sou Collection*, No. 008.1052, 2125, v. 7, 1937, reel 17.

[10] *Ibid.*

merchants, and capitalists were to be brought before a crowd and asked for donations of up to 40 percent of their capital. Those classified as "reactionary" rich peasants were to be treated more harshly: their property was to be confiscated. However, it was explained that only those rich peasants who had *serious* counterrevolutionary behavior and not all who belonged to reactionary groups were to be classified as "reactionary."[11]

Lo-an Hsien, where over 700 landlords and rich peasants were arrested in one morning, was cited as an example of the proper procedures to be used against landlords and rich peasants.[12] Thirty were shot as counterrevolutionaries and the rest were forcibly removed from the area. The Political Security Bureau was in charge of advance planning and held meetings to explain the new policy to the *ch'ü* and *hsiang* level personnel.

On the appointed day, cadre were sent to each village in Lo-an Hsien to direct the masses in arresting people. The arrests were made early in the morning so that the landlords and rich peasants would not have an opportunity to escape. Red Guards escorted the prisoners, forcing them to carry their food and personal belongings with them. Any who resisted were shot. After the arrested were led away, representatives and Party members explained the necessity of such action to the remaining villagers. The property confiscated from the counterrevolutionary landlords and rich peasants was then distributed to the masses.

The arrested landlords and rich peasants were sent to detention centers in rear areas where they were registered and

[11] "The Central Government's Decisions Concerning Some Questions in the Land Struggle," passed by the Council of People's Commissars, October 10, 1933. In the *Shih-sou Collection*, No. 008.743, 4047, 1166, reel 17.

[12] "Raise Class Awareness and Increase Suppression of Counterrevolutionaries in the New Border Areas: the Red Terror's Reply to the Enemy's White Terror," *Sheng-wei t'ung-hsun* (Bulletin of the Provincial Committee), March 30, 1934. In the *Shih-sou Collection*, No. 008.2105, 9023, 1156, reel 17.

divided into different categories (i.e., male-female, old-young, etc.). A piece of bamboo was hung on the prisoner to identify him as a landlord or rich peasant. The strong were organized into labor groups (*lao-i-tui*) and sent to the tungsten mines. Some were fined, and others were forced to plow virgin land.

Chang Wen-t'ien's orders reflected a change in Communist policy necessitated by the increased KMT pressure. No longer was punishment reserved for those who committed overt acts in opposition to Communist rule. Instead, in strategic areas, preventive action was to be taken against potential enemies *before* they had committed any counterrevolutionary activities. In all areas, the landlords and rich peasants were expected to play an increased role in meeting the critical supply shortages resulting from the KMT encirclement.

Vacillating between a hard- and soft-line approach, Chang was critical of both right-wing and left-wing mistakes in applying his policy. He cautioned that in such critical times all who were lenient, permissive, particular about procedure, or legalistic were no different from the counterrevolutionaries. He urged a policy of "Red Terror" against all counterrevolutionaries, whereby anyone even suspected of counterrevolutionary activities would be arrested. If there was proof of serious criminal activity, the criminal was to be executed immediately, with no need for a detailed trial. Workers, peasants, or poor people who were important counterrevolutionaries were to be treated likewise.[13] Thus, in addition to extending punishment to potential enemies, the Communists responded to the crisis by sanctioning harsher treatment of actual counterrevolutionaries. Judicial cadre who did not quickly punish these counterrevolutionaries were to be severely criticized and even arrested and tried, if the mistakes continued.[14]

On the other hand, excesses of the opposite nature were equally condemned. Chang warned that the Communists' policy was definitely not aimed at creating terror. On the contrary, its purpose was motivating the masses to participate

[13] Chang Wen-t'ien, "Only Hatred . . . ," *loc.cit.*
[14] *Ibid.*

actively in the revolution by mobilizing them to go to the front. Thus, creating disturbances or indiscriminately killing people was considered counterproductive and could only terrify the masses. Chang warned that the policy of "Red Terror" would be successful only if it was selectively and precisely applied.[15]

The vagueness of Chang's criterion, even on paper, naturally resulted in both types of mistakes in application. The left wing's use of excessive terror seems to have been the most frequent. In some places cadre arrested and detained all landlords and rich peasants. Instead of asking donations from the rich peasants, some cadre simply confiscated their property.[16]

In part, the excesses were due to the inability of the cadre to control the aroused crowds. In one *ch'ü*, reportedly, mass groups without authority sealed houses for confiscation and posted false orders. These groups, and sometimes even judicial cadre, kept the money that was confiscated and did not turn it over to the government.[17]

At the opposite extreme, in some places the Communists were still not successful in overcoming peasant apathy, as evidenced by low attendance at public trials. At one trial only twenty people attended; twelve of them were landlords and rich peasants who were immediately reclassified as middle and poor peasants by the embarrassed cadre.[18] The people who did attend the trials did not always understand the significance of the event. Of the 200-300 people who attended one meeting, reportedly only seven or eight gave an opinion.[19] It was stated

[15] *Ibid.*

[16] Chang Wen-t'ien, "Is Critically . . . ," *loc.cit.*

[17] "A Review and Discussion of Po-sheng Hsien's 3rd Joint Meeting of Judicial Department Heads." In the *Shih-sou Collection*, No. 008. 54105, 1732, 0658, reel 6.

[18] "Actively Develop the Land Investigation Movement and Without Mercy Suppress the Landlord and Rich Peasant Counter-attack," *Hung-se Chung-hua* (Red China), March 20, 1934. In the *Shih-sou Collection*, No. 008.1052, 2125 v. 6, 1937, reel 17.

[19] Hsiang Ying, "The Circumstances and Experiences of the Accusation Movement in Yü-tu," *Hung-se Chung-hua* (Red China), March 29, 1934. In the *Shih-sou Collection*, No. 008.1052, 2125 v. 6, 1937, reel 17.

that the common people did not understand that the courts functioned to protect workers and peasants; rather, they feared the judicial personnel, whose primary function appeared to be killing people.

Not all Communist attempts to arouse, organize, and control the masses were unsuccessful. Newspapers of the period report many successful mass trials (*kung-shen*) like the one in Yün-chi Ch'ü attended by 3,000 people.[20] Mass trials differed from ordinary court trials, which were open for public attendance. Mass trials were usually reserved for very important criminals clearly guilty of counterrevolutionary activities punishable by the death penalty. Since the defendant's guilt was not at issue, the primary purpose of the mass trial was to stimulate and involve the common people in eliminating counterrevolutionaries. Jerome Cohen characterizes mass trials as "morality plays."[21] To achieve this purpose, extensive advertising in the form of billboards, wall posters, banners, parades, and slogans was employed. Examples show that the agenda of the trial was carefully planned and organized.[22] Because of the size of the crowd attending, mass trials were frequently held outdoors or in large meeting halls. The trial usually began with the entry of the judge and assessors, followed by the reading of the accusation by the clerk. After added details of the crime were given by the prosecution, the accused was allowed to testify and answer questions from the judge and assessors. One identifying characteristic of all mass trials was the participation of the audience. They were encouraged to give evidence or relevant experiences and finally to shout out their verdict. The trial ended when the judge pronounced the sentence and the

[20] "Victory of the Sudden Attack Month in Juichin," *Tou-cheng* (Struggle), January 19, 1934, p. 12. In the *Shih-sou Collection*, No. 008.2105, 7720 v. 4, 1133, reel 18.

[21] Jerome Cohen, *The Criminal Process in the People's Republic of China 1949-1963: An Introduction* (Cambridge, Mass.: Harvard University Press, 1968), p. 13.

[22] "A Counterrevolutionary Sentenced to Five Years in Prison," *Hung-se Chung-hua* (Red China), January 13, 1934. In the *Shih-sou Collection*, No. 008.1052, 2125, 1139, reel 17.

masses showed their approval by applauding and yelling slogans. The decision was posted publicly to inform others of the results. Frequently, the court adjourned to the execution area, where the crowds watched the immediate implementation of the sentence.

While newspapers report many mass trials in the years 1933-1934, they give less frequent reports of ordinary judicial procedures conducted by the judicial departments than in the 1931-1932 period. In response to the more critical situation and in accord with the new procedures, the Political Security Bureau personnel often conducted the mass trials or simply executed criminals without trials.[23] Since the decision as to guilt or innocence was usually made by the Political Security Bureau and not by the judge, trial procedures were rather superfluous from the viewpoint of the system's efficiency and thus were logically eliminated during crisis periods. Nevertheless, from the viewpoint of the individual, reexamination of the case by the judicial department did furnish the possibility of correcting any errors of the Political Security Bureau. The elimination of this opportunity for reexamination resulted in loss of the limited protection afforded the accused. The lack of the right of appeal for members of the landlord and gentry class, coupled with the immediate execution of sentences, left most "counterrevolutionaries" wholly at the mercy of the Political Security Bureau.

Deserters and Runaways

With the increasingly critical situation, two other problems arose to plague the Communists. They involved deserters and runaways (masses who ran away and changed sides [*fan-*

---

[23] For examples see the following articles: "Increase the Work of Suppressing Counterrevolutionaries," *Hung-se Chung-hua* (Red China), March 19, 1933; "Four Counterrevolutionaries are Executed," *Hung-se Chung-hua* (Red China), May 2, 1933; and "The State Political Security Bureau Arrested Four Counterrevolutionaries," *Hung-se Chung-hua* (Red China), February 20, 1934. All are located in the *Shih-sou Collection*, No. 008.1052, 2125, 1937, reel 17.

shui]). In a five-month period of 1934 the First Army Corps had 203 deserters, the Third Army 98, and the Fifth Army 110.[24] In one place, 80 percent of the troops ran away.[25] The explanations for the high desertion rates ranged from class deviates hidden in the Red Army to incorrect and coercive leadership by Red Army officers. One of the main reasons for desertion appears to have been that most of the new recruits had been forcefully conscripted (for example, had their name called at a meeting) and thus were not personally dedicated to the cause. Also, living conditions on the front were difficult. At some places runaways were told they would be shot if they returned, and sometimes their families were arrested and their property confiscated. These tactics merely scared the runaways, thereby decreasing the chances of their return. Red Army officers who were bureaucratic and who mistreated the soldiers were held personally responsible for the problem and were considered as counterrevolutionaries and severely punished.[26]

As part of the Enlarging the Red Army Movement, the Communists organized a Sudden Attack Movement and a Return to the Troops Movement to entice soldiers back. The program had two parts. Leniency and propaganda were used to win back the majority of the deserters and runaways, while strong measures were ordered toward their leaders and firm counterrevolutionaries.

To arouse the masses at the beginning of the movement, one of the leaders of the deserters or runaways was usually tried and shot in front of the local people. The masses laughed

[24] "Instructions on Questions Concerning the Struggle to Oppose Runaways from the Army," signed by Commander Chu Teh, June 21, 1933. In *Ch'ih-fei wen-chien hui-pien*, Vol. 8. Also in the *Shih-sou Collection*, No. 008.2129, 4074, reel 21.

[25] "A Large Number of Soldiers Run Away in Yü-tu," *Ch'ing-nien shih-hua* (True Words of Youth), September 20, 1934. In the *Shih-sou Collection*, No. 008.2105, 5083, 1143, reel 18.

[26] "The Central Committee: Decisions Concerning the Results of the Sudden Attack Month," *Tou-cheng* (Struggle), January 19, 1934. In the *Shih-sou Collection*, No. 008.2105, 7720, v. 4, 1132, reel 18.

at and ridiculed the deserters to make them feel ashamed. To mold public opinion, newspapers, operas, and posters extolled the glory of the Red Army. The dependents of Red Army soldiers and returned deserters formed Sudden Attack Patrols (*t'u-chi tui*) that went out at night to find other deserters. These groups conducted "thought struggle and education" in order to persuade the deserters to return. Those who were willing to return were congratulated and their families encouraged by being praised at mass meetings or by having a red cloth or paper put on their gate. The masses were also organized to cheer the soldiers along the way as they returned to the troops. Thus, recognizing that their primary need was to get soldiers back to the front, the Communists were generally willing to allow past mistakes to go unpunished in return for future service. Also, they realized the necessity of relying on propaganda and peer-group pressure to persuade the deserters rather than on physical force.

Soldiers who refused to return were publicly tried by a Comrades Adjudication Committee. They were forced to return all blankets, clothing, supplies, etc., received from the army and to repay any kindness done for their family. In addition, they were assigned double the normal amount of public land to cultivate. After they were dismissed from military and political membership and disfranchised, their names were publicly posted on bulletin boards in their village.[27]

More serious action was demanded against certain types of deserters who were considered counterrevolutionaries. Those who ran away with their weapons were ordered shot as soon as they were captured. Those who organized runaways or who led a squad or company to run away were to be shot after a mass trial. Anyone who ran away twice or more was to be tried by the military judicial department. Furthermore, anyone who did not carry out these orders was to be considered guilty

[27] "How to Develop the Movement to Oppose Deserters," *Hung-se Chung-hua* (Red China), April 11, 1933. In the *Shih-sou Collection*, No. 008.1052, 2125 v. 3, 1937, reel 17.

of "approving the runaways and thereby destroying the Red Army."[28]

A typical trial of deserters took place on April 26, 1933 at 9 a.m. in Jui-chang Hsien.[29] The trial was attended by representatives from more than thirty *hsien* and from eighty Model Regiments. To begin the meeting, the significance of the mass trial was explained. Then all the people in the hall yelled out in a high voice, "Oppose deserting," "Deserting is the biggest shame," "Eliminate the Social Democratic Party and all kinds of counterrevolutionaries," and other slogans.

The representative of the Public Security Bureau reported the evidence against the four criminals, and each one was tried in turn. Two Social Democrats confessed that they had created rumors among the masses, had organized secret armed forces, and had plotted to kill all revolutionary workers when the White Army came. The other two criminals were poor peasants who sincerely admitted their mistakes.

Next, the representatives from different places spoke, one right after another, pointing out the shame and danger of deserting. They said deserting equaled helping the enemy and they pledged to go back and work diligently to oppose all deserters.

The crowd demanded that the two Social Democratic counterrevolutionaries be killed by the traditional method of beheading. Under the request of the masses, the court sentenced the two to death, by the common Communist method of a firing squad. One of the peasants was sentenced to one year of hard labor and the other to long-term hard labor.

Immediately after the trial, everyone formed two lines and followed the firing squad through town, yelling slogans and

[28] "Order #25 of the Central Executive Committee of the Chinese Soviet Republic Concerning the Problem of Deserters from the Red Army," signed by Chairman Mao Tse-tung on December 15, 1933. In the *Shih-sou Collection*, No. 008.542, 4424 v. 2, 1146, reel 16.

[29] "Mass Trials of Criminals Who Led Deserters," *Hung-se Chunghua* (Red China), May 5, 1933. In the *Shih-sou Collection*, No. 008.1052, 2125 v. 3, 1937, reel 17.

singing songs. The newspaper reports that the noise shook the city and people hurried into the streets, blocking traffic. The two criminals were then executed in front of the crowd.[30]

The Communist policy toward civilian deserters was similar. In addition to the pressure from mass meetings, relatives and friends were urged to coax runaways to return. To further this policy, the dependents and property of runaways were protected and not mistreated. Whenever runaways returned, a celebration was held.[31]

A similar policy of trying to win over the majority and to isolate and punish only the firm counterrevolutionaries was also followed toward prisoners of war. Some POW's, especially those with special skills, were even allowed to serve in the Red Army.[32] The Communists needed manpower and supplies during this critical period and could ill afford to feed and care for a large number of prisoners. Thus, economic and military considerations necessitated overlooking minor crimes.

Summary

In response to the deteriorating political, economic, and military situation of 1933 and 1934, the Communists sanctioned more severe punishment for counterrevolutionaries, e.g., death without trial or a superior's approval. While dangerous enemies were treated with increased severity, increased leniency was offered to entice minor offenders into the Communist camp. The policy of combining suppression with leniency was primarily applied to deserters, runaways, and prisoners of war in an attempt to recruit soldiers for the Red Army from among the most combat-ready segment of the society.

Paradoxically, the laws dealing with counterrevolutionaries

---

[30] *Ibid.*

[31] "Hsing-kuo Hsien Soviet Government Circular Concerning the Discussion, Facts and Decisions of the 30th Meeting of the Standing Committee." In the *Shih-sou Collection*, No. 008.631, 3039, 0889, reel 10.

[32] "Three Secret, Hidden Counterrevolutionaries," *Hung-se Chung-hua* (Red China), August 16, 1933. In the *Shih-sou Collection*, No. 008.1052, 2125 v. 4, 1937, reel 17.

were finally formalized in a 1934 statute; yet, at the same time judicial organization and procedures were becoming less rigorous and consistent in practice. Judicial organs were increasingly replaced by the Political Security Bureau. On balance, as the crisis increased, all non-essential procedures were eliminated in favor of a speedy and unhindered achievement of short-run objectives.

The clear objective that emerges from a study of the Kiangsi Soviet period is governmental control of territorial sanctuaries by the CCP. The continuation of the Communist Party as a serious political force in China depended upon the successful achievement of this objective. The preeminence of this objective helps to explain the legal attitude of the Communists. As we pointed out in Chapter II, the Communists did not appear to consider law inherently bad and, in fact, they seemed to appreciate its utility in ordering society. However, law was considered a tool and not an end in itself. Formal laws and procedures were considered secondary to the achievement of an objective, and the utility of the rule of law was closely tied to an environment characterized by stable governmental control of a territory.

CHAPTER IV. Yenan, 1935-1944

Introduction

FOLLOWING the bitter campaigns of 1934 and the losses of the Long March, the Communists found themselves in a position of comparative weakness. While trying to reorganize and to establish governmental control over their new base areas in the northwest, they were hindered by another factor: the war with Japan. Growing in scope and intensity, the war against the Japanese dominated the 1935 to 1944 period. To augment their weak position, as well as to repel the advancing Japanese, the CCP wisely adopted a united front strategy that permeated all policies. Translated into actions against counterrevolutionaries, the united front policy signaled an increased emphasis on leniency for all except important war criminals. Temporarily shelving the cry for class warfare, the Communists switched to a policy of a War of National Resistance that required class unity and the largest possible united front against Japanese attack. This change in policy was reflected by a narrowing definition of counterrevolutionary activity.

The united front proved to be a wise maneuver for the Communists. The CCP gained legitimacy, publicity, and a variety of potentially useful contacts. In addition, the united front arrangement gave the Communist Party time to achieve its primary objective: local governmental control of territorial sanctuaries. The necessity of unity also encouraged the more radical members to temper their dogma with practicality. One of the most significant developments arising from the united front policy was in the area of judicial policy. The expanded program of leniency, which provided an incentive to neutralize the enemy and possibly even to transform former enemies into dedicated cadre, aided the Communists not only in the defeat of the Japanese but also in their subsequent liberation of China.

The remainder of the chapter will trace the significant

changes from the Kiangsi period to the Yenan period. First, major changes in the environment will be described and then related to changes in judicial organization, definition of counterrevolutionaries, laws and their practical application.

Environment (1935-1944)

Chiang Kai-shek's Fifth Extermination Campaign forced the Red Army of about 90,000 to leave Kiangsi on October 16, 1934. The 6,000-mile "Long March" that followed finally ended in northern Shensi a year later with the Communist forces reduced to less than 20,000 men. The emergence of Mao Tse-tung as the firm leader of the CCP during the Long March brought a unified, pragmatic approach to policy as the Communists attempted to rebuild their forces in their barren new base, Yenan. Success did not come easy, but by the end of the first period (1944), the CCP controlled nineteen Communist enclaves scattered from Hainan Island to Manchuria with a total population estimated at 160,000,000, an eighteen-fold increase over that of the Kiangsi Soviet.[1]

During this period the main problem to plague China was Japanese aggression. Japanese officers had taken over Manchuria in the Mukden Incident of September 1931 and had proclaimed the state of Manchukuo on March 1, 1932. Despite the Japanese incursions, Chiang Kai-shek continued his anti-Communist campaigns with a slogan of "Unification before Resistance." Meanwhile, the Communists, taking advantage of a huge groundswell of nationalism, reacted to Japanese aggression by declaring war in April 1932. To meet this new situation, as well as to prevent their own annihilation by the KMT, the CCP inaugurated a new policy espousing a united front.

At first, Chiang Kai-shek was unwilling to accept the idea of a united front, but he was convinced to begin negotiations

[1] Chalmers Johnson, "Chinese Communist Leadership and Mass Response: The Yenan Period and the Socialist Education Campaign Period," in Ping-ti Ho and Tang Tsou (ed.), *China in Crisis* (Chicago: The University of Chicago Press, 1968), I, 1, p. 412.

when two commanders, Marshall Chang Hsüeh-liang and Yang Hu-ch'eng, kidnapped him at Sian. The understanding announced by the KMT and accepted by the Communists on March 15, 1937 included the following conditions: (1) abolition of the Red Army and its incorporation into the government's Central Army; (2) dissolution of the Soviet Republic; (3) cessation of all Communist propaganda; and (4) suspension of the class struggle. No formal agreement seems to have been signed, but the Red Army base was designated as a garrison area comprising twenty-three *hsien* and named the Shensi-Kansu-Ninghsia Border Region. The Red Army was reorganized as the Eighth Route Army under the command of Chu Teh and P'eng Te-huai. On September 22, 1937, the Communists issued a proclamation from Yenan, formally dissolving the Soviet Republic and affirming their unity with the Kuomintang.

Following the occupation of Peiping in July 1937, Japanese forces advanced rapidly through North China, for the Chinese provincial and Central Government armies north and east of the Yellow River had virtually collapsed by the end of 1937. The Japanese set up Chinese puppet administrations to maintain order in the occupied zones, but their control rarely extended beyond the cities. In the countryside, most of the officials, merchants, and wealthy families fled as the government troops withdrew, leaving the villagers to organize self-defense units to protect themselves against the Japanese, bandit groups, and roving units of disorganized Chinese troops. It was into this chaotic situation that the Communist Eighth Route Army moved and began to restore order. The people looked to the Communists for protection from the Japanese and their policies of looting, raping, beating, and killing.

At first the united front brought a degree of unity. On January 30, 1938 Chiang Kai-shek approved the formation of a second border region called the Shansi-Chahar-Hopei Border Region. The break in the civil war provided a period for organization and legislation in the Communist-controlled border regions, which were temporarily secure from the Japanese because of their northwestern location. It was during this period that the majority of the laws dealing with counter-revolutionaries were first enacted.

The truce began to break down in 1938 since the KMT suppressed the Communist groups in the cities under their control. Finally, open fighting broke out between KMT and Communist forces, and in the summer of 1939 the Chungking government began a strict military blockade of the Shensi-Kansu-Ninghsia Border Region.

Matters became worse when Chungking forces attacked the headquarters of the Communist New Fourth Army in January 1941, inflicting heavy casualties. The Central Government cut off subsidies both for the maintenance of the Eighth Route Army and for administration of the border regions. During 1940-1941, no military supplies from the Central Government reached the Communists. At the same time the Japanese directed their offensive against the Communist areas. They initiated a scorched-earth policy called "the three all policy"— kill all, burn all, loot all. This assault was said to have reduced the population of the Communist areas by half and decreased the Eighth Route Army from 400,000 to 300,000 men.[2]

In 1941 the Communists were forced to impose severe taxation and military conscription on the people. The tax levy was more than double that of the previous year. To aggravate the hardships, drought and locust plagues caused diminished agricultural production in 1942-1943. In an attempt to combat these problems, the CCP turned its attention from politics to economics with the launching of the Great Production Movement. Also, the Party was streamlined and reformed during the Cheng-Feng Movement of February 1942. The situation improved after 1943, when the Japanese diverted their efforts from the Communists to the KMT areas.

Organization (1935-1944)

The judicial systems of the border regions were nominally under the jurisdiction of the Nationalist Supreme Court be-

[2] Ho Kan-chih, *A History of the Modern Revolution* (Peking: Foreign Language Press, 1960), pp. 373-374.

cause of the united front arrangement. In actuality, the judicial system of each border region operated as a separate entity. Communist policy was that: "A large part of the old bourgeois democratic judicial system is being used, but whatever violates the fundamental rights and interests of the peasants and working proletariat should be eliminated."[3]

Sometimes the Communists simply adopted and implemented the Nationalist laws, but more frequently they promulgated their own laws and regulations. In cases where the two conflicted, the Communists relied on their own "Separate Statutes."

The "Organic Regulations of the High Court of the Shensi-Kansu-Ninghsia Border Region," promulgated on April 4, 1939,[4] established the High Court (*kao-teng fa-yuan*), which for all practical purposes was the highest court in each border region. The High Court was the organ of first trial for important criminal cases and the organ of appeal in other cases. The president of the High Court was elected by the Border Region People's Political Council. The departments under the High Court were the Procuracy, Civil Court, Criminal Court, Secretariat, Detention Centers, and General Affairs. Judicial personnel were appointed by the president of the High Court with the approval of the border region government.

At the bottom of the judicial system were the local courts (*ti-fang fa-yuan*). If the local courts had not been established, justice bureaus of the *hsien* government (*szu-fa ch'u*) handled the cases. For example, the Shensi-Kansu-Ninghsia Border Region had three branch courts, twenty-nine *hsien* justice

[3] Lu Pi-min, "A Few Opinions Concerning the Judiciary of the Border Region," translated in Allyn Rickett, *Legal Thought and Institutions of the People's Republic of China: Selected Documents* (University of Pennsylvania Institute for Legal Research, Mimeographed, 1963-1964), Supplementary Materials, p. 41.

[4] *K'ang-jih ken-chü-ti cheng-ts'e t'iao-li hui-chi, Shen-Kan-Ning chih-pu* (Compendium of Policy Statements and Statutes of the Anti-Japanese Border Regions, Shensi-Kansu-Ninghsia Section), (Shensi-Kansu-Ninghsia Border Region Government, July 18, 1942), Vol. 1, pp. 43-49.

bureaus, and one local court.[5] Judicial committees (*ts'ai-p'an wei-yuan-hui*) consisting of Party, government, and court officials were established on the *hsien* level to discuss the judges' opinions. In cases of disagreement, the judicial committee could report the decision directly to the High Court.[6]

The judicial system described above functioned as a three-level system with a Border Region Government's Trial Committee (*shen-p'an wei-yuan-hui*)[7] superior to both the local courts and the High Court. In March 1943, this system was modified by the establishment of branch courts (*fen-t'ing*) on the special commissioners' level.[8] These second-level trial organs were to handle appeals from local courts or justice bureaus. Criminal cases decided by the branch courts involving sentences of three years or more imprisonment were automatically sent to the High Court to be recorded and approved. Other decisions by the branch courts could be appealed to the High Court. By 1944, this system was further modified when the Border Region Government's Trial Committee was abolished temporarily. The local courts or *hsien* justice bureaus were still the level of first trial, but the High Court or its branch courts were considered the final trial organ.[9]

Also in March 1943, the *hsien* level justice bureaus were reorganized so that the *hsien* magistrate served concurrently as

[5] Ma Hsi-wu, "The People's Judicial Work in Shensi-Kansu-Ninghsia Border Region during the State of the New Democratic Revolution," *Cheng-fa yen-chiu* (Studies in Political Science and Law), Peking, No. 1, 1955, p. 8.

[6] *Ibid.*

[7] "Directive from the Shensi-Kansu-Ninghsia Border Region High Court Concerning Each Hsien's Judicial Work," May 10, 1941. Located in *Compendium . . . Shensi-Kansu-Ninghsia, op.cit.,* Vol. 3, p. 750.

[8] "Draft Organic Regulation on Branch Courts of the Shensi-Kansu-Ninghsia Border Region High Court," March 1943. Located in *Compendium . . . Shensi-Kansu-Ninghsia, op.cit.,* Supplement, pp. 96-98.

[9] "Summary of One Year's Work of the Border Region Government," January 6, 1944. Located in *Compendium . . . Shensi-Kansu-Ninghsia, op.cit.,* Supplement, p. 54. Also reported in "The Border Government's Correct Decision on Two Level Courts," *Chieh-fang jih-pao* (Liberation Daily), February 25, 1944, p. 2.

head of the *hsien* justice bureau.[10] This move helped to alleviate the manpower shortage and to strengthen the already significant political control over the courts that resulted from government approval of judicial appointments and from the system of judicial committees.

The judicial organs were aided in dealing with traitors by the Public Security Bureau (*kung-an chü*). The Public Security Bureau and its branches were under the joint direction of the governments of their respective levels and of the Public Security Bureau system.[11] Thus, this Bureau was not an independent, vertically controlled system like the powerful Political Security Bureau in the Kiangsi Soviet.

Once a traitor was detected, the Public Security Bureau, as well as the judiciary, could issue a summons or arrest warrant. The Public Security Bureau also had the right to investigate the case, question the suspect, and detain him for longer than the usual twenty-four-hour limit.[12] In general, the procedures for the Public Security Bureau's preliminary investigation and for the judicial cadre's handling of the case were similar to those formally prescribed in the Kiangsi Soviet.

However, the Public Security Bureau had a more limited function in these judicial proceedings than did its counterpart, the Political Security Bureau of the Kiangsi Soviet. In the Kiangsi period, the Political Security Bureau was given the right to try, sentence, and *execute* criminals in special circum-

[10] "Draft Organic Regulation of the Shensi-Kansu-Ninghsia Border Region Hsien Justice Bureaus," March 1943. Located in *Compendium . . . Shensi-Kansu-Ninghsia, op.cit.,* Supplement, pp. 99-100.

[11] "Temporary Statute of the Public Security Bureau of the Shansi-Chahar-Hopei Region," April 10, 1941. Located in the *K'ang-jih ken-chü-ti cheng-ts'e t'iao-li hui-chi, Chin-Ch'a-Chi chih-pu* (Compendium of Policy Statements and Statutes of the Anti-Japanese Border Region, Shansi-Chahar-Hopei Section), pp. 454-456.

[12] "Directive Concerning the Relationship of the Public Security Organs with the Judicial Organs and the Division of Labor in the Cities," February 20, 1946. Located in *T'ai-hang ch'ü i-chiu-ssu-liu nien chung-yao wen-chien hui-chi* (Collection of the Most Important Documents of T'ai-hang Ch'ü in 1946), pp. 134-136.

stances. Evidence substantiates the frequent use of this right, and the Political Security Bureau, rather than the judicial organs, became the principal organ for handling counterrevolutionary cases in Kiangsi. Such an overlap of functions did not occur in the Yenan period.

Despite the limitations of police power, judicial functions were often carried out by other extrajudicial officials. For example, mass trials were frequently conducted by governmental cadre or by a special elected presidium, with no mention of judges, assessors, or other judicial personnel. One source criticized people for thinking a case could not be decided without a formal court trial. He explained that whenever the accuser accuses, the witnesses testify and the accused replies, it is the same as a court.[13] Thus, in Kiangsi and in Yenan, the Communists established a precedent for their post-1949 practice of imprecisely defining procedures and of using a variety of structures to perform judicial functions.

The Weed-Out Traitors Committees (*ch'u-chien wei-yuan-hui*) were another tool specifically designed to deal with traitors. These committees were voluntary mass groups organized at the *hsiang* or city level. In addition to collecting and reporting intelligence information, they were responsible for educating and organizing the masses to discover traitors. To achieve this aim they organized small groups consisting of three to nine members from a given village or city street. The committees could not examine, investigate, or arrest anyone without permission from the police; however, they could apprehend and escort counterrevolutionaries to the Public Security Bureau.[14] Thus, they had little judicial authority and did not become as powerful as their counterparts in the Kiangsi Soviet, the Committees for Suppression of Counter-revolutionaries.

[13] *T'ai-hang ch'ü szu-fa kung-tso kai-k'uang* (Report on the General Situation of Judicial Work in T'ai-hang Ch'ü), (T'ai-hang Administrative Office, May 1946), p. 16.

[14] "Draft Organic Regulation for the Shensi-Kansu-Ninghsia Border Region Weed-Out Traitors Committee" (no date). Located in *Compendium . . . Shensi-Kansu-Ninghsia, op.cit.*, Vol. 3, pp. 746-750.

Who Were the Counterrevolutionaries? (1935-1944)

One of the main differences between the Kiangsi and Yenan periods was the definition of counterrevolutionaries. As noted in the previous chapter, during the Kiangsi period the term was applied to all class enemies (such as the landlords and bourgeoisie) as well as anyone who did not sympathize with the leadership of the Communist Party. In the 1935-1944 period such terminology was reserved solely for military enemies—Japanese aggressors, Chinese traitors, and spies.[15]

Mao's theory of contradictions helps to explain this shift. According to Mao, many contradictions exist in society, but "at every stage in the development of a process, there is only one principal contradiction which plays a leading role."[16] The Japanese aggression against China clearly was the principal contradiction of this period and overshadowed the contradictions of the class struggle predominant in both the period before and after the war. To combat this contradiction, the formation of "a dictatorship of all revolutionary classes over the counter-revolutionaries and collaborators"[17] was suggested. The required government was a "new democracy" in the form of an anti-Japanese united front. Mao explained: "The zigzag course of the Chinese revolution has again led to a united front of four classes with, however, a much wider scope than before, including many representatives of the ruling circles in the upper classes, the national bourgeoisie and the petty bourgeoisie in the middle classes, and all propertyless people in the lower classes so that all classes and social strata of the nation have become members of the alliance and have

[15] For more precise definitions of these terms see "Draft Statute of the Shensi-Kansu-Ninghsia Border Region Governing Punishment of Traitors During War Times," Appendix D, and "Revised Statute Concerning Punishment of Traitors," Appendix K.

[16] Mao Tse-tung, "On Contradiction," August 1937, translated in *Selected Works . . . , op.cit.*, Vol. I, p. 332.

[17] Mao Tse-tung, "On New Democracy," January 1940, translated in *ibid.*, Vol. III, p. 120.

fought resolutely againt Japanese imperialism."[18] Even the bourgeoisie had a dual nature that allowed them to be revolutionary in some circumstances.

The Chinese Communist Party had been greatly weakened in its flight from Kiangsi, and Chiang's proposed Sixth Extermination Campaign against the new base in Yenan might have eliminated them as a meaningful force. From a position of weakness, the Communists needed the widest possible appeal, and Japanese aggression provided them with an appropriate issue. As Van Slyke explains, "The united front defined the enemy in terms as manageable as possible and sought to isolate him. It sought allies and neutrals."[19]

Laws and Punishments (1935-1944)

During the Yenan period the general policy direction was made more specific by promulgation of laws and regulations. In October of 1941, the Border Region Judicial Conference stressed that "our past guerrilla methods cannot be applied to the present situation because everything needs to be formalized; the laws also need to be formalized."[20] It was pointed out that at some places the Party, military units, or mass groups were still arresting people and making decisions based on personal feelings rather than on the law. Furthermore, as one writer pointed out, "Some comrades are stubborn and want to keep the old ways. They think that the border regions are special circumstances and that most of the bourgeoisie laws are not applicable. Therefore, they hope to preserve their past method—guerrillaism."[21] He suggested more education and the use of legal specialists.

[18] *Ibid.*

[19] Lyman Van Slyke, *Enemies and Friends: The United Front in Chinese Communist History* (Stanford: Stanford University Press, 1967), p. 115.

[20] "Oppose Chaos and Establish the Revolutionary Order," *Chiehfang jih-pao* (Liberation Daily), October 12, 1941, p. 4.

[21] Lu Pi-min, *loc.cit.*

In response to the calls for formalization, several types of regulations dealing with counterrevolutionaries were drafted. The most general type was a statute protecting the human and property rights of all inhabitants of the border regions.[22] This gave all people who resisted the Japanese certain rights: freedom of speech, publication, assembly, association, residence, movement, thought and belief (Article 2), and private ownership (Article 3).

People's rights were even protected from encroachment by judicial organs. In contrast to the directives of the Kiangsi period, Article 7 provided that "besides the judicial organs and the public security organs carrying out their responsibilities according to the law, no organ, military unit, or group can arrest, interrogate or punish any person." This restriction did not apply when a criminal was discovered in the act of committing a crime. In such circumstances, others could arrest the criminal and escort him to the Procuracy or Public Security Bureau within twenty-four hours (Article 9). Another directive said specifically that *hsiang* and *ch'ü* heads could arrest criminals only under special circumstances and then they had to turn them over to judicial personnel. Contrary to the practice in the Kiangsi Soviet, *ch'ü* and *hsiang* level personnel could not decide a case or carry out punishment on their own.[23] In dealing with criminals, the judicial organs and the public security organs were to follow legally prescribed measures (Article 8) and were not permitted to insult, to beat, to torture, to force testimony, or to coerce a confession (Article 10). Evidence was to be stressed rather than a reliance solely on testimony (Article 10). To avoid the suffering caused by excessive delay, cases were to be handled within thirty days (Article 11). All cases of the death penalty were to be reported to the border region government for inquiry and approval (Article 19), and in other cases the right of appeal was provided (Article 18).

[22] See Appendix C for translation.
[23] "Directive from the Shensi-Kansu-Ninghsia Border Region High Court . . . ," *op.cit.*, p. 751.

The Shansi-Chahar-Hopei Border Region had a similar, although less specific, policy of protection.[24]

While the general tone of these statutes was of regularization and protection, a few loopholes did exist to allow more judicial discretion. For example, although trials were to be held within thirty days, Article 11 stipulated that "special circumstances when the trial cannot be carried out immediately should not be restricted under this article." Also, approval of the border region government was necessary in all cases of the death sentence, but, according to Article 19, "emergency situations in war times are not restricted under this." Thus, the Communist favorite principle of flexibility was retained.

Other regulations dealt more specifically with traitors (Appendix D, Appendix J, and Appendix K). The "Revised Laws Governing Emergency Crimes Endangering the Republic," translated in Appendix J, was first issued by the Nationalist government and then reissued by the Shansi-Chahar-Hopei Border Region Government. Judicial workers were instructed to follow the Nationalist law so long as it did not conflict with their own statutes. The Nationalist and Communist laws dealing with traitors were quite similar during this period, varying only in minor respects.

One area of modest difference was the penalties. For the most serious crimes, the Nationalists demanded the death penalty, while the Communists added the option of imprisonment. Another small difference was that the Nationalists prescribed a minimum of five years in prison for knowing and concealing traitors (Appendix J, Article 2), while the Communists required a maximum penalty of life imprisonment or a minimum of seven years (Appendix K, Article 4). In addition, the Nationalists, but not the Communists, explicitly stated certain acts that were punishable even if not done

[24] "A Report to the Compatriots of the Border Region on the Accomplishments of the Shansi-Chahar-Hopei Border Region Government in Three Years," January 18, 1941. Located in *Compendium . . . Shansi-Chahar-Hopei, op.cit.*, pp. 7-12.

purposely to help the enemy. Such unintentional crimes included making propaganda for the enemy, transmitting untrue news, and sending letters to enemy countries without permission.

The Communists in both border regions had property confiscation as a supplementary penalty for traitors (Appendix D, Article 4, and Appendix K, Articles 8-13). The Shansi-Chahar-Hopei area even passed a specific regulation for dealing with traitors' property.[25] The general principle was to confiscate only the traitor's property and not that of his family. The confiscated goods and property were to be distributed to the poor and to families of Red Army soldiers.

Comparison of the two Communist statutes dealing with traitors[26] reveals that generally they followed the example set by the 1934 "Statute of the Chinese Soviet Republic Governing Punishment of Counterrevolutionaries." As in Kiangsi, the Communist statutes for the Shensi-Kansu-Ninghsia Border Region and for the Shansi-Chahar-Hopei Border Region both provided punishment for attempted but unaccomplished crimes (Appendix D, Article 6, and Appendix K, Article 6). Those who incited, abetted, or assisted in a crime were treated in the same manner as the main criminal (Appendix D, Article 5, and Appendix K, Article 3). Both statutes contain provisions for special handling of those who voluntarily surrendered and confessed before being discovered (Appendix D, Article 8, and Appendix K, Article 18).

The statute for Shensi-Kansu-Ninghsia[27] contains several provisions adopted from the 1934 statute but not found in the one for Shansi-Chahar-Hopei. For example, reduced punishment was provided for those who were coerced (Article 7) and for those who were fourteen and under (Article 10). The Shensi-Kansu-Ninghsia statute for the first time introduces provisions for reduced or remitted punishment for persons

[25] "Revised Method of Handling Traitors' Property," January 1, 1939. Translated in Appendix F.

[26] See Appendix D and Appendix K.

[27] Appendix D.

eighty or above (Article 10) or for offenses reported before the damage was done (Article 9). This latter provision is akin to the traditional Chinese practice of not requiring punishment in cases where the cosmic harmony had not been disturbed or could be restored.[28]

In the Shansi-Chahar-Hopei Border Region, traitors were to be tried by an organ or military unit having the right of trial by military law (Article 14) and decisions were to be sent to the highest central organ of military affairs for approval. While the statute for the Shensi-Kansu-Ninghsia area does not specify what organ should try the cases, "The Shensi-Kansu-Ninghsia Border Region Statute on Protecting Human and Property Rights" guarantees that "Except in periods of martial law, non-military personnel who commit crimes will not be tried by military law."[29]

Generally, the border region laws concerning traitors were similar to those of the earlier Kiangsi Soviet and to those of the Nationalist government. However, the border region laws were more specific than the Kiangsi laws, as evidenced by the exclusion of the all-encompassing analogy clause.

While leniency was applied in some cases in the Kiangsi Soviet,[30] it became a more important policy instrument in Yenan. Article 8 of the "Draft Statute of the Shensi-Kansu-Ninghsia Border Region Governing Punishment of Traitors During War Times" stipulated that a separate statute con-

[28] Derk Bodde and Clarence Morris, *Law in Imperial China* (Cambridge, Mass.: Harvard University Press, 1967), p. 4.

[29] See Appendix C, Article 13.

[30] Leniency was first mentioned in connection with the A-B League and appears to have been applied mainly to members of the A-B League who revealed valuable information, who had only minor crimes, or who had needed technical skills. Leniency was excluded from the principal laws drafted from 1932 and 1933, including the "Draft Statute of the Chinese Soviet Republic Governing Punishment of Counterrevolutionaries." However, an article dealing with *tzu-shou* was included in the final version of the statute in 1934. The "Written Decisions" published in the newspapers of the period reveal that the Communists faced a problem of recurring crimes among criminals who have been allowed to *tzu-shou*.

cerning voluntary surrender and confession would be enacted.[31]
While no such statute appears in any of the material available
to this author, a statute for the Shansi-Chahar-Hopei Border
Region was available.[32] Moreover, the Shansi-Chahar-Hopei
Border Region Administrative Committee promulgated the
Nationalist government's statute concerning voluntary surrender and confession.[33] However, the editor added a note
saying the border region's own "Separate Statute" was the
main document to be followed.

China had a long tradition of leniency in cases of voluntary
surrender and confession that went back at least as far as the
Former Han dynasty (206 B.C.–A.D. 8).[34] Usually, the term
tzu-shou meant voluntary surrender and confession before
discovery of the offense. As the previously cited study by
Rickett demonstrates, this traditional institution underwent
fundamental changes over time. In traditional codes leniency
was given only in cases such as robbery, where the harmonious
balance in human and cosmic relations could be restored by
repentance, restitution, or compensation. Once harmony was
restored, punishment was unnecessary; therefore, the reward
for voluntary surrender and confession was freedom from
punishment. This aspect of the concept vanished in Republican,
Nationalist, and Communist codes, for *tzu-shou* was applied
even to cases involving death where the harmonious balance
could not be righted. Rickett points out that in Republican
codes remission of punishment largely gave way to mere reduction: "The institution of *tzu-shou* became little more than
a formal statement that an offender who cooperated with the
authorities and made it easy for them by voluntarily surrendering and making a confession would be granted some degree
of leniency. In this sense the institution differs little from the

[31] See Appendix D, Article 8.

[32] Translated in Appendix G.

[33] Translated in Appendix I.

[34] W. Allyn Rickett, "Voluntary Surrender and Confession in Chinese
Law: The Problem of Continuity," *Journal of Asian Studies*, August
1971, p. 798.

informal practice of granting leniency to cooperative offenders in the West."[35]

The articles concerning *tzu-shou* in the "Draft Statute of the Shensi-Kansu-Ninghsia Border Region Governing Punishment of Traitors During War Times"[36] and in the "Revised Laws Governing Emergency Crimes Endangering the Republic"[37] follow this pattern by providing for a reduction of penalty for those who voluntarily surrender and confess. However, the specific statutes dealing with this problem passed both by the Nationalists and by the Shansi-Chahar-Hopei Border Region speak more in the traditional manner of a remittance or suspension of punishment.

Voluntary surrender and confession prior to discovery was usually not sufficient to insure lenient treatment. In addition, the Nationalist and Communist statutes both insisted on some redemptive action as proof of the criminal's repentance. To receive leniency, the Nationalists required the traitor to report evidence concerning other traitors, to report beneficial enemy intelligence, or to surrender carrying arms.[38] The Communists broadened the list of possible redeeming actions to include such activities as helping to retake areas, killing puppet officials, sabotaging the enemy's work, aiding the border region in mobilizing supplies, or making propaganda for the Communists. Finally, the minimum condition necessary for leniency was a sincere confession and repentance substantiated by subsequent behavior. It was promised: "As for those who, because there was no alternative, participated in the puppet propaganda teams, puppet newspapers, puppet New People Associations, and other traitor organizations, regardless of the evilness of their past deception, if they can forsake darkness and surrender to light, correct past crimes, return from the enemy territory, and write a sincere confession, and if their behavior proves they are truly repentant, they will be assigned appropriate work after they are educated."[39] The vagueness of the language

[35] *Ibid.*, p. 814.
[37] Appendix J, Articles 1 and 2.
[39] Appendix G, Article 4.

[36] Appendix D, Article 8.
[38] Appendix I, Article 1.

leaves the exact punishment uncertain. "Education" was often provided in prison and "appropriate work" could have been a synonym for hard labor.

Since part of the success of the leniency policy was due to the indebtedness the criminal felt toward the government, the criminal's attitude, as well as his actions, was considered a measure of repentance. Criminals who said they deserved leniency or implied they felt the government was obligated to treat them leniently were often denied leniency.[40]

Repentance, substantiated by the criminal's actions and attitude, was a necessary but not a sufficient condition for leniency. While not so stated, the nature of the crime appeared to be another variable. Some crimes were so serious that they could not be forgiven. Presumably, the Communists felt they could not trust those who had committed serious crimes against the regime for fear they might repeat such activities.

In addition, the particular circumstances of the case and the environment of the times could also affect the decision. For example, the Communists were more likely to grant leniency for criminals who had served the enemy "because they had no alternative"[41] or because of "a moment's foolishness"[42] under the assumption that traitors who were not dedicated to the enemy's cause could be easily enlisted in the anti-Japanese defense effort. The timing of a case could also be significant, for economic imperatives, more than abstract standards of repentance, motivated the early release of prisoners during much of the Yenan period. Also, after 1935 the united front policy precluded the punishment of groups (e.g., landlords and capitalists) that were severely suppressed in both the Kiangsi and post-war periods. Thus, the Communists used the degree of repentance (as evidenced by the criminal's attitude and actions), the seriousness of the crime, and the circumstances of the case and of the times as the criteria for deter-

[40] This trend was continued in the post-1949 period, see Rickett, "Voluntary Surrender and Confession in Chinese Law," *op.cit.*, p. 811.

[41] Appendix G, Articles 2, 3, and 4.

[42] Appendix G, Article 6.

mining when and how the leniency policy should be selectively applied.

Furthermore, the Communists enlarged the idea of leniency to include reform. Leniency was also offered those who had not confessed prior to discovery, but who later repented and reformed into new men (*tzu-hsin*). In these cases, the criminal's confession, attitude, and actions while in prison were taken as determinants of the degree of reform. The Communists' aim was to obtain all possible information concerning the crimes and then to release the prisoners without fear of repetition of their crimes.

In part, the leniency policy was motivated out of practical necessity. Faced with a rapidly increasing rate of criminal activity due to the war and economic disaster, and forced to rely on local leaders who had been connected with the old regime, the Communists found it impossible to arrest and punish everyone who had committed crimes.

Under these circumstances, leniency served several functions for the Communists. First, it decreased the power of the enemy by neutralizing potential opponents. As explained in one directive, "To win over to the side of the revolution, a criminal who has formerly opposed and harmed the revolution is to decrease to some extent the strength of the counterrevolution and increase that of the revolution."[43] The common people were not sufficiently motivated to run away or to actively oppose the Communist regime as long as they were promised leniency and freedom from punishment. To neutralize the ex-convicts and the more active opposition, they were made to feel that they had been punished more leniently than they would have been otherwise. Whether or not these people were *in fact* treated more leniently is an academic question; the critical factor for the success of the leniency policy was that the people *felt* that they were treated leniently.

A second related function of leniency was to stabilize the social order. By granting leniency to many, the Communists

<hr />

[43] "Directive from the Shensi-Kansu-Ninghsia Border Area High Court Concerning Each Hsien's Judicial Work," *op.cit.*, p. 756.

were able to take control from the old regime with a minimum of confusion, fear, and disruption.

In addition, leniency increased the Communists' flexibility of action, for it allowed them to alter their position for individual cases without changing general policy. Jerome Cohen suggests that leniency is sometimes given as justification for releasing criminals when all the requisites of conviction are not met.[44] Such a use preserved the credibility of the regime while allowing flexible responses to individual situations.

Leniency also functioned to motivate prisoners to participate in education and production efforts. One Westerner imprisoned by the Chinese observed: "It is not the fear of sanctions that stimulates the prisoners; there is little punishment because of work. The method is positive. The administration keeps alive the hope of being rewarded, of having one's sentence reduced; it hints at the possibility of an amnesty for good workers. This arouses competition among the more energetic prisoners."[45]

More importantly, leniency functioned to conserve scarce resources. Many minor criminals and informants were simply released after a warning against continuation of their activities, while others obtained substantially reduced prison terms. While conserving resources, the policy of leniency provided important by-products—useful intelligence information, a list of possible offenders, and a feeling of gratitude among the affected criminals.

To turn from leniency to the unique problems of prison maintenance in war areas, a special statute specified special procedures for treating counterrevolutionaries during periods of martial law.[46] Two areas that were subject to attack during periods of fighting could come under martial law—areas that came under alert and areas contiguous to the war zone (Article

[44] Jerome Cohen, *The Criminal Process in the People's Republic of China, 1949-1963: An Introduction* (Cambridge, Mass.: Harvard University Press, 1968), p. 41.

[45] *White Book on Forced Labour and Concentration Corps in the People's Republic of China* (Commission Internationale Contre le Regime Concentrationnaire, 1954), p. 198.

[46] "Draft Statute of the Shensi-Kansu-Ninghsia Border Region Concerning Martial Law During War," 1939, translated in Appendix E.

3). Once martial law was proclaimed, the military judicial organs had the right to handle several varieties of cases, including traitor cases (Article 5). As in most Western societies, certain civilian rights could be interrupted, such as the freedoms of assembly, press, speech, and written communications. A residence could be searched and property could be destroyed, but compensation was required (Article 6).

Furthermore, the fighting necessitated special provisions for temporarily handling prisoners.[47] Paroling and releasing prisoners with someone's guarantee[48] were encouraged (Article 2) since it was impossible to protect the prisoners in the midst of battle. The list of criminals who could be so treated was broadened to include those with an original sentence of five years or less, those with remaining terms of less than three years, and those over sixty who were sick (Article 3). When the fighting made guarding the prisons impossible, prisoners with a maximum sentence of ten years were to be temporarily released, while those convicted for life or more than ten years were to be moved to prisons in rear areas (Article 4). However, if there was not sufficient time to move them, they too could be released temporarily. Prisoners temporarily released under these provisions were to surrender to authorities within ten days after the suspension of martial law or be considered escaped convicts. People held in detention centers were to be treated analogously (Article 5).

Information on the punishments given for specific counter-revolutionary crimes was difficult to obtain since the statutes did not specify exact punishments. Furthermore, while some sources discuss punishments, the data generally are not classified according to punishments for a given crime.

According to one source, the punishments given in the border regions included death, life in prison, prison terms,

[47] "Method for Temporarily Handling Criminals in Prison in Extraordinary Times," translated in Appendix H.

[48] Guaranteeing allowed a criminal to be released before completing his sentence, provided a certain number of people would sign a guarantee for his behavior. This practice, which followed a pre-modern example, had been temporarily suspended by the Communists in Kiangsi during the 1933-1934 crisis period.

detention, confiscation of property, hard labor, fines, and reprimands.[49] Evidently life in prison was a possible penalty, especially in the Shansi-Chahar-Hopei Border Region; however, reportedly it was seldom used. Most other sources indicate that in the Shensi-Kansu-Ninghsia Border Region five years was the maximum prison sentence until 1943, when it was changed to ten years.[50] This latter policy was consistent with the practice in the Kiangsi Soviet. Fines were imposed infrequently, for it was felt that paying a fine had very little educational value and often stimulated the criminal to commit another crime to redeem the lost money. Also, fines did not give equality in punishment since the rich were more able to pay than the poor.[51]

The statistics for this period are less than optimal, since they come from varying geographic areas and time periods and from limited sample coverage, all of which makes comparison difficult. Because of these problems and the inadequate reporting techniques used in most areas, results often do not cluster in predicted patterns, and conclusions are tenuous at best. Nevertheless, the statistics are interesting and do suggest a few observations.

Table 4.1 shows a breakdown of the criminal cases in more than 20 *hsien* of the Shensi-Kansu-Ninghsia Border Region from 1939 through the first six months of 1941. Although only 44 individuals were classified as traitors, several of the other crimes are included in the description of traitorous activities in the "Draft Statute of the Shensi-Kansu-Ninghsia Border Region Governing Punishment of Traitors during War Times." The author's calculation[52] shows 553 cases, or 12 per-

[49] Yang Ch'i, "A Preliminary Discussion of the Development of the People's Criminal Law during the New Democratic Stage," *Fa-hsüeh* (Jurisprudence), Shanghai, No. 3, 1957, p. 43.

[50] Ma Hsi-wu, *op.cit.*, p. 8.

[51] Chu Ying, "Special Points Concerning Punishment in the Border Regions," *Chieh-fang jih-pao* (Liberation Daily), October 26, 1941, p. 4.

[52] The following categories were included in this calculation: traitor, banditry, sabotage of the border region, obstructing military units, obstructing mobilization, endangering public affairs, offenses against secrets, endangering national currency, and concealing criminals.

TABLE 4.1
Types of Criminal Cases[53]

Crime	1939	1940	First Half 1941	Total
Traitor	28	15	1	44
Banditry	48	85	24	157
Sabotage of the border region	0	99	29	128
Obstructing military units	0	21	3	24
Obstructing mobilization	0	27	11	38
Running away	88	126	33	247
Corruption	84	115	36	235
Opium	361	644	153	1,157
Gambling	164	230	303	697
Violation of laws and decrees	56	91	68	215
Larceny	104	175	150	429
Fraud	29	34	16	79
Bodily injury	60	53	54	167
Homicide	15	45	26	86
Neglect of duty	20	34	9	63
False charges	15	21	23	59
Looting	0	12	27	39
Criminal appropriation	18	15	18	51
Disobeying military discipline	24	8	4	36
Obstructing freedom	24	70	33	127
Interfering with marriage and family	35	56	56	147
Damaging public mores	24	40	27	91
Endangering public affairs	52	10	10	72
Offenses against reputation or credit	3	9	6	18
Offenses against secrets	0	7	2	9
Endangering national currency	18	15	9	42
Disturbing public order	1	19	1	21
Counterfeiting seals	4	10	3	17
False measurement	2	0	1	3
Concealing criminals	25	11	3	39
Causing damage	2	6	3	11
Public danger	1	2	0	3
Deserting	0	1	1	2
Totals	1,304	2,106	1,143	4,553

[53] Hai-yen, "The Border Region Judiciary," *Chieh-fang jih-pao* (Liberation Daily), October 13, 1941, p. 4.

cent of the total, which could be categorized as traitorous. Another source claimed that the Shensi-Kansu-Ninghsia High Court reported that 30 first-trial organs under it handled 10,112 cases from 1938-1943, and 26 percent of the criminal cases reportedly involved traitors.[54] In part, this greater percentage may be explained by the longer time period covered. Apparently the number of traitors increased markedly in 1942 and 1943. For example, in T'ai-hang Ch'ü cases involving traitors increased to 2,681 in 1942 and to 7,853 in 1943.[55] This increase in the number of traitors coincided directly with the Japanese scorched-earth policy against the border regions. As the Japanese turned their offensive against the KMT-controlled areas in 1944, these cases declined to 1,779.

According to this limited data, the number of traitors brought before the courts apparently varied between 12 and 26 percent of all criminal cases. This percentage is significantly less than the 70 percent accounted for by counterrevolutionary cases in the Kiangsi Soviet, and probably reflects the narrower definition of counterrevolutionary activity under the united front policy. Also, the difference may be attributable to the use of the judicial system to deal with a wider range of criminal activity.

Table 4.2 shows the punishments given for the crimes listed in Table 4.1. Since the crimes and punishments are not cross-classified, the specific punishments given traitors are unclear. The fact that the innocent category represented only 3 percent of the total cases tried by the judiciary substantiates the earlier conclusion that the Public Security Bureau was the primary decision-maker in determining the guilt or innocence of criminals.

By assuming that only cases of traitors and homicide were punishable by death and that all cases of homicide were punished by death, one can estimate that 60 out of the 553 traitors

[54] Ma Hsi-wu, *op.cit.*, p. 8.

[55] Even considering the intense struggle for control of this strategic area, these numbers appear rather large for such a small geographic area; see *T'ai hang Ch'ü szu fa . . . , op.cit.*, p. 19.

TABLE 4.2

Punishments in Criminal Cases[56]

Punishments	1939	1940	First Half 1941	Total
Innocent	6	59	84	149
Education and criticism	414	407	213	1,034
Exiled	0	12	8	20
Disenfranchised		(unclear)		
Fined	69	119	122	310
Confiscated	34	63	15	112
Imprisonment				
Half year or less	547	894	507	1,948
One year or less	102	230	104	436
Two years or less	53	124	36	213
Three years or less	13	67	17	97
Four years or less	5	10	10	25
Five years or less	12	30	15	57
Death	49	91	6	146
Other	0	0	6	6
Total	1,304	2,106	1,143	4,553

(or 11 percent) were punished by death. On the other hand, if we assume that only traitors were given the death sentence, then, at the maximum, 26 percent of the traitors were punished by death. Data from the Shansi-Hopei-Honan-Shantung Border Region for 1938-1942 showed that 25.5 percent of the cases involved the death penalty. Furthermore, it was stated that most of these cases involved traitors and enemy spies.[57]

Accepting the above analysis, one concludes that probably 11 to 26 percent of the counterrevolutionary cases resulted in the death sentence. Since the data from the Kiangsi period suggested that 25 percent of the counterrevolutionaries received

[56] Hai-yen, "The Border Region Judiciary," *Chieh-fang jih-pao* (Liberation Daily), October 14, 1941, p. 4.

[57] Yang Chi, *op.cit.*, p. 43.

death, the percentage appears to be somewhat lower during the united front period. Nevertheless, the percentage remained numerically significant, which suggests that the Communists found a sizable minority of the counterrevolutionaries to be non-reformable.

Also of interest is the introduction of a category called "education and criticism," which accounted for 23 percent of the total punishments. While not clearly defined, this category, together with imprisonment, which accounts for 61 percent of the total, substantiates the Communists' increased emphasis on education and reform of criminals. Because of the frequency of such reform methods, they must have been used for a wide range of crimes, including counterrevolutionary activity. While statistics for hard labor were not differentiated, they were probably included in the imprisonment category, a fact reflecting the increased emphasis on prison production.

In summary, the data suggest that the Communists adopted a dichotomous policy toward the punishment of counterrevolutionaries. The majority, who were considered educable, faced punishments of education and criticism, disenfranchisement, confiscation, or reform through labor in prison. Moreover, the terms of imprisonment were short. The minority, probably constituting 11 to 26 percent of the counterrevolutionaries, were considered uneducable and were exterminated. Thus, the frequency of punishments of counterrevolutionaries in terms of severity tended to form a bi-modal distribution rather than the more common uni-modal distribution, with counterrevolutionaries either being treated leniently or being suppressed.

Laws in Practice (1935-1944)

In counterrevolutionary cases the courtroom trial was frequently bypassed in favor of the mass trial (*kung-shen*), which had been developed during the Kiangsi period. The term *kung-shen* had been broadened to include at least three methods of conducting a mass trial. At the mass public trial (*ch'ün-*

chung kung-shen-hui) everyone was encouraged to attend and to express opinions, but not given an actual vote in the decision. The second type was a meeting to announce the decision (*hsüan-p'an ta-hui*) and to inform people of the nature of the crime and the reason for the prescribed punishment. The third was a mass trial attended by representatives of mass groups or military units (*tai-piao kung-shen-hui*). These representatives were to return and report the events of the trial to their comrades. Of course, these three methods were different from a public trial (*kung-k'ai shen-p'an*), which was simply judicial procedures open for public attendance.[58]

Chieh-fang jih-pao includes some vivid examples of such mass trials. These meetings were often held in connection with the Guard Against Traitors Movement launched in 1943 in response to the increased number of traitors. To publicize the Guard Against Traitors Movement, mobilization meetings were held, such as the one attended by over 1,000 at a normal school in Sui-te.[59] At the nine-day meeting, teachers, parents, and students were told how young people were forced to make propaganda, yell slogans, spread rumors, and write wall posters for the secret agents. The meeting ended with the signing of a petition urging a struggle against the secret agents. The targets of this particular meeting were KMT secret agents, rather than the Japanese. The KMT was charged with sending secret agents into the border regions to disrupt and often to join with the Japanese in attacking the Communists.

The first mobilization meeting was usually followed by a second meeting to conduct mass trials of the captured secret agents. In Sui-te the follow-up meeting was held in an open field under a huge white canvas.[60] Twenty-five hundred and eighty people, mainly representatives from surrounding local governments, military units, schools, and mass organizations,

[58] Ma Hsi-wu, *op.cit.*, p. 12.

[59] "A Demonstration of the Leniency Policy of the Party," *Chieh-fang jih-pao* (Liberation Daily), September 22, 1943, pp. 1-2.

[60] "The Masses of Sui-te *Fen-ch'ü* Hold a Representative Assembly," *Chieh-fang jih-pao* (Liberation Daily), October 2, 1943, p. 1.

attended the week-long meetings. Banners of all colors deco-
rated the streets leading to the meeting. The meeting tent was
draped with a huge cloth with red letters proclaiming the title
and purpose of the gathering. To the left of the platform was
hung a large painting that depicted people in a swamp laying
down their weapons and reaching for the Communists to pull
them out. To the right of the platform, another painting
showed KMT secret agents kicking large numbers of youth
into a deep, bottomless pit.

The meeting began at 9 a.m. with the election of a nineteen-
man presidium. One member of the presidium was made
chairman; he explained the significance of the meeting, prom-
ising that anyone who confessed and repented would not be
punished but would be released. After many people had gone
to the stage to confess, the audience demanded that the mayor
also confess. At first the mayor reported only minor crimes but
finally he made a full confession. The chairman praised the
mayor's sincere confession, but explained that since his crimes
were very serious, he would be dismissed as mayor and other
punishment would be considered later.[61]

Similar meetings were held elsewhere. For example, Kao
Kang spoke to a rally of 5,000 in Yenan.[62] He promised guns
for the area most successful in finding spies. His speech was
reportedly interrupted continually by replies, slogans, and ap-
plause from the audience. Twenty-three secret agents seated
next to the platform came forward one after another to give
confessions. This emotional meeting showed the common
people's lack of understanding of the leniency policy, for they
demanded death for a spy, Huang Liu, who had given a
complete confession. When Huang described his specific
crimes, the soldiers raised their red-tasseled spears toward him
and yelled, "Kill him, kill him!" The *hsien* magistrate had to

[61] "Wang Yü-ch'i Utilized His Position as Mayor to Develop the
Special Agents' Betrayal of Youth," *Chieh-fang jih-pao* (Liberation
Daily), October 2, 1943, pp. 1-2.

[62] "Yenan Hsien Opens the Guard Against Traitors Movement,"
Chieh-fang jih-pao (Liberation Daily), September 21, 1943, p. 1.

explain the leniency policy to the people several different times to calm them. The main purpose of these mass rallies was to correct this type of policy misunderstanding. At the conclusion of the testimonies, those who had confessed and promised to reform were asked to provide a written confession. Practical methods for discovering spies and secret agents were then discussed. Finally, since it was getting dark, the meeting ended with a review of the troops.

Some meetings were conducted more like regular trials with a judge and assessors.[63] This type of meeting usually began with a specially selected chairman announcing the purpose of the meeting. After the judge and assessors were seated, representatives from the masses and military units would accuse the criminal, who could then stand and confess his crimes. For example, a young man, Liu Ch'ing-yun, stood before the judge, too afraid to speak. Finally, he said brokenly: "I was wrong. What I did as a traitor dishonored my ancestors. From now on I will change, I swear."[64] He then revealed the crimes he had committed while young and promised to reform and carry out the laws of the government and resist the Japanese until death. Liu vowed that if he did not do this he was willing to be punished by death and to have all his property confiscated. The audience shouted that Liu should be treated leniently. It was common practice for the spectators to voice their opinions before the verdict was read by the chairman.

Other trials of traitors were simply conducted publicly in military courts.[65] While the masses did not yell and shout slogans, as in the mass trials, they were free to question the criminal during the proceedings. The defendant and witnesses testified and the judge questioned them. Agnes Smedley describes the chief judge of one such court as a young officer with five years of regular schooling. His chief education had been in the army. She says, "Of ordinary law he knew nothing, but

[63] "A Mass Trial of Important Special Agents and Traitors," *Chieh-fang jih-pao* (Liberation Daily), September 7, 1943, pp. 1-2.

[64] *Ibid.*

[65] Agnes Smedley, *Battle Hymn of China* (New York: Alfred A. Knopf, 1943), p. 483.

he knew patriots, he knew traitors, and he knew politicians who would be traitors if they could."[66]

Other methods besides trials were used during the Guard Against Traitors Movement. In one village, groups of ten families were organized in a manner similar to the old *pao-chia* system, to guarantee that no spies existed among them.[67] At another place, repentance statements of people who voluntarily surrendered and confessed were posted on proclamation stands at major intersections. Also, people were encouraged to drop anonymous opinions concerning the proper punishments for traitors into conveniently placed opinion boxes. In addition, government personnel were sent among the people to listen to their opinions.[68]

Mistakes in application of the law were attributed to the limited legal knowledge of the judicial cadres.[69] The High Courts of the Shensi-Kansu-Ninghsia Border Region accused the judicial workers of beating and cursing the masses, making random arrests, occupying land and houses at will, and conducting investigations by beating the suspect.[70] One judicial worker who used corporal punishment during questioning of a suspect was sentenced to only one month of hard labor.[71] Cases of the people killing secret agents and traitors rather than turning them in to authorities were also reported.[72]

In a few cases, cadre were accused of being too lenient. For

[66] *Ibid.*

[67] "Ten Thousand Assemble in T'ai-hang, Wu-tung Hsien for a Mass Trial of Surrendered KMT Special Agents," *Chieh-fang jih-pao* (Liberation Daily), August 16, 1943, p. 1.

[68] "Under Our Leniency Policy Puppet Personnel in P'u-yang Continuously Return," *Chieh-fang jih-pao* (Liberation Daily), December 26, 1944, p. 1.

[69] Lu Pi-min, *loc.cit.*

[70] "Directive from the Shensi-Kansu-Ninghsia Border Region High Court . . . ," *op.cit.*, p. 751.

[71] "Border Region Judicial Organs Strictly Enforce the Protection of Human and Property Rights," *Chieh-fang jih-pao* (Liberation Daily), December 31, 1942, p. 1.

[72] Nym Wales, *Red Dust* (Stanford: Stanford University Press, 1952), p. 106.

example, in 1940 after the "Statute for the Protection of Human and Property Rights" had been promulgated, a large number of traitors with serious crimes were mistakenly released.[73] Fewer mentions are made of mistakes during the 1935-1944 period, which implies either that fewer were made or that their behavior had become accepted.

Summary

Two of the main differences between the treatment of counterrevolutionaries in the Yenan and the Kiangsi periods are an increased emphasis on both leniency and regularization. During the 1935 to 1941 period, the Communists enjoyed a relatively secure environment, as a result of the unified leadership of the CCP under Mao, a united front with the KMT, and remoteness from Japanese attacks. In this environment, the Communists organized a judicial system and promulgated specific statutes for dealing with traitors. With the increased demand for formalization and regularization, law was no longer simply defined as the wishes of the masses. While there was still some reliance on extra-judicial organs, their functions were much more limited than in the Kiangsi period. For example, the power of the Public Security Bureau was restricted considerably.

Learning from the Kiangsi experience, the Communists were more cautious not to offend large or powerful segments of the population. The terminology changed from talk of counterrevolutionaries to the more specific definition of traitors. Moreover, traitors were selectively punished under a policy of leniency for those willing to cooperate with the Communists. By continuing to kill those deemed too politically dangerous, the Communists succeeded in inculcating a feeling of leniency among those spared. Leniency served the dual purpose of obtaining greater cooperation from the spared prisoner and of picturing the Communists as lenient, paternalistic leaders.

From 1941 to 1943 the breakdown of the united front and

[73] *T'ai-hang Ch'ü szu-fa* . . . , *op.cit.*, p. 30.

the Japanese attacks left the Communists besieged by both the KMT and the Japanese. As in Kiangsi, the Communists stressed mass line techniques, especially mass trials for traitors during crisis periods. In contrast to the earlier examples from Kiangsi, the mass trials showed much greater organization and leadership. The trials frequently ended with lenient punishment rather than with immediate execution, as in the Kiangsi Soviet. Rather than sticking stubbornly to past methods, the Communists appeared to learn and experiment during the Yenan period. While there was a definite continuity in both organization and methods between the two periods, the difference was mainly in maturity—the student revolutionary was becoming a political pro.

CHAPTER V. Civil War, 1945-1949

Introduction

THE IMMINENCE of the civil war became apparent in 1946 following a brief interlude (1944-1946) during which the uncertainty of the post-war situation stifled drastic policy changes. The Communists were once again involved in a bitter struggle for political and territorial control of much of China. The civil war period offers a critical test of the role of the environment in affecting the law. As noted in previous periods, the definition of counterrevolutionary activity changed to reflect the political and economic environment. It is important to consider what definitional differences occurred as a consequence of the renewed struggle with the KMT. To ascertain whether the environment is a sufficient explanation for changes, the following types of questions will be examined in this chapter. With the eruption of the civil war, did the Communists by-pass their laws and revert to an ad hoc legal approach, as in Kiangsi? To what degree did they appear to have modified their methods in response to past experiences? Did the trends toward regularization and leniency fall prey to temporary exigencies or did they exhibit some permanence?

Environment (1945-1949)

Even before the war with Japan ended in August 1945, attention turned to consideration of post-war KMT-CCP relations. The Seventh Congress of the CCP, which was held from April to June 1945, adopted a flexible policy of "coalition government"—which could mean either coalition *with* the KMT, or with minor parties and liberals *against* the KMT. At the end of World War II, Nationalist troops outnumbered the Communists 3 million to 1 million, and American war aid of $1.5 billion also gave the KMT superiority in military equipment.

From 1945 to 1948 the United States provided another $2 billion in aid.[1]

President Truman sent General Marshall to China in December 1945 to negotiate an end to the civil war. The Chinese were tired of war and longed for peace, and at first Marshall's efforts appeared successful. On January 10, 1946 a cease-fire agreement was announced. The Political Consultative Conference, which met January 10-31, 1946, with the CCP represented, adopted a program for political reform unfavorable for the KMT. On February 25, 1946 reorganization of the military and integration of the Communist forces into the national army was announced.

It soon became evident that more than paper agreements were necessary to end the civil war. The implementation of the above policies stalled, and gradually both sides became more and more intransigent in their demands. In April the Russian troops withdrew from Manchuria and the Communist and Nationalist troops clashed in an attempt to take over this strategic area. Finally, the Nationalists openly attacked the CCP and defiantly convened the National Assembly. On November 19, 1946, the Communists' chief negotiator, Chou En-lai, departed for Yenan, and with him all hope of a peaceful settlement of the civil war. As one authority on this period summarizes, the attempts at settlement were doomed to failure, for the impasses between the CCP and KMT "reflect an absence of principles shared by the two sides and showed the existence of basic conflicts of interest."[2]

By June 1948 the CCP roughly equaled the Nationalists in men, rifles, and cannons. The showdown of the civil war was a battle at the end of 1948 for control of the Huai River basin, where four Nationalist armies were surrounded and forced to surrender. Tientsin and Peking surrendered in January 1949. In April the Communists crossed the Yangtze; in

[1] John K. Fairbank, Edwin O. Reischauer, Albert Craig, *East Asia: The Modern Transformation* (Boston: Houghton Mifflin Co., 1965), p. 859.

[2] Tang Tsou, *America's Failure in China* (Chicago: University of Chicago Press, 1963), Vol. 1, p. 403.

May they took Shanghai; in October, Canton; and finally in November, Chungking, thereby forcing Chiang Kai-shek and the National Government leaders to flee to Taiwan.

Organization (1945-1949)

With the end of World War II, the necessity for the mask of the united front and the subservience of the border regions to the National Government ended. As the civil war progressed, the Communists expanded their control into other "liberated areas," setting up courts that were regional in nature with no central supreme judicial organ. Usually the courts were on a two-trial, three-level system. An example is the North China region's judicial system, which consisted of the following three grades: (1) *hsien* or municipal courts, (2) provincial or directly controlled municipal courts, and (3) the North China People's Courts. Each court, as in the past, still had a judicial committee to discuss and examine important cases.[3] A similar court structure was also in effect in the northeast.[4] In T'ai-hang Ch'ü the courts were organized on a three-trial, three-level system. Cases could be tried or appealed at each of the following levels: *hsien* or municipal, commissioner's office, and administrative office.[5]

Rather than relying on the above judicial organs, the Communists established a separate organizational structure to deal with Japanese war criminals. In Yenan on November 5, 1945, a Chinese Commission of Inquiry Concerning War Criminals (*chan-fan tiao-ch'a wei-yuan-hui*) was formed with 22 representatives from various areas.[6] Branches of this commission

---

[3] *Hua-pei jen-min cheng-fu fa-ling hui-pien* (Compendium of Laws of the North China People's Government), Vol. 1, pp. 11-12.

[4] Shao-chuan Leng, *Justice in Communist China* (Dobbs Ferry, New York: Oceana Publications, 1967), p. 22.

[5] *T'ai-hang ch'ü i-chiu-ssu-liu nien chung-yao wen-chien hui-chi* (Collection of the Most Important Documents of T'ai-hang Ch'ü in 1946), p. 147.

[6] "The Establishment of a Chinese Commission of Inquiry Concerning War Criminals," *Chieh-fang jih-pao* (Liberation Daily), November 8, 1945, p. 1.

were to be established by local governments to deal with war criminals. In the Shansi-Chahar-Hopei Border Region a similar Committee for Handling War Criminals (*chan-fan shen-li wei-yuan-hui*) was established and empowered to call special tribunals (*t'e-pieh fa-t'ing*) to try Japanese war criminals.[7] In Shantung province, war criminals were to be tried by military tribunals.[8]

Other special judicial organizations were formed to handle cases involving land reform. With the switch from a united front policy calling for class unity to a civil war policy of class struggle, the moderate land reform program of rent and interest reduction that the Communists followed during the war was replaced with a policy of radical agrarian reform similar to that of Kiangsi days. The "Outline of the Land Law" of October 10, 1947 called for "land to the tillers" (Article 1) and confiscation of landlords' and rich peasants' property without compensation (Article 8). "People's tribunals" were set up as ad hoc judicial organs to punish the enemies of the land policy (Article 13).[9] Their main function was to conduct mass trials, struggle meetings, and accusation rallies.

Who Were the Counterrevolutionaries? (1945-1949)

As the Communist Party reverted from a war of national resistance to a revolutionary struggle, it likewise reverted to the

---

[7] "A Trial to Suppress Nine Japanese War Criminals Who Under Kuomintang Special Agents' Orders, Hid and Committed Sabotage," *Chieh-fang jih-pao* (Liberation Daily), September 25, 1946, p. 2.

[8] "The Political Department and the Headquarters of the Shantung Military Region Announces Organic Regulations of Shantung Province for All Levels of Court Martial Tribunals," August 17, 1945. Located in *Shan-tung sheng cheng-fu chi Shan-tung chün-ch'ü kung-pu chih ko-chung t'iao-li kang-yao pan-fa hui-pien* (Collected Statutes, Regulations, and Outlines Issued by the Shantung Provincial Government and the Shantung Military Region), (Shantung Ch'ü Administrative Office, August 29, 1945), pp. 38-39.

[9] Leng, *op.cit.*, p. 20.

counterrevolutionary terminology of the Kiangsi Soviet. The CCP was involved in an armed struggle to seize political control of the nation, and all who opposed this attempt, such as KMT members, were considered counterrevolutionaries. Furthermore, the Communists considered their land reform program a vital part of their revolutionary strategy; therefore, those (i.e., landlord, gentry and bourgeois classes) who opposed the land revolution were also considered counterrevolutionaries. Finally, as in the 1935-1944 period, the term "counterrevolutionary" also encompassed war criminals and traitors. This category included Japanese agents, Chinese agents for the Japanese, and Chinese who served in the puppet regimes established by the Japanese in the areas under their control.

War criminals were specifically defined in the "Temporary Statute of Shantung Province for Punishing War Criminals and Traitors."[10] Generally speaking, only those who were commanding officers, principal conspirators, or instigators in serious activities that sabotaged the resistance effort were to be severely punished. Such activities included the following: organizing feudalistic societies and superstitious groups to work for the enemy; causing loss to military, political, economic, cultural, and communication facilities; organizing surrender; stealing secret information; seizing men to work for the enemy; plundering military weapons and supplies; and running away. Also included as war criminals were those who had taken advantage of the situation to burn, kill, or otherwise harm the masses, to create internal disorder, or to massacre or mistreat prisoners of war.

Laws and Punishments (1945-1949)

New regulations similar to those of the border regions in the previous period, but more specific in content, were passed in the newly liberated areas to deal with war criminals and traitors. These regulations dealt with protection of human and

---

[10] See Appendix L, Article 2.

property rights,[11] punishment of counterrevolutionaries, confiscation of property, and voluntary surrender and confession.

As in the previous period, only the leaders and those with especially serious crimes were to be punished severely. Their punishment could range from death to ten[12] or fifteen[13] years in prison and disenfranchisement. Those who were coerced, who had been motivated by economic difficulties, or who later made a contribution to the resistance were to be freed from punishment and disenfranchisement.[14] The similarity to earlier policies on this subject is seen in the "Temporary Statute of Shantung Province for Punishing Criminals and Traitors" (Appendix L). One exception was that those who concealed, hid, or abetted criminals were sentenced to three to ten years in prison, while in both the Kiangsi and Yenan periods, they had been treated equally with the main criminal (see Appendix B, Article 30; Appendix D, Article 5; Appendix A, Article 3; and Appendix L, Article 4). Also in contrast to previous policy, *any* person was given the right to report, investigate, and arrest war criminals (Appendix L, Article 5).

As in the past, criminal sentences were not considered sufficient punishment, and the criminal was also forced to suffer humiliation. Before serious war criminals were punished, they were to go before a mass accusation meeting during which they had to admit their mistakes and compensate people for their losses. Even those whose crimes were not serious enough

[11] "Provisional Draft Regulation for the Protection of Human and Property Rights in the Northeast Liberated Area," May 8, 1948. Located in *Kung-fei fan-tung wen-chien hui-pien* (A Collection of Bandit Reactionary Documents), June 1948, pp. 125-128.

[12] "Temporary Statute of Shantung Province for Punishing War Criminals and Traitors," August 15, 1945. Translated in Appendix L.

[13] "Directive Concerning Handling of War Criminals," December 10, 1945. Located in *T'ai-hang ch'ü i-chiu-ssu-liu nien . . . , op.cit.*, p. 140.

[14] "Principles for Handling Members of Puppet Troops and Puppet Organizations and a Directive Regarding Matters of Importance During the Implementation Period," April 8, 1946. Located in *T'ai-hang ch'ü i-chiu-ssu-liu nien . . . , op.cit.*, p. 137.

to warrant imprisonment had to confess their crimes before their peers and receive approval for their release. However, specialists with needed skills were not thus humiliated.[15]

In contrast to the infrequent use of fines during the united front period, fines were levied more often in the civil war period. Those whom the masses did not find offensive could pay a fine instead of serving a prison sentence, and those who were guilty of profiteering from the war were *ordered* to pay fines instead of serving in prison.[16] In part, greater economic scarcity may account for the change in policy. However, another explanation is that wealth redistribution was not a primary objective during the united front; consequently, fines were not frequently imposed. On the more practical side, people could not as easily flee to avoid the fines during the civil war period as during the united front period.

During this period, appeals were granted and encouraged for all except traitors, special agents, and local despots. While denied the right of appeal, these criminals were given some protection by the requirement that all cases involving sentences of ten years or more were to be reported to a higher level for inquiry and approval. Traitors sentenced to less than ten years had five days to request that a superior examine the case. If no request was made, the judgment was considered correct.[17] However, as usual an exception was made for areas of intense struggle or areas involved in the *fan-shen* movement.[18] In these

[15] "Directive Concerning Handling of War Criminals," *op.cit.*, pp. 140-142.

[16] *Ibid*.

[17] "Communique on Renewed Regulations for the Trial and Inquiry System," August 11, 1946. Located in *T'ai-hang ch'ü i-chiu-ssu-liu nien . . . , op.cit.*, pp. 147-149.

[18] William Hinton defines this term in his book, *Fanshen: A Documentary of Revolution in a Chinese Village* (Vintage Books, 1968). He says it literally means "to turn the body," or "to turn over." To the Chinese peasants it meant "to stand up, to throw off the landlord yoke, to gain land, stock, implements and houses. But it meant much more than this. It meant to throw off superstition and study science, . . . to do away with appointed village magistrates and replace them with elected councils. It meant to enter a new world."

cases the commissioner's office could authorize lower level cadre to conduct immediate executions upon the approval of the *hsien* magistrate. A report to superiors after the fact was considered a sufficient check. If a mistake was made in such cases, the *hsien* magistrate would be held responsible.[19]

Also in the tradition of previous periods, leniency was promised for those who voluntarily surrendered and confessed before discovery (*tzu-shou*).[20] The leniency could be either a reduced or remitted sentence. As in the past, some positive action of redemption was required, the minimum being to tell all one knew about the enemy or puppet organizations and to reveal thoroughly all the facts of one's crime. One provision, not seen previously, provided for release, after serving half their sentence, for those who had voluntarily surrendered, confessed, and shown themselves to be repentant.[21] Furthermore, people who had surrendered voluntarily and confessed were not simply released but were placed under the supervision of their spouse or a lineal relative, plus two or more persons who signed a guarantee for them.[22] Guarantors were held personally accountable for the actions of the released and could even be arrested in their place.

Confiscation was considered appropriate for any property directly occupied by the Japanese or the puppet personnel,[23] any private wealth that was used in enemy activities,[24] and wealth obtained by plunder or blackmail under the protection

[19] "Communique on Renewed Regulations for the Trial and Inquiry System," *loc.cit.*

[20] "Temporary Statute of Shantung Province Concerning Traitors Who Voluntarily Surrender and Confess (*tzu-shou*) and Reform Themselves into New Men (*tzu-hsin*)," August 15, 1945. Located in *Shan-tung sheng cheng-fu . . .* , *op.cit.*, pp. 33-35.

[21] *Ibid.*, Article 4.

[22] *Ibid.*, Article 5.

[23] "Method for Handling Enemy and Puppet Property," August 15, 1945, Article 2. Located in *Shan-tung sheng cheng-fu . . .* , *op.cit.*, pp. 35-37.

[24] *Ibid.*, Article 3.

of the enemy or puppet power.[25] Criminals convicted of the crimes under Article 2 of the Shantung Statute concerning war criminals and traitors (Appendix L) were to have their property confiscated. Anyone who tried to hide property or to run away would be punished more severely and have more wealth confiscated.[26] On the other hand, those traitors who voluntarily surrendered and confessed might have less confiscated.[27] In general, all confiscated items were to be handled by the local government and immediately put to use by the new regime.[28]

Laws in Practice (1945-1949)

The statistics for the 1945-1949 period are even more limited than for the earlier periods, thereby precluding any definitive statements. The critical question concerning the civil war period is the degree to which conflicting policies were followed. During the 1945-1949 period, legal policies were a mixture of past techniques. Curiously, the special tribunals, mass trials with immediate execution and broad powers of arrest—all methods similar to those utilized in the Kiangsi Soviet—occurred simultaneously with the right of appeal, leniency, and superior approval prior to execution of sentence. Accurate judgment on the relative significance of these practices would necessitate a quantitative analysis of the frequency of each technique. Unfortunately, the data to support such an analysis were simply not available. Thus one is left with an imprecise view that characterizes the civil war period as partially a continuation of the major trends from Yenan, but also with some reversion to the tactics of the Kiangsi Soviet. Perhaps the

[25] "Temporary Method for Handling Traitor's Property," August 15, 1945, Article 8. Located in *Shan-tung sheng cheng-fu . . . , op.cit.*, pp. 27-37.

[26] *Ibid.*, Articles 4 and 7.

[27] *Ibid.*, Article 3.

[28] "Method for Handling Enemy and Puppet Property," *loc.cit.*, Articles 6-8.

dominant impression gained from existing statistics and from the frequency of newspaper reports on the Anti-Traitor Accusation Movement (*fan-chien su-k'u*) is that the public assumed a much more active role than in previous periods. For example, during the Anti-Traitor Accusation Movement, alternatively referred to as the Revenge and Complaint Movement (*fu-ch'ou k'ung-su*), one *ch'ü* in North Kiangsu claimed that more than 12,000 "anti-traitor" and "anti-despot" meetings were organized with the participation of some two million people.[29] The movement began in November and December 1945 and by March 1946 the Border Region High Court reported considering 178 cases involving traitors. Of these, 25 (14 percent) were executed and 66 were given prison sentences.[30]

The usual form for the movement was to call an accusation rally at which the masses were encouraged to disclose traitors and war criminals. Either at this meeting, or at another, the High Court would establish a special tribunal to conduct mass trials of the main criminals. During 1946, the pages of *Chieh-fang jih-pao* (Liberation Daily) are full of reports of mass trials that were very similar to those of the Kiangsi and Yenan periods. The masses were probably even more enthusiastic than in earlier periods, for they sometimes jumped to the stage and threatened to kill or beat the criminal.[31] The accused were usually puppet military leaders, puppet magistrates or mayors, puppet police chiefs, puppet judges, secret agents, bandits, or war profiteers. Frequently, they were charged with cooperating with the Japanese and carrying out activities detrimental to the Communists or to the masses. Contrary to the formally established approval system, most of these criminals were executed on the spot following the mass trial, with no mention of approval from superior organs.[32]

[29] Leng, *op.cit.*, p. 21.

[30] "Twenty-five Major Puppets Have Already Been Punished," *Chieh-fang jih-pao* (Liberation Daily), March 8, 1946, p. 1.

[31] "Seven Thousand People Gather in the Rain in Ning-wu to Try War Criminals," *Chieh-fang jih-pao* (Liberation Daily), August 6, 1946, p. 2.

[32] However, since the guilt of a suspect was decided secretly, prior

Plays, operas, parades, small group meetings, and wall posters were other techniques used to indoctrinate people during the campaign. One source reported that the main participants in these events were students and teachers who paraded with the masses and helped arouse them.[33]

Not all who had worked for the puppet or Japanese regimes were punished. In fact, the majority were encouraged to surrender and confess voluntarily and then to reform. After making his confession, the individual's sincerity was evaluated by his fellow villagers. Activists would organize an "Honestly Reform into a New Man (*tzu-hsin*) Meeting" for those who had not been candid in their first confession. Colored lists of names were posted to encourage criminals to reform. Those who had cooperated with the enemy were first listed on the green list, but if they repented and reformed, they recovered their citizenship rights and were transferred to the red list. Those who confessed but were not completely reformed went on a yellow list, while the very evil ones were put on the white list.[34] The posting of these lists clearly established everyone's position and brought family and group pressure for change.

As the Anti-Traitor Accusation Movement developed, the Reduce Rents and Interest Movement was initiated. Landlords were encouraged to reduce rents and interest "voluntarily." This movement served as a prelude to the Settlement Movement, during which the peasant associations formed settlement committees to consider all the past debts of the traitors, war criminals, landlords, and local despots. "Debts" was broadly interpreted to include mental and physical as well as monetary

---

to organizing the mass trials, prior approval could have been obtained and not mentioned. Such a procedure is stated in one case.

[33] "Shantung's Settlement and Reduce Rent Movement," *Chieh-fang jih-pao* (Liberation Daily), May 28, 1946, p. 2.

[34] "All the Masses in the New Liberated Areas of China Join the Punishing Traitors Movement," *Chieh-fang jih-pao* (Liberation Daily), May 12, 1946, p. 2.

debts. Property and wealth were confiscated and distributed to pay monetary debts. In addition, those who had beaten people were made to kowtow to their victims. Murderers were ordered to wear funeral clothes, to hold a public funeral ceremony, and sometimes to stand trial in front of the graves of their victims. Robbers were ordered to return the stolen property to the original owners publicly with great fanfare. Those who had blackmailed or cheated people were ordered to compensate them.[35] These methods again illustrate the Communists' preference for the traditional Chinese concept of "loss of face" as an auxiliary punishment rather than relying solely on monetary and judicial punishment.

During the period of settlement, education about the next phase, the Production Movement, was to be carried out.[36] The peasants were taught that the lower rents and interest and the property obtained through settlement were not sufficient to change their lives. Increased production was necessary before the results of years of poverty could be overcome. The Communists feared that the sudden wealth would result in laziness and loss of much-needed production. The primary goal during this movement was to win the support of the masses in order to mobilize the entire nation for the increased production necessary to win the civil war and to restore the war damage.

As in the Kiangsi period, most of the mistakes made in applying the law were caused by over-zealous masses. For example, on several occasions in the western part of Chekiang province mobs beat villagers and *pao* leaders, burned their homes and furniture, and sometimes even killed their relatives.[37] In another area the judicial cadre were accused of

---

[35] "Five Hundred Thousand Peasants Turn Their Heads During the Anti-Traitor Accusation Movement in the Ch'iao-tung, Chang-i Plain," *Chieh-fang jih-pao* (Liberation Daily), April 11, 1946, p. 2.

[36] "The Experiences of the Shantung Peasant Movement," *Chieh-fang jih-pao* (Liberation Daily), June 7, 1946, p. 2.

[37] "Thousands of Peasants in Western Chekiang Spontaneously Carry Out the Anti-Traitor Movement," *Chieh-fang jih-pao* (Liberation Daily), May 26, 1946, p. 1.

kidnapping[38] because they made a practice of seizing people and secretly detaining them. Mao Tse-tung, speaking before the Cadres' Conference of Shansi-Suiyuan Liberated Area on April 1, 1948, admitted that not only had many landlords and rich peasants been killed unnecessarily in the land reform campaign, but that also a number of workers had been killed by those who seized the opportunity for personal revenge.[39]

Summary

The close relationship between environmental conditions and judicial policy is particularly evident from a study of the civil war period. When their goal of territorial control seemed obtainable only through a civil war, the Communists reinstated their call for class warfare. They changed their tactics to reflect the new situation by orienting laws and punishments toward wealth redistribution. Some reversion to Kiangsi tactics occurred as the definition of counterrevolutionaries was broadened and ad hoc organizations, rather than normal judicial channels, were employed to deal with counterrevolutionaries. However, in contrast to the Kiangsi experience, extrajudicial organs, such as the special tribunals for war criminals and for land reform, were more cautiously and selectively empowered. The practice of granting leniency, which had been widened during the Yenan period, was also continued.

The return to many of the tactics of Kiangsi may lead one to question the long-run effects of the trends toward leniency and regularization noted in the summary of the Yenan period. Were not these changes only temporary and primarily a propaganda ploy necessitated by the CCP's weakness? The similarity between the laws of the Nationalists and the Communists during the united front period suggests that some laws and organizational structures were passed for propaganda purposes with little concern for actual implementation. To the

---

[38] "The Border Region Council Discusses Judicial Work," *Chieh-fang jih-pao* (Liberation Daily), April 10, 1946, p. 2.

[39] Leng, *op.cit.*, p. 21.

degree that propaganda considerations did influence the legal system, the emphasis on regularization and leniency in Chapter IV may be somewhat overstated.

However, regularization can be viewed as a direct response to the Kiangsi experience. The problem of controlling aroused mobs of peasants in Kiangsi had vividly illustrated the necessity of more legal structure and consistency. While definitely of some propaganda value, the policy of leniency is probably best understood as a lesson learned from Kiangsi. The Kiangsi experience underscored the importance of defining the enemy in manageable terms. Given the Communists' position of weakness, the policy of leniency allowed them to punish only a restricted segment while espousing a more general definition of socially unacceptable behavior for educational purposes. The Communists' appeal for support from important groups— such as uncommitted third parties and the national bourgeoisie —illustrated their continued application of a restricted united front.

In conclusion, since regularization and leniency were continued into the civil war period to an undetermined degree, they appear to have become a permanent aspect of the legal policies of the Chinese Communists. To judge from their rhetoric, it appears that the experience in Kiangsi and Yenan had showed the Communists that laws and a legal system could be functional in controlling and educating people, particularly in periods of stability. However, laws and formal procedures were viewed as only one of a variety of tools useful in the struggle against counterrevolutionaries. Moreover, the utility of law appeared closely tied to the objectives sought and to the environmental conditions.

Chapter vi. Prison Management*

Introduction

PREVIOUS chapters provide a chronological description of the legal process from the definition of what constitutes counterrevolutionary activity through the arrest-and-trial process. There is a somewhat natural reaction to merely halt the analysis at this point, thereby overlooking the process that begins with the prisoner's incarceration and ends with his release. An implicit assumption underlying such a decision is that the latter process is unimportant since prisons merely serve their traditional function of removing the criminal from society. The Chinese Communists would vehemently reject such an assumption, for they consider imprisonment only the beginning of the criminal's "reform." Therefore, it seems necessary to extend the examination into the treatment of counterrevolutionaries during their imprisonment.

With their view that penal policies were a vital part of the revolutionary process, the Communists defined three functions prisons could play in the revolutionary struggle. First, prisons could continue to fulfill the traditional function of control of criminal elements and political deviates through physical incarceration. Second, because the extreme scarcity of resources limited the capacity to imprison, prisons could serve an auxiliary function of production, thereby augmenting the capacity to imprison. Despite prison production efforts, the prison facilities were inadequate to incarcerate permanently the large number of prisoners during a revolution. Consequently, prison facilities were expected to perform a third function of education or political socialization. It was theorized that reform would turn counterrevolutionaries into revolutionaries, thereby reducing their stay in prison and decreasing the number of second offenders. The amount of attention given penal

* This material is reprinted from *The China Quarterly*, April-May 1974.

theories by the Communist leaders clearly shows that they viewed events within the prisons as important variables in the ultimate success of the revolution.

In addition, penal policies are interesting because in a sense prisons serve as a microcosm of society. In winning and holding power in a backward, impoverished, and hostile country, the Chinese Communists needed to perform the same three functions of control, production, and education. Since many of the techniques evolved through experimentation in the prisons of Kiangsi and Yenan were later applied to society as a whole, a knowledge of the environment in which these policies evolved is most helpful in understanding current Chinese society.

Prison management is considered in a separate chapter to emphasize the evolution of the Communists' concepts concerning the function of prisons. To reinforce the temporal aspect, chronological descriptions of the prison policies in Kiangsi and then in Yenan are presented. This chronological framework allows one to observe the learning ability of the Communist leaders. It is interesting to consider to what extent policy changes were initiated in response to feed-back from previous experience.

A chronological presentation also provides a convenient format for linking prison policies to environmental conditions. Throughout the chapter the effects of environmental conditions on the decision-making process are studied. The question of primary importance is the degree to which the environment circumscribed the policy options open to the Communists. Were their policy decisions rational responses, given the limitations imposed by their environment?

Following this general description, particular sections describe in greater detail specific policies. These policies include release, production, democratic management, education, and thought reform. The interrelatedness of these policies is particularly important to note. Some policies may be direct substitutes, while other policies may be complementary. Tradeoffs exist so that the use of a policy to attain one objective may mean the sacrifice of competing objectives.

Kiangsi Period

Available information concerning prisons in the Kiangsi Soviet indicates that two types of facilities were maintained. Detention centers (*k'an-shou-so*) detained people prior to their trials and housed some short-term criminals after sentencing. Labor reformatories (*lao-tung k'an-hua-yuan*) served as prisons for criminals with longer sentences.

During their initial experiments with prison management, the Communists admitted that the primary function of prisons was the control of political enemies. Restraining devices, such as handcuffs and leg irons, were used on the prisoners, and informers were planted among them. Since most of the former prison guards had joined the enemy, the new guards were all of peasant origin and evidently considered the convicts as slaves. The Communists acknowledge that beatings, cursings, discrimination, corruption, and exploitation were common occurrences in the prisons.[1]

Attempts to control counterrevolutionaries by imprisonment were hindered by security and sanitation problems. It was reported that prison records were not always kept accurately, with the resulting uncertainty as to the identity and number of those imprisoned. Many places lacked full-time guards or were forced to use women, so that the escape rate was high.[2] Failure to watch the prisoners closely also provided the prisoners with a chance to commit suicide or to beat other prisoners to death.[3] Sanitary conditions were reportedly so bad that

[1] *T'ai-hang ch'ü szu-fa kung-tso kai-k'uang* (Report on General Situation of Judicial Work in T'ai-hang Ch'ü) (T'ai-hang Administrative Office, May 1946), p. 33.

[2] "The Circuit Victory and the Work Experiences of the *Hsien* Judicial Departments," *Hung-te Chiang-hsi* (Red Kiangsi), October 14, 1932. In the *Shih-sou Collection*, No. 008.1052, 2123-2, 0817, reel 1.

[3] "A Review and Discussion of the Third Joint Meeting of Judicial

many died or contracted diseases. For example, in Kiangsi Province, ninety-two prisoners died of diseases from May through October of 1932.[4]

The People's Commissariat of Justice, under the leadership of Chang Kuo-t'ao and Liang Po-t'ai, issued a directive in June 1933 that offered suggestions for improving penal conditions.[5] To correct the security problems, they advised hiring guards on a twenty-four-hour basis. Only people with permission from the judicial departments were to be allowed to visit prisoners, and all letters and packages sent or received by prisoners were to be inspected. In detention centers, criminals involved in the same case were to be held in separate areas to prevent collaboration concerning their testimony. For added security, they suggested that more informants be placed among the prisoners. To improve the sanitary conditions, the directive recommended that prisoners be given a specific time each day to wash and to have fresh air.

Failure of the Communist prisons even to maintain consistent control over the inmates is a variable partially explaining the Communists' policy of Red Terror in the Kiangsi Soviet. Essentially unable to control political opposition through imprisonment, they turned to the option of mass executions. However, this policy proved counter-productive, for the resulting terror and chaos turned many people against the CCP. Desiring to increase the capacity of their prisons, the Communists attempted to reduce the high cost of maintaining prison facilities by putting prisoners to work producing necessary

---

Department Directors in Po-sheng Hsien," 1933. In the *Shih-sou Collection*, No. 008.54105, 1732, 0658, reel 6.

[4] Kiangsi Provincial Soviet Government, "Summary Report of Six Months' Work, May through October, of the Kiangsi Provincial Soviet Government," November 2, 1932. In the *Shih-sou Collection*, No. 008.61026, 3119, 0269, reel 10.

[5] "The People's Commissariat of Justice Directive No. 14 Concerning the Work of Judicial Organs," dated June 1, 1933. In the *Shih-sou Collection*, No. 008.548, 3449, 0759, reel 6.

supplies. Prisoners in the labor reformatories worked to produce such items as ink, paste, paper, and envelopes. In other labor reformatories inmates manufactured clothing such as hats, grass shoes, and belts.[6] With the hope that all labor reformatories would soon become self-sufficient, in 1934 the People's Commissariat of Justice ordered that prisoners who were not skilled in other work be required to plow virgin land or to aid in agricultural production.[7] However, production and distribution were often poorly planned; the result was chronic gluts and shortages. A Management Committee for Enterprises in Labor Reformatories was suggested to coordinate production, sales, and distribution.[8]

Only minor attention was given to the option of reforming the prisoners. Lenin rooms, libraries, and clubs were provided to educate the prisoners. However, because of a shortage of staff, political and literacy classes were not conducted on a regular basis; consequently, prisoners were left to read on their own.[9]

Yenan Period

Under the influence of the united front policy, emphasis shifted during the Yenan period toward the third function of prisons—political socialization. Turning to the problem of reforming criminals, the High Court advocated a slogan of democratization of prison management in 1941. The term "convict" was changed to "reformed person" (*tzu-hsin*)[10] and

[6] "One Year's Work of the People's Commissariat of Justice," *Hung-se Chung-hua* (Red China), November 7, 1932. In the *Shih-sou Collection*, No. 008.1052, 2125, v. 2, reel 16.

[7] Chang Kwei-chao, "Opening New Land Movement in the Labor Reformatories," *Hung-se Chung-hua* (Red China), April 3, 1934. In the *Shih-sou Collection*, No. 008.1052, 2125, v. 6, 1937, reel 17.

[8] "The People's Commissariat of Justice Directive No. 14," *op.cit.*, p. 23.

[9] "One Year's Work of the People's Commissariat of Justice," *loc.cit.*

[10] The term "tzu-hsin" is usually translated as one who has reformed himself into a new man. As the translation implies, it denotes one who

beatings, cursings, and exploitation were prohibited. Law-breaking cadre were to be punished severely. The slogan of the period proclaimed that "education is primary and punishment is secondary,"[11] with education being defined broadly to include all thought reform. Early release and leniency were promised to those who took advantage of the opportunity to reform. The new policies blended well with a continued stress on production, for production was viewed as serving the dual function of providing supplies and of aiding in the reformation of the prisoner.

In line with the new policies, all sentenced criminals had to spend at least some time in detention centers (*k'an-shou-so*) or prisons (*chien-so*), where they would have the opportunity to reform. Even those sentenced to hard labor (*k'u-i*) were first sent for a period of detention. If a prisoner showed "true repentance" during the detention period, the *hsien* judicial committee could decide to parole him. On the other hand, if he showed a "serious mistake in his thinking," his sentence could be increased. In the case of criminals originally sentenced to prison, the approval of the High Court was necessary before a sentence could be changed.[12]

Reports on the actual application of policies are often conflicting. In 1941 the Shensi-Kansu-Ninghsia High Court reported that sanitary conditions in the prisons had been badly neglected. Prisons were described as damp, dark, foul-smelling caves in which many prisoners had become ill. The High Court suggested that windows be built and prison walls con-

---

has reformed or is in the process of reforming. However, in the *T'ai-hang Report* the term seems to be used simply as a synonym for convict.

[11] "Conciliation in Civil Cases and Education in Criminal Cases," *Chieh-fang jih-pao* (Liberation Daily), August 1, 1946, p. 2.

[12] "Directive from the Shensi-Kansu-Ninghsia High Court Concerning Each *Hsien's* Judicial Work," May 10, 1941. In *K'ang-jih ken-chü-ti cheng-ts'e t'iao-li hui-chi, Shen-Kan-Ning chih-pu* (Compendium of Policy Statements and Statutes of the Anti-Japanese Border Regions, Shensi-Kansu-Ninghsia Section), Shensi-Kansu-Ninghsia Border Region Government, July 18, 1942, Vol. 3, p. 752.

structed so that the prisoners could enjoy fresh air and sun-shine for an hour or two daily. Even prisoners held in isolation were to be taken out into the air three times each day. Sports and recreational activities were also ordered. To improve sani-tary conditions, human waste containers were to be provided and were to be cleaned daily. Medical care and isolation were prescribed for sick prisoners.[13] Since the need for such improve-ments was specified in the report, it appears these were fairly widespread problems.

In contrast to this bleak picture, in 1939 Ch'i Li described prisons as schools. He said they were not dark dungeons as they had been previously. Prison personnel reportedly shared the prisoners' food and work and were not allowed to insult or to beat the prisoners. He mentioned literacy classes and small group study sessions for the prisoners.[14] A similar but more detailed account of "Life of a Criminal in the High Court Prison" was reported in *Chieh-fang jih-pao*.[15] According to this account, upon entering the prison, the criminal had private conversations with the prison staff, during which they asked his opinion of his sentence and explained the prison rules. Then he was assigned to a cell with seven or eight other people. The newspaper explained that since the primary pur-pose of the prison was reform, there was no need to make the prisoner's life difficult. Consequently, the prisoners who did not eat meat were given vegetables, and sick prisoners were given medicine and hospital care. If necessary, aid was given to support the prisoner's family or, with permission, the pris-oner was allowed to return home to visit or to help with fam-ily affairs. The account mentions that these prisoners also at-tended political and literacy classes, and, in addition, this prison was equipped with a library. The prisoners reportedly demo-cratically elected prison association officers, who made sug-

[13] *Ibid.*, p. 753.

[14] Ch'i Li, *Shensi-Kansu-Ninghsia pien-chü shih-lu* (A True Account of the Shensi-Kansu-Ninghsia Border Region), (Liberation Press, 1939), p. 36.

[15] "Life of a Criminal in the High Court Prison," *Chieh-fang jih-pao* (Liberation Daily), January 16, 1945, p. 4.

gestions concerning prison entertainment, wall-posters, hygiene, food, and production. The prisoners spent an unspecified amount of time working in the fields, vegetable garden, lumber mill, or at other productive tasks. After dinner they were free to play chess, to read books or newspapers, to play the Chinese violin, or to participate in other leisure activities.

Another newspaper account described the regional prison in a small city ten miles south of Yenan.[16] This prison consisted of five one-story buildings enclosed by a low wall. The author stated that while there were no locked gates or iron bars, there was a guard, "who is practically a doorkeeper." According to the newspaper, most of the prisoners were permitted to go out of the compound unguarded. This account also mentions the election of prison officers. The warden assisted some of the prisoners' families in settling in the area and, after release, the ex-convicts stayed on to form a new village. The account reports that by the end of 1944 the prison, which operated three farms, a lumber mill, a charcoal works, and a ranch, was self-supporting.

In part, the discrepancy between these reports may be explained by differences in time and location. The first report was dated May 1941 and the Communists admit that their prison policies were reformulated in 1941 and not implemented until 1944 and 1945 in most prisons.[17] The newspaper stories both appeared in 1945, well after the implementation of policies. However, Ch'i Li's account was dated 1939, prior to the 1941 High Court directive. In addition, conditions could be expected to vary in different locations, and the *Chieh-fang jih-pao* story concerning the High Court Prison probably represented the best possible conditions.

The similarity between the newspaper accounts and the policies reiterated in the *T'ai-hang Report* suggests another possible explanation. In propagandizing their image as lenient reformers, the Communists may have been utilizing the con-

[16] Tseng Ke, "Prison in the Border Region is a School: Warden Tang Hung-k'wei," *Hsin Hua jih-pao* (New China Daily), January 23, 1945.
[17] *T'ai-hang ch'ü szu-fa . . . , op.cit.*, p. 33.

trolled press to present their espoused policies as accomplished facts. Therefore, while some parts of the stories probably are accurate, the newspaper accounts cannot be accepted as purely descriptive.

Turning from the practical to the theoretical, the remaining portion of this chapter will examine in greater detail the organization and policies the Communists outlined for their penal system during the 1935-1949 period.

Prison Organization

In Yenan, prisons continued to be an integral and important part of the judicial network. Because of the united front arrangements, the border regions' judicial system was nominally under the jurisdiction of the Nationalist Supreme Court. In actuality, the judicial system of the border regions operated as a separate entity, with the High Court (*kao-teng fa-yuan*) being the highest judicial body in each border region. The High Court was the organ of first trial for important criminal cases and the organ of appeal in other cases. The Detention Center Department under the High Court operated the prison facilities connected with the High Court and exercised vertical authority, mainly of a supervisory nature, over prison facilities established at lower levels. At the bottom of the judicial system were the local courts (*ti-fang fa-yuan*). Before these local courts were established, cases were handled by the justice bureaus of the *hsien* governments (*szu-fa ch'u*). The justice bureau might or might not operate a detention center and/or a prison, depending upon the *hsien*'s size, location, and length of time under Communist control. To assure political control of the judicial system, judicial committees (*ts'ai-p'an wei-yuan-hui*) consisting of Party, government, and court officials were established at the *hsien* level to discuss cases and to report injustices to the High Court. In 1943, branch courts (*fen-t'ing*) were established as an intermediary court between the local courts and the High Court.

The Chinese followed an inquisitory trial procedure similar

to that in Continental countries. The Public Security Bureau carried out an extensive preliminary investigation before turning a case over to the judicial department for further investigation and trial. Thus, a suspect might be held in a special detention center operated by the Public Security Bureau during the initial investigation. He then could be transferred to a detention center operated by the *hsien* justice bureaus or to a prison if no detention center was located in the area. A person could thus be incarcerated for a long period of time in a variety of institutions before ever coming to trial. Some attempt was made to protect the individual during this pre-trial imprisonment. For example, the Public Security Bureau was asked to initiate its investigation within twenty-four hours after apprehending the criminal[18] and the judicial organs were requested to bring a case to trial within thirty days.[19] As usual, this provision contained the standard Communist loophole, which exempted "special circumstances" from these restrictions. Thus the regulations were only model targets, and evidence suggests the Communists were usually far short of these goals. After 1949, it appears that limitations on the duration of post-trial confinement were dropped,[20] possibly revealing their ineffectiveness in the pre-1949 period. Resource shortages, not legal provisions, were the primary restraints against long periods of detention.

Release

The Chinese Communist policies concerning release of prisoners are clearly a direct response to the critical supply shortage. Releasing prisoners freed the government from the necessity of providing for the prisoners and also it allowed the

[18] "The Shensi-Kansu-Ninghsia Border Region Statute Protecting Human and Property Rights," Article 9, *Chieh-fang jih-pao* (January 1, 1942), p. 4.

[19] *Ibid.*, Article 11.

[20] Jerome Cohen, *The Criminal Process in the People's Republic of China 1949-1963: An Introduction* (Cambridge, Mass.: Harvard University Press), p. 33.

prisoners to return to productive labor. Parole after serving half of one's sentence was the most common form of release. One account stated that eighty percent of the criminals were paroled[21] and another source estimated that only ten percent of the prisoners served their full term.[22] Parole for prisoners with long-term sentences required the approval of the Border Region government. To minimize the potential danger for the revolution of these parolees, the deciding factor in granting a parole was the degree of repentance revealed during the educational process within the prison.

With the increasing impact of the KMT blockade and the Japanese attacks, the categories of prisoners eligible for release were expanded. The criteria for release were broadened to include seriousness of the offense and willingness to participate in production, in addition to the former criteria of time served and repentance. Thus, some minor criminals were released without serving a sentence and without any definite sign of repentance, especially if they were willing to participate in production.

In 1944 the Shensi-Kansu-Ninghsia Border Region government directed that all vagrants who had not committed any counterrevolutionary actions should be released under guarantee.[23] Furthermore, criminals convicted of minor criminal offenses (excluding counterrevolutionary offenses, banditry, and homicide), who showed evidence of repentance and reform, could be released under guarantee. If their remaining sentence was two years or more, the High Court had to approve the release.[24]

[21] Ch'i Li, op.cit., p. 35.

[22] Yung Ying Hsu, *A Survey of the Shensi-Kansu-Ninghsia Border Region* (New York: Institute of Pacific Relations, 1945), p. 82.

[23] Guaranteeing allowed a criminal to be released before completing his sentence, provided a certain number of people would sign a guarantee for his behavior. This practice, which followed a pre-modern example, had been temporarily suspended by the Communists in Kiangsi during the 1933-1934 crisis period.

[24] "Shensi-Kansu-Ninghsia Border Region Government Directive No. 48," dated February 18, 1944. Located in *Compendium . . . Shensi-Kansu-Ninghsia, op.cit.*, Supplement, pp. 271-273.

In April 1943 the Shansi-Chahar-Hopei Border Region's Administrative Committee decided to decrease the number of people detained in its prisons by releasing four categories of prisoners.[25] One category allowed some minor criminal offenders to be released while awaiting trial. Other categories applied to sick people, who were allowed to return to the villages for treatment, and to thieves, who on their first offense stole out of economic necessity. These thieves were allowed to return to the villages to do labor service (*lao-i*)[26] in place of their prison terms. Such labor service was similar to the traditional corvee labor, for it involved constructing and repairing public works, digging irrigation canals, and plowing fields for the families of soldiers or for the poor. This forced labor assured that the government would gain production from the prisoners' release.

Under a fourth category, prisoners with good behavior, whether their sentences were long- or short-term, were eligible to return to their villages to help with the plowing for a three-month period. Before they returned, village officials or relatives had to sign a guarantee. Those released under this category also had to do labor service for a period not to exceed five days a month. However, traitors who had *voluntarily* served the enemy were not eligible for release under this provision.

Other sources mention a final category under which prisoners were allowed to return to the villages to serve their sentences (*hui-ts'un chih-hsing*).[27] This practice was alternatively referred to as serving one's sentence outside of prison (*chien-wai chih-hsing*) or returning to the village to perform service (*hui-*

[25] *Hsien-hsing Fa-lü hui-chi* (Compendium of Current Laws) (Administrative Committee of Shansi-Chahar-Hopei Border Region, 1945), pp. 702-703.

[26] This term differs from *k'u-kung, ch'iang-po lao-tung*, and *k'u-i* which have all been translated "hard labor." As in English, these terms signify forced punishments and have bad connotations. *Lao-i* simply means "to do labor" and is not accompanied by such a stigma.

[27] Yang Ch'i, "A Preliminary Discussion of the Development of the People's Criminal Law during the New Democratic Stage," *Fa-hsüeh* (Jurisprudence), Shanghai, No. 3, 1957, p. 44.

ts'un fu-i). This category is similar to, and may not be distinct from, the fourth category since both applied to the same border region (Shansi-Chahar-Hopei) and to all criminals except traitors. However, the fourth category was applicable only for a temporary period (three months) and specific labor (plowing and labor service). This method of returning prisoners to the villages to serve their sentence under the supervision of local residents was continued by the Communists after 1949 under the name control (*kuan-chih*).

There were two ways of applying this latter category. In the Shansi-Chahar-Hopei Border Region it was applied to all criminals except traitors. Other areas limited it to prisoners originally sentenced to five years or less who also showed repentance. T'ai-hang Ch'ü was an example of the latter application and of the 2,072 people returned to the villages under this category, reportedly eighty percent proved to have been truly reformed.[28]

Two misapplications of this approach were noted. In some cases the released prisoners were allowed to move freely with no supervision at all. In other places, they simply became servants to the village cadre, spending all their time running errands for the cadre.[29]

In summary, motivated by expediency, the Communists initiated a program of releasing prisoners to augment the labor force. To insure increased production, release often was conditional upon participation in labor projects. Utilizing the traditional practice of group responsibility, the people in the villages were to assist in controlling the criminal element, thereby relieving the shortage of prison personnel and facilities. The success of such a program was dependent upon the level of political awareness among the villagers and on the degree of repentance of the criminals. Understandably, some people did not comprehend the rationale for deliberately returning criminals to their villages. One source reported that the random release of criminals necessitated by the shortage of sup-

[28] *T'ai-hang ch'ü szu-fa . . . , op.cit.,* p. 50.
[29] *Ibid.,* p. 51.

plies caused people to doubt the relationship between crime and punishment in the Communist-controlled areas.[30] To minimize the danger from releasing criminal elments into society, major offenders, especially counterrevolutionaries, were not eligible for release, and prisoners in most categories were released only with the guarantee of reliable local people. However, as resources became more scarce, the Communists were willing to take greater risks by redefining the categories of prisoners eligible for release.

Production

Just as the policy of releasing low-risk prisoners was an attempt to alleviate the shortages of prison supplies, this problem also motivated a general movement calling on all prisoners to be productive within the prisons. As indicated previously, the scarcity of food was hindering the entire judicial process, since prison sentences frequently either were not being given or were not being administered. To remedy such problems, the production movement was instituted with the goal of making the prison budget self-sufficient.

During the production movement, high-risk prisoners who could not be released were to work within the prison or as a supervised group, while low-risk criminals were to do agricultural work. Even before sentencing, criminals were expected to perform light tasks within the prison compound, e.g., spinning and cleaning. Criminals with a needed specialty, such as carpenters or blacksmiths, were to use their trade.[31]

While the original function of the movement was the production of supplies, a second and potentially more important function was realized as a by-product when the Communists recognized that production could also play an essential part in

[30] "Circular of the Shansi-Chahar-Hopei Border Region Administrative Committee," February 16, 1944. In *Hsien-hsing fa-lü hui-chi, op.cit.*, p. 696.

[31] "Directive from the Shensi-Kansu-Ninghsia Border Region High Court . . . ," *op.cit.*, p. 757.

reforming the prisoner. They enumerated three benefits, in addition to the production of goods, which could result from a prison labor program.[32] First, laboring would show whether a person was diligent, careful, honest, and positive, or lazy, selfish, vain, opportunistic, and negative. Second, it was claimed that working each day would develop an appreciation for labor and a "labor habit" so that after release the prisoner would become an industrious and productive member of society. Third, the Communists expected production to help reform the prisoner by teaching him a skill or trade with which he could earn a living after release from prison. For example, in the Shansi-Chahar-Hopei Border Region, any healthy male from ages eighteen to fifty who showed good behavior and who was willing to mine coal was sent to a special training school, regardless of the nature of his crime.[33] In 1940, a special Reformed Persons Trade School (*tzu-hsin hsüeh-i so*) was established to train prisoners.[34] Construction, coal mining, farming, and weaving formed the main part of the curriculum, which also included politics and cultural subjects.

To increase the productivity of the convicts, different systems of incentive were employed. A profit-sharing system in which the prisoners received 20 to 30 percent of the profits was suggested.[35] Of the remaining 70 to 80 percent, 60 percent would be reinvested to keep the prison and production project operating, while 20 percent would go to improve the living conditions of the prisoners.[36]

Reduction of sentences was another incentive tried by the Communists. For example, those who worked in the coal mines

[32] *T'ai-hang ch'ü szu-fa . . . , op.cit.*, pp. 36-39.

[33] "Decisions of the Shansi-Chahar-Hopei Border Region Government Committee for Criminals to Participate in Production," *Chieh-fang jih-pao* (Liberation Daily), May 7, 1942, p. 2.

[34] Chang Chen, "Reformed Persons Trade School," *Chieh-fang jih-pao* (Liberation Daily), May 8, 1944, p. 3.

[35] *T'ai-hang ch'ü szu-fa . . . , op.cit.*, p. 40.

[36] "Circular of the Shansi-Chahar-Hopei Border Region Administrative Committee," *op.cit.*, p. 698.

were examined every three months. A merit equivalent to one month in prison was awarded for good work. Three merits could be substituted for six months in prison and a life sentence eventually could be reduced to eight years.[37] In the Reformed Persons Trade School, prisoners were evaluated every three months on learning (cultural, political, and technical courses), thought (recognizing personal mistakes and improving political awareness), and work (mood and sense of responsibility), and were granted a reduction of sentence on the basis of total points earned.[38]

Successes in the production movement were frequently reported in the *Chieh-fang jih-pao*. At one cotton mill, prisoners earned enough to provide for themselves and to send some money back home to their families. In the month of March they reportedly initiated a competition, vowing to increase production by 10 percent.[39] As another example, Chu Yüan-ts'ai, who had been an orphan and a thief all his life, was reportedly so impressed with life in the prison that he refused to leave when the court decided to free him early. He was given the job of keeper of the prison and became a model for other thieves.[40] The Reformed Persons Trade School reported that of their 400 graduates, including former traitors and spies, only six again committed serious crimes.[41]

Failures and mistakes were reported along with successes. At some places, transportation was not coordinated and thus products sat idle. The fixed costs of equipping a prison was sometimes prohibitive. Apparently not all prisoners were motivated by the incentives, for low productivity was reported. One frequently cited cause of low morale was the cadre's failure to take part in production. Although the cadre were

[37] "Decisions of the Shansi-Chahar-Hopei Border Region Government Committee for Criminals to Participate in Production," *loc.cit.*

[38] Chang Chen, *loc.cit.*

[39] "Labor Reforms Criminals," *Chieh-fang jih-pao* (Liberation Daily), March 25, 1946, p. 2.

[40] "Transformation of an Orphan," *Chieh-fang jih-pao* (Liberation Daily), August 1, 1946, p. 2.

[41] Chang Chen, *loc.cit.*

ordered to participate and live with the prisoners, they reportedly sometimes simply ordered work done.[42]

The production movement attempted to make a virtue out of necessity by producing rehabilitated criminals as well as supplies. The Communists took the view that prisons must prepare individuals to be economically productive, law-abiding citizens. To accomplish this, they showed understanding of the prisoner's motivation by offering incentives for high achievement. Vagrants and counterrevolutionaries formed the two largest categories of criminals. In the old society, neither group had developed the skills or the custom of laboring with their hands; in fact, the intellectuals and bourgeoisie who had committed counterrevolutionary crimes viewed physical labor with disdain. The assumption behind the production movement was that prisoners could exchange their old attitudes for a new proletarian consciousness only through participation in actual labor. After learning a skill, acquiring the habit of working, and, most important, gaining a proletarian viewpoint, the ex-convict would supposedly become a productive member of society.

The Communists use of prison labor has been a very controversial part of their program. Whether it was therapeutic or simply an excuse for slave labor is largely an unanswered empirical question depending upon the actual physical and mental conditions under which the prisoners labored. Unfortunately, available data suggest a wide variance in prison conditions and provide little basis for generalization. In contrast to some Communist sources, refugee accounts reveal that conditions were intolerable enough in some camps to engender animosity rather than to foster the proletarian viewpoint. Probably the critical element in explaining the wide variance of accounts is the varying relative importance of production versus education between prisons and within a prison over time. In some periods, the need to increase productivity clearly overshadowed any interest in education. Given the critical

[42] Ning Hsien, "Prison Work in Shansi-Chahar-Hopei," *Chieh-fang jih-pao* (Liberation Daily), May 8, 1944, p. 3.

nature of the struggle in Yenan, it is somewhat surprising that the long-term educational function of prisons received so much attention.

Democratic Management

During the production movement, a policy of democratic management of the prisons was formulated in an effort to increase productivity. It was reasoned that if the prisoners could be convinced that the Communists were truly concerned for them and that the labor was for the prisoner's mental and physical improvement, productivity could be improved.

Democratic management was first tried in the areas of production and leisure activities.[43] All aspects of production—from planning to the incentives and division of profits—were to be discussed by the group. In the area of extracurricular activities, the prisoners were allowed to organize a prison association and elect its officers. In the Shensi-Kansu-Ninghsia High Court Prison, the prisoners also elected one person to be responsible for each of the following areas of prison life: entertainment, wall-posters, hygiene, food, and production. The prisoners could reportedly make suggestions or complaints concerning any of these subjects to their representative, who would then discuss the problem with prison officials.[44] It was suggested that clubs be organized around sciences or the arts (such as literature, fine arts, or the art of Chinese boxing and calisthenics). Also, the report said prisoners were allowed to publish wall newspapers in which they could freely make suggestions or criticisms concerning any of the institutions in the detention facilities.

While allowing democratic management, the Communists stressed the necessity of democracy under the guidance of

[43] *T'ai-hang ch'ü szu-fa* . . . , *op.cit.*, pp. 41-45.

[44] "Life of a Criminal in the High Court Prison," *loc.cit.* Similar democratically elected committees in a post-1949 prison were described by Father Mark Tennien, *No Secret Is Safe* (New York: Farrar, Straus and Young, 1952), p. 116.

centralism. It was explained that democratic management meant "control by many" rather than "control by a few" but should not be interpreted as a "renunciation of control."[45] They pointed out that, due to the large number of counterrevolutionaries in prison, the element of centralism in detention facilities had to be larger than in general society. For instance, the disciplinary regulations were determined by the leadership *prior to* the democratic discussion. The right to organize clubs and to elect officers was democracy, but the necessity of having both the club and its officers officially approved was centralism. Thus, democracy was allowed only within the scope of centralized supervision.

Education

With the increasing emphasis on reform, during the Yenan period the Communists enlarged the educational programs within the prisons. The literacy classes that had been started in conjunction with the production movement took on added significance in the reform process. In addition to providing the minimal literacy prerequisites for production, it was anticipated that literacy training would also engender a feeling of dignity and worth among the prisoners, since education had been associated with high social status in traditional China.

In their classes, the Communists taught the simplified modern language called "pai-hua." During his stay in prison, an illiterate was expected to learn 500 to 700 characters[46] so that he would be able to read a newspaper or to write a letter by the time of his release.[47] In addition to the classroom instruction, other supplementary teaching devices, such as small study groups, private tutoring by the judicial cadre, and using other prisoners as teaching assistants, were suggested. Even the prisoner's free time was to be utilized efficiently, for the prison-

---

[45] *T'ai hang ch'ü szu-fa . . . , op.cit.*, p. 41.

[46] Ch'i Li, *op.cit.*, p. 36.

[47] "Directive from the Shensi-Kansu-Ninghsia Border Region High Court . . . ," *op.cit.*, p. 757.

ers were encouraged to attend lectures and to print their own wall posters.[48]

Political indoctrination was also an important aspect of the prison curriculum; prisoners learned political ideas as well as characters from the reading materials chosen for study in literacy classes. Current events and biographies of revolutionary heroes were two types of materials selected to stimulate patriotism, especially among traitors. Later, classes discussed the government and laws of the border regions, in the hope that every prisoner would understand what crime he had committed. In the Yenan High Court Prison, politics and military science were the topics of small group sessions each day.[49]

Education was broadly defined to include other areas of the prisoner's life in addition to literacy and politics. For example, in the Shensi-Kansu-Ninghsia High Court Prison, the curriculum included three types of education—practical, political, and cultural. Practical education concerned both daily life and occupational training. According to the newspaper account, the prisoners had a set period every evening for discussing the problems of cell life, attending free lectures, or discussing prison conditions with the warden. Law, government, and current events were studied as part of the political education program, while cultural education included reading, writing, arithmetic, and hygiene.[50]

Thought Reform

During the Yenan period, the Communist emphasis on education grew from a few literacy classes into a dynamic attempt to remold the total personality. All aspects of the prisoner's environment—from productive labor to democratic management of the prison—were viewed as components of the process of education. It was realized that even the attitudes of the guards and cadres toward the prisoners were crucial variables

[48] *Ibid.*   [49] Ch'i Li, *loc.cit.*
[50] "Life of a Criminal in the High Court Prison," *loc.cit.*

in teaching the prisoners respect for the new government. Consistent with their new educational theories, the Communists considered thought reform as the final goal of all educational efforts within the prison. The assumption underlying thought reform was that political attitudes can be learned and unlearned and thus are not irrevocably fixed by class origins. While of dubious Marxian origin, this assumption has been a consistent foundation of Maoism and has been applied in Chinese society as a whole as well as in the prisons.[51]

It is particularly interesting to note that the Communists refused to rely solely on ad hoc methods of reform, choosing instead to formulate a systematic theory of thought reform. While they consistently recognized the need for flexible adaptation within these theoretical guidelines, the *T'ai-hang Report*,[52] which forms the basis of our subsequent discussion, is primarily a detailed elucidation of theory.

The *T'ai-hang Report* gives instructions on the treatment of prisoners from the moment they enter the detention facilities until their release. Neglecting details concerning procedures, food, clothing, etc., the report concentrates on the prisoner's mental attitude and how he is affected by his environment. Anticipating the defensiveness of a prisoner upon entering a detention facility, the Communists advised prison officials to be especially attentive to the prisoner's welfare and to stress the democracy and leniency of the government. A newly arrived prisoner was not to be asked to engage in self-examination immediately. It was feared that in his distress the prisoner might reveal falsities that would only hinder his true confession later. At this stage, other prisoners were not supposed to discuss his case for fear of increasing the prisoner's defensiveness. This initial caution was abandoned in the post-1949 period, for

[51] See Ezra Vogel, "Voluntarism and Social Control," in Donald W. Treadgold (ed.), *Soviet and Chinese Communism: Similarities and Differences* (Seattle: University of Washington Press, 1967), pp. 168-184. Also see Donald J. Monro, "The Malleability of Man in Chinese Marxism," *The China Quarterly*, October-December 1971, pp. 609-640.

[52] See *T'ai-hang ch'ü szu-fa . . . , op.cit.*, pp. 46-50.

prisoners often were subjected to all-night interrogations immediately after arrest and were urged to confess.[53]

The principal method for influencing the prisoner was by establishing rapport between the criminal and the prison cadre. Through a series of private conversations the cadre were to learn of the prisoner's personality and social background. Even at this stage, these discussions were not supposed to concentrate on the case, and the cadre were warned not to interrogate the prisoner or to take notes.

After the prisoner's thinking had been stimulated by these talks, the cadre were told to expect that the prisoner would become confused and troubled. The report calls this period of mental uncertainty the "fleeting opportunity" for reform. At this point positive factors (value of his own future, regret for his crime, and gratitude toward the Communists) were to be encouraged. The cadre were instructed to reemphasize leniency and to encourage discussions with other people (other prisoners, judicial policemen, friends, and relatives) in order to allay the prisoner's fears and misgivings.

Also at this stage, self-examination was to be begun. While the report does not explain what this "self-examination" entails, post-1949 accounts elaborate in greater detail.[54] Adele Rickett explains that a prisoner was expected to analyze his way of thinking by questioning why he thinks in a certain way and what his motivations are. Then, the prisoner is expected to scrutinize his thoughts from the Communist point of view. The yardstick for determining right and wrong is socialist morality. That is to say, "what is best for the greatest number of people in a special historical context determines right from wrong."[55] The psychologist Robert Lifton, studying the process, describes it as an assault upon identity, during which an individual feels guilt because his past actions do not coincide with

[53] For examples see Harold Rigney, *Four Years in a Red Hell* (Chicago: Henry Regnery Co., 1956) and Allyn and Adele Rickett, *Prisoners of Liberation* (New York: Cameron Associates, 1957).

[54] Rickett and Rickett, *op.cit.*, p. 169.

[55] *Ibid.*, p. 200.

his new identity. If the process is successful, the individual reintegrates his actions and standards to form a new self-image.[56] In practice, self-examination consisted of the prisoner writing a series of confessions in which he was to analyze his past attitudes and actions from the Communist point of view. In many cases, the prisoner's primary dilemma was to ascertain what crime he had committed. These confessions provided the Communists with a procedure for evaluating the prisoner's level of reform. The cadre were cautioned not to be too hasty in urging self-examination but to consider the individual factors affecting the timing of each case.

If the individual's self-examination was not thorough and if he continued to give superficial and evasive answers after several periods of questioning, the cadre were advised to call a discussion meeting. At this meeting, following the prisoner's report on his own self-examination, other prisoners were to give their opinions concerning his problem. To assure spontaneity, the head of the judicial department was not supposed to take part in the discussions, and the other prisoners were not to be briefed beforehand. The Communists cautioned that discussion meetings were not appropriate for everyone and should be used only under special conditions. The report further admonished that these discussion meetings were not designed to turn into the more advanced form of "struggle meetings" in which the struggle often reached the point of physical violence.

In the pre-Liberation period, the Communists placed much less emphasis on the use of other prisoners as a means of reform than in the post-1949 period. One group studying the Chinese Communist post-1949 thought reform process concluded that "the period of being 'struggled' by cellmates in a group cell was a *necessary* condition for being influenced to confess and change attitudes. . . . It was the single most effective device used to influence the prisoners."[57] In the *T'ai-hang Report*

[56] Robert Lifton, *Thought Reform and the Psychology of Totalism: A Study of Brainwashing* (New York: Norton, 1961), p. 66.

[57] Edgar Schein, *Coercive Persuasion* (New York: Norton, 1961), pp. 176, 193.

Communist policy-makers seemed unsure of the political reliability of their "reformed" prisoners, and preferred to leave the tedious task of reform to the more seasoned judicial workers. Given the newness of Communism in these areas, such an assessment was probably not unrealistic.

Once the prisoner became repentant for his errors and his self-examination had reached an acceptable level, judgment was to be pronounced in his case. Thus the main thought reform occurred prior to the trial at which sentence, most of which had already been served, was passed. This timing was similar to that experienced by most Westerners in China in the 1950's. They were usually taken to court only after having been detained for several years and having written an acceptable confession. In most cases their sentences had already been served and they were immediately deported.

The report urged that continued attention be paid to the prisoner even after judgment had been announced. The cadre were counseled to point out model prisoners and parolees to counteract the prisoner's pessimism over his sentence.

The most striking aspect of the *T'ai-hang Report* is the sophistication of the psychological methods suggested. The origin of these ideas is highly speculative since there is no evidence indicating that the Chinese Communist leadership or their Russian advisers had specialized training in this field. A more plausible explanation is that much of the theory and many of the techniques of thought reform were developed by the Red Army as part of their guerrilla warfare in Kiangsi and Yenan. The Red Army lived among the population and depended on them for food, protection, and information. Consequently, they had to treat people in a manner consistent with winning support. A Communist soldier told of groups of troops in Kiangsi, and later in Yenan, sitting around campfires in the evenings discussing standards of conduct and methods of winning popular support.[58] These small-group discussions may have been the origin of criticism and other thought reform techniques.

[58] This incident was related to Allyn Rickett while in Chinese Communist prison and relayed to this author in a recent conversation.

After having undergone the thought reform process, Allyn Rickett notes: "Strong similarities between the methods used in helping . . . [us] reform through criticism and self-criticism and those used in group therapy in the U.S. Yet, it was clear from my experience with the authorities and the prisoners themselves that none of these people had any systematic training in psychology. Rather the entire process seems to have developed in a rule-of-thumb manner based on a common-sense insight into human character, something for which the Chinese have always been noted, a concept of self-criticism borrowed from general Marxian practice and techniques which grew out of the need to reform the troops and intellectuals in the early days of the revolution."[59]

Regardless of origin, the process of ideological education outlined by the Communists was a delicate and complicated one that would naturally involve difficulties in implementation. For example, the report stated that many cadre continued to use a bureaucratic style. Lacking understanding, the cadre did not carry out the thought reform process with sincerity and patience. Instead, they were slipshod, quick-tempered, impatient, and dogmatic. It was reported that such attitudes were quite prevalent before the Great Rectification Movement (*cheng-feng*) of 1942, which focused on overcoming this bureaucratism.

The Communists recognized that the crucial variable in the success of thought reform was the quality of the cadre, who had to apply it creatively. Application required thorough and painstaking work that was subtle and complicated. In addition, since human nature differs among individuals, the methods had to be adapted flexibly for each case. The intricacies of the process raise the question of whether such techniques could ever be successfully applied on a large scale by untrained personnel. The personal interaction necessary for genuine reform defies generalization and the appropriate techniques are not likely to be taught in a few seminars for cadre. Furthermore, the nature of the revolution, requiring regimentation and orthodoxy, may have predisposed the cadre to have a militant,

[59] Rickett and Rickett, *op.cit.*, p. 199.

dogmatic attitude that was incompatible with thought reform. The harsh treatment of some prisoners in the early 1950's suggests that the cadre's inflexibility was a continuing problem.

Conclusions

Perhaps the most general observation arising from a study of the Kiangsi and Yenan material is that prison policies appear to be rational responses to environmental conditions that to a large extent circumscribed policy alternatives. The process by which the function of prisons evolved from one of control to one including production and education is understood primarily as a reaction to the changing environmental situation and secondarily as a learning process by the Communists. Facing economic rationing and military attacks, the Communists sought to achieve immediate, short-term solutions that, if successful, often became institutionalized. For example, the programs of release and production appear as direct responses to economic shortages and limited prison capacity. Similarly, these conditions also precluded a highly centralized prison system with elaborate facilities. When the political situation stabilized, the Communists exhibited an ability to shift their attention from short-term to long-term considerations. In Yenan, when it became more likely that the Communists would gain permanent control of vast areas, they showed concern for the long-term problems of political control by initiating programs designed to impart skills, literacy, and especially political socialization.

The evolution of policies over time also reveals that the 1927-1949 period was a learning experience for the Chinese Communist leaders. They learned to rely more on political socialization and less on execution and long-term imprisonment. Furthermore, the Communists perceived and utilized secondary benefits from their programs of production and education. Their emphasis on the reform potential of these programs, even if only a rationalization to justify their policies, demonstrates a systemic awareness of the interrelatedness of policies. In theory, at least, the Communists demonstrated a high comprehension of human motivation and persuasion.

Finally, it is interesting to note how ad hoc, short-term solutions motivated by expediency became institutionalized as permanent features of the penal system. While detailed enumeration and documentation are beyond the scope of this book, in general, all the major techniques of prison management outlined in this chapter—i.e., release, production, democratic management, education, and especially thought reform—are still important aspects of the penal policies of the People's Republic of China.

CHAPTER VII. Conclusions

Introduction

AT THIS POINT, it is necessary to extricate one's self from the aforementioned details in order to pose some important questions suggested from this data and to give at least partial answers, while at the same time realizing the risks in constructing a house from straw. One major question of interest is "What are the principal determinants of the Chinese Communists' policies for dealing with counterrevolutionaries over the sample period?" In the following three sections of this chapter, we hypothesize that the three principal variables that seem capable of explaining policy changes over the period are the environment, ideology, and leadership experience. The next section asks the related question, "What is the primary attribute of the Chinese Communist legal policy?" Stated alternatively, "What was the most outstanding feature characterizing the Communist legal system?"

It is not enough to look only backward and to ask the statistician's questions, such as what are the explanatory variables and what weights should be attached to each, etc. The analysis is then extended by exploring possible ramifications of the Communist legal approach. The legal policies adopted by the Communists are examined for possible inherent contradictions that may have led to inevitable problems for the regime. In the concluding section, we consider the implications of the 1924 to 1949 experience for the post-1949 period. It is important to ask what relevance the data presented in this study has for understanding the more recent legal policies of the People's Republic of China.

The reader is prewarned that the explanations offered here are based on casual empiricism and, in the case of the last two questions, reach well beyond the material presented. Nevertheless, such speculation seems justified by the importance of the issues raised and by the hope that, even if incorrect, this discussion may have the salutary effect of generating viable alternative hypotheses.

Environment

Certainly the most obvious conclusion arising from the preceding three chapters is the significance of the environment in explaining the legal approach developed by the Chinese Communists in their dealings with counterrevolutionaries from 1924 to 1949. The environment was the binding constraint that limited the feasibility of certain policy options. In part, the Communists merely did what was expedient, given the difficult circumstances in which they operated. During the 1924-1949 period, the environment was essentially characterized by economic scarcity, by the continuous possibility of guerrilla warfare, by a poor communication and transportation system, and by a generally apathetic populace. Coupled with these external environmental difficulties, the CCP found itself torn by internal dissension during the Kiangsi period, leaving it rather ineffective in formulating and implementing consistent policies. In Yenan, the unified Party leadership, under Mao, brought relative stability and the opportunity to establish a more formal legal system (1935-1941); however, even these efforts were interrupted by Japanese and KMT attacks. Under such chaotic conditions, a centralized, well-integrated, and efficient judicial system was impossible. The lack of adequate transportation and communication facilities alone necessitated a decentralized legal system. Furthermore, the rapidly changing political, economic, and military situation required a flexible set of laws and procedures. Absence of a corps of trained legal specialists further circumscribed the Communists' choice set by necessitating the use of simple guidelines rather than detailed legal codes.

Nor should the impact of the wartime atmosphere be overlooked. When immediately threatened, as during a war, most regimes react with extreme measures of control. There are striking similarities between CCP policies from 1924 to 1949 and the Nationalists' policies toward political offences in Taiwan.[1] The Nationalists govern Taiwan by martial law under a "national emergency" policy that allows for retroactive laws, no parole, and indefinite internment without judicial procedures for political offenders. Even in the United States, the Japanese-Americans were incarcerated on purely racial grounds during World War II. These examples serve to illustrate the importance of the crisis variable.

In sum, the environment, defined as the economic, geographic, military, political, and social situation, constrained the legal options open to the Communists in their campaign against counterrevolutionaries. In turn, the legal actions taken against counterrevolutionaries affected the environment by periodically either bolstering public confidence or creating fear.

Importance of Ideology

Environmental constraints were not the sole determinants of the legal approach of the Chinese Communists. An equally significant factor was their own legal philosophy which viewed law as a political tool to serve the interests of the state rather than of the individual. Implicit in this viewpoint is the idea that law is not revered per se but has value only to the extent that it aids in the achievement of objectives. Following a strictly utilitarian viewpoint toward law, the Communists could establish a fairly complex legal system during periods of tranquillity without any compulsion to adhere to its laws and procedures during periods of turmoil. This philosophy seems consistent with both Communist and traditional Chinese views toward law.[2] Chinese Communist leaders who favored a

[1] Ming-min Peng, "Political Offences in Taiwan: Laws and Problems," *The China Quarterly*, No. 47, July-September 1971, pp. 471-493.

[2] This viewpoint appears consistent with the traditional Chinese attitude toward law. Jean Escarra has pointed out that occidental civilizations consider law sacrosanct, but this characteristic "tends to disappear in proportion as one advances toward the east," where law and justice have been given an inferior place. See Jean Escarra, *Chinese Law*, translated by Gertrude Browne, p. 578.

stricter adherence to legal formality during the 1924-1949 period were branded as "mechanistic" and "legalistic." Liang Po-t'ai charged that such people "did not understand that law develops in accord with the needs of the revolution, and whatever benefits the revolution is law. Legal procedures can be changed and must not become an obstacle to the interest of the revolution."[3]

Since the primary function of the legal system was to crush opposition to the regime (i.e., counterrevolutionaries), those few procedures which did protect the individual (e.g., centralized authorization of arrest, consideration of cases by the judicial departments, pre-execution review and appeal) were suspended in periods of crisis, such as 1934. Even during periods of relative stability (e.g., 1931-1933 and 1935-1941), formalization was accompanied by a series of "special provisions" to insure that procedural inadequacies would not restrict the priority of suppressing counterrevolutionaries. Since the responsibilities for arrest and investigation, as well as the determination of guilt, were largely vested with one organ, the police, there were no effective checks to avoid unwarranted arrests and punishments.

Furthermore, to insure consistency between the regime's ideology and judicial actions, an independent judiciary was rejected in favor of political control over the courts. Judicial personnel were approved by the local government, and important decisions were reviewed by a judicial committee consisting of government and Party leaders. The Communist legal system that evolved over the 1924-1949 period appears to be an efficient form of organization, given their goal of maximizing the interest of the state.

Because of the close connection between ends and means in the Communist ideology, naturally laws (means) varied with changes of the political objectives of the regime (ends). For example, in the Kiangsi period a broad definition of counterrevolutionary activity was needed to coincide with the objective

[3] Liang Po-t'ai, "The Judicial Organs' Important Task of Suppressing Counterrevolutionaries," *Hung-se Chung-hua* (Red China), March 1, 1934. In the *Shih-sou Collection*, No. 008.1052, 2125, v. 6, 1937, reel 17.

of the class struggle. When the objective changed to national resistance against the Japanese, the CCP adopted a narrow definition of counterrevolutionary activity as well as many of the KMT's laws in an effort to show political unity. As the CCP objectives reverted to a class struggle in the post-war period, the definition of counterrevolutionary activity was again expanded to include economic crimes.

Leadership Experience

While the environment of Kiangsi and Yenan and the Communists' own philosophy toward law appear to delineate the policy constraints, they do not appear sufficient to explain an improved ability to optimize over the period which must be attributed to improved leadership. Even given the environmental constraints, the Communists were left with a range of policy options, all of which were ideologically acceptable. Thus, the environment and ideology, while constraining the options open to the Communists, did not completely *determine* their choice of legal policies. In this light, the Kiangsi and Yenan period can also be viewed as a learning process for the Communist leaders. By a trial-and-error approach, they matured in their understanding of the legal system and of the options available to them.

An example of the Communists' improved ability to select from the relevant choice set is their changing interpretation of the mass line. In order to appease the masses during the Kiangsi period, the cadre frequently interpreted the mass line as simply obeying the wishes of the majority. For example, Chang Wen-t'ien advised judicial personnel not to study legal procedures and precedents but to listen to the demands of the people: "Even to the point where if the masses demand a criminal shot, take your gun and shoot him, even if you can find no law so specifying."[4]

---

[4] Lo Fu (alias for Chang Wen-t'ien), "Show Mercilessness Toward our Class Enemies," *Tou-cheng* (Struggle), March 2, 1934. In the *Shih-sou Collection*, No. 008.2105, 7720, v. IV, 1133, reel 18.

The practice of defining law as whatever the people demanded resulted in a situation of "red terror." Such an interpretation fulfilled the first part of the mass line theory (i.e., learning from the masses), but did not accept the responsibility implied by the second part (i.e., teaching the masses). In the Kiangsi Soviet, the mass line degenerated to simple guerrillaism.

During Yenan the interpretation of the mass line shifted as the judicial cadre were told that "following the mass line does not mean that whatever the masses say goes or that the masses are completely correct, so that we are the masses' tail."[5] It was recognized that the masses might not always understand what was in their best interest. When the demands of the masses did not coincide with CCP objectives, the cadre were instructed to rely on "education," whereby the people learned and internalized socially accepted values and norms.[6] For example, it was not sufficient simply to kill an enemy. Rather he first had to be discredited through humiliation at mass trials in order to destroy not only the man but old values and attitudes as well.

The mass line was translated into several precise techniques of criminal law. In the Kiangsi Soviet, the principal technique involving counterrevolutionaries was the mass trial (*kung-shen*), which educated the spectator as well as intensified the criminal's punishment through humiliation before his peers. Even regular trial proceedings functioned more as public announcements than as a decision-making apparatus. Chang Wen-t'ien pointed out that the main reason for trying a criminal was "to make the masses clearly understand the counterrevolutionary plots and to increase the enthusiasm of the masses in protecting the Soviet regime."[7] Also during this period Committees for the Suppression of Counterrevolutionaries were organized to enlist the populace in controlling

[5] *T'ai-hang ch'ü szu-fa kung-tso kai-k'uang* (Report on the General Situation of Judicial Work in T'ai-hang ch'ü) (T'ai-hang Administration Office, May 1946), p. 29.

[6] Victor Li, "The Role of Law in Communist China," *The China Quarterly*, October-December 1970, pp. 66-72.

[7] Lo Fu (alias for Chang Wen-t'ien), *loc.cit.*

deviants. Other mass line techniques, such as the use of assessors, circuit courts, and on-the-spot executions, also functioned to involve and to educate the people.

The above mass-line techniques were continued and refined in Yenan while others were initiated. For example, villagers assisted in supervising and controlling prisoners who returned to their villages to render service. The emphasis on mediation, while rooted in Chinese tradition, also mirrored the use of the mass line in judicial work. Non-judicial organizations were to act as mediators in solving many crimes without the necessity of judicial action.[8]

The emphasis on the educational function of the law is another area in which the Communists learned over the 1924 to 1949 period. The publicity and audience participation in mass trials increased markedly over the period. Since this increased participation was paralleled by increased organization and control of the proceedings by the CCP leaders, the decision-making function of the masses decreased as mass trials became clearly an educational device. Moving from Kiangsi to Yenan, we observe an increased emphasis on reforming the criminal as well as the populace. Education was broadly defined to include teaching the prisoners literacy, productive skills, and even new values and attitudes.

Finally, the Communists matured in their awareness of political realities. In contrast to the idealistic, dogmatic, theoretical approach of Kiangsi, during Yenan the Communists adopted policies (e.g., the United Front) that were consistent with the balance of power. They sought to define the enemy in manageable terms with only secondary consideration for ideology. This improved political sophistication is one of the primary distinctions between the Kiangsi and Yenan periods.

---

[8] This subject will not be discussed in detail since mediation was not permitted in serious cases, such as those involving counterrevolutionaries. For a discussion of mediation, see Jerome Cohen, "Chinese Mediation on the Eve of Modernization," *California Law Review*, August 1966, pp. 1201-1226, or see Stanley Lubman, "Mao and Mediation: Politics and Dispute Resolution in Communist China," *California Law Review*, 1967, p. 1284.

Flexibility

Perhaps the most encompassing word describing the legal policies of the Chinese Communists during the 1924-1949 period is flexibility. A flexible approach to legal policy was, of course, suggested by the three determinants discussed above. By maintaining flexibility, the Communists could easily alter the legal system in response to changes in the environment or in political goals. Furthermore, their experience, which had been primarily with local government in rural areas, reenforced their tendency toward a flexible, ad hoc legal approach.

During the Kiangsi and Yenan periods, a variety of techniques were employed to give judicial cadre flexibility of action. To begin with, contrary to the very detailed codes of traditional China, the Communists seldom published codes of law,[9] depending instead on general directives and circulars. Because such directives did not have the sanctity of codified law, they could be more easily and rapidly changed.

When statutes were passed, the wording was ambiguous. Part of the ambiguity stemmed from the impreciseness of the Chinese language. However, as one author suggests, this ambiguity was not wholly unwelcome to the Communists: "If the Chinese Communist leadership in fact does not want the legal language to be used precisely, it is most likely because too much precision would tie down the policy-makers for whom law is but another weapon in the service of continuing revolution."[10]

Moreover, loopholes allowed for the flexible application of even the more specific articles. These loopholes were in the form of "under special circumstances . . ." clauses, which left the "special circumstances" undefined. The statutes of the

[9] Arthur Stahnke argues that precise legal codes are inconsistent with the Chinese Communist theoretical foundations and historical experience (i.e., pre-liberation). See "The Background and Evolution of Party Policy on the Drafting of Legal Codes in Communist China," *The American Journal of Comparative Law*, 1966-1967, p. 513.

[10] David Finklestein, "The Language of Communist China's Criminal Law," *Journal of Asian Studies*, Vol. 27, May 1968, p. 512.

Kiangsi period had even greater flexibility through the analogy clause.

Furthermore, flexibility was provided by the overlapping of functions between agencies. During the Kiangsi period, either the State Political Security Bureau or the judicial departments could decide most cases, and the Political Security Bureau personnel were not encumbered by normal judicial procedures. While procedures were regularized during the Yenan period, a great deal of flexibility remained, and mass trials were conducted frequently without the leadership or even the knowledge of the judicial personnel.

Additional flexibility was provided by allowing for differentiated treatment for special categories of criminals. For example, lenient treatment was permitted for people who voluntarily surrendered and confessed prior to discovery (*tzu-shou*) or who repented and reformed (*tzu-hsin*).

Through the class line another large group of criminals was promised special treatment because of economic class. The landlords and bourgeoisie were considered suspect purely because of their class origin, while workers and peasants were promised more lenient treatment.[11] For example, the "Draft Statute of the Chinese Soviet Republic Governing Punishment of Counterrevolutionaries" stated: "Those workers and peasants who commit the criminal activities stipulated in Articles 3-25 may have the punishment reduced one degree from that set by the said article."[12]

The class line was a particularly flexible tool, since the criterion of economic class could remain latent, only to be selectively applied when convenient for political purposes. For example, the above draft was modified in the final statute to read: "Workers and peasants who commit an offense *but are*

[11] For an example of the application of the class line see the Sung T'ieh-ying case in which his sentence was decreased from ten to five years solely because of his worker background, while Ch'en Tsung-chun, a landlord, received a more severe sentence. See "The Soviet Court," *Hung-se Chung-hua* (Red China), March 2, 1932. In the *Shih-sou Collection*, No. 008.1052, 2125, v. 1, reel 16.

[12] Appendix A, Article 28.

not leaders or major offenders shall have their punishment reduced from that stipulated in the various articles of this statute compared to elements from the landlords and bourgeoisie who commit the same class of offenses [italics added]."[13] This modification signifies a decreasing emphasis on the class line in the face of immediate danger from the opposition since by 1934 it was necessary to suppress *all* counterrevolutionary leaders and major offenders, regardless of class background. Class was particularly significant in defining counterrevolutionaries during periods of redistribution of wealth (e.g., Kiangsi Soviet, and civil war periods), but not in periods of unity (e.g., united front period).

Flexibility was further expanded by the rejection of the idea that economic class is the sole determinant for treatment. Mao was critical of cadre who did not realize that actions were not necessarily dictated by class origin. The more decisive criterion for Mao seems to have been class stand which in practice involved acceptance or rejection of his policies.

The Communists extended the flexibility inherent in the class-line technique by setting up separate laws and legal machinery to deal with crimes committed by different classes, e.g., the special tribunals of the early peasant movement in Kiangsi and Hunan and the separate special tribunal for landlords and for war criminals during the civil war period. This dual legal system provided flexibility in dealing with the "enemy" while maintaining relative stability in the laws and organs affecting the "people."

Contradictions in the Legal System

At least three interesting problems arise from the Chinese Communists' choice of a legal system during the period 1924 to 1949. First, by directly involving the people in the legal process through the mass-line techniques, the Communists faced the additional problem of controlling the aroused masses. Secondly, the local cadre were a critical element in the success

[13] Appendix B, Article 34.

of a decentralized legal system. Yet, not having their own corps of trained specialists, the Communists were forced to rely on illiterate peasants and former KMT officials. Finally, the Communists faced the fundamental dilemma of balancing stability and flexibility in their legal system.

Beginning in 1924 and continuing to a lesser degree throughout the sample period, the Communists faced the problem of making the generally apathetic peasants aware of their role in the revolution. To gain popular support the CCP interpreted law as the wishes of the masses. Paradoxically, while such an interpretation succeeded in awakening the populace, it contributed to the Communists' difficulties in the Kiangsi Soviet. The "red terror" resulting from the harsh indiscriminate action of uncontrolled groups is one factor accounting for the rejection of the Communists in 1934. Apparently, they recognized this problem because they redefined the mass line to include leading the masses during the Yenan period. Nevertheless, the activism of the masses during the Civil War, the Land Reform, and, more recently, the Cultural Revolution suggests that direct mass involvement in the legal process inherently created the risk of uncontrolled violence.[14]

The Communists were faced with a second problem of being forced by the environment to depend on a decentralized legal system, which delegated primary authority to the local cadre, who in general were either illiterate or potentially disloyal. The lack of trained personnel may be a partial explanation for the reliance on simplified legal proceedings since the emphasis on common sense and general custom, rather than on codified law, helped to alleviate the need for trained legal specialists.[15]

[14] For some current theories concerning conflict management and the Chinese political culture, see Lucian Pye, *The Spirit of Chinese Politics* (Cambridge, Mass.: M.I.T. Press, 1968) and Richard H. Solomon, *Mao's Revolution and the Chinese Political Culture* (Berkeley: University of California Press, 1971).

[15] Apparently even the top Party leadership lacked legal knowledge. Of the few leaders named during this period only Tung Pi-wu, who studied law in Japan in 1916, appears to have had formal legal training. Lower level Party workers were seldom mentioned by name; thus their legal competence is unknown.

Also, the fact that the Communists emphasized political education in their legal system may be attributed to the need to indoctrinate the cadre as well as the criminals. The quality of cadre was especially critical for the success of reform efforts in the prisons. Consequently, the wide variation in the quality of prison personnel is probably a major variable in explaining the mixed reports about prison conditions and techniques. In a broader context, personnel deficiencies are a principal factor in explaining the previously noted gap between theory and practice. Moreover, this gap appears to have narrowed in the Yenan period as the cadre gained experience.

The most fundamental dilemma facing the Communists revolves around the degree of legality necessary for the functioning of society. Legality can be defined as "rule-following, resulting in the reduction of arbitrariness of officials."[16] In effect, legality involves a reduction, not an elimination, of arbitrariness. As the distinguished jurist Dean Pound said, "Law must be stable and yet it cannot stand still."[17] Therefore, in all societies laws must have a degree of flexibility; however, "change is never a net gain, but always purchased at some cost to stability."[18] In other words, the dilemma involves the trade-off between flexibility and stability,[19] since the optimal legal system is neither one of complete stability nor of complete change. Failure to adapt laws to changing circumstances may result in injustice and coercion and may stifle innovation and improvement of the system. On the other hand, too much flexibility may deny the minimum degree of order necessary for the economic system to function. Extreme flexibility also denies the individual stable rules of conduct, thereby under-

[16] Richard Pfeffer, "Crime and Punishment: China and the United States," in Cohen, *Contemporary Chinese Law* (Cambridge, Mass.: Harvard University Press, 1970), p. 263. Also in *World Politics*, No. 152 (1968), pp. 163-173.

[17] Harry Jones, "The Creative Power and Function of Law in the Historical Perspective," *Vanderbilt Law Review*, December 1963, p. 139.

[18] *Ibid.*, p. 145.

[19] For a discussion of this trade-off see Lucian Pye, "Law and Dilemma of Stability and Change in the Modernization Process," *Vanderbilt Law Review*, December 1963, pp. 15-27.

cutting the foundations of social order. As one author points out: "The observance of law is largely habit and undue change in legal rules may deprive law of the precious support of moral obligation and make law enforcement a matter of pure coercion."[20] Thus the optimal trade-off lies somewhere on a continuum between complete stability and complete flexibility.

From a Western viewpoint the stability/flexibility dilemma may be exaggerated by a comparison of Chinese Communist legal practice and an idealized view of the Western legal system. Richard Pfeffer points out that in practice the U.S. legal system is much more flexible than its theoretical model would suggest. He concludes: ". . . the criminal process in China is neither as unlike its American counterpart as a comparison of our stated ideas with China's operational reality would indicate, nor as similar as a comparison of the regularized abuses of our process would suggest. Truth, as usual, elusively lies somewhere between the poles."[21]

By focusing on law as applied to counterrevolutionaries, this study probably further exaggerates the flexibility of the Chinese system. The data from the Kiangsi and Yenan periods suggest that the degree of flexibility increases in crisis periods, when it is imperative that nothing hinder the expedient achievement of objectives. Since political deviates, as dangerous enemies of the state, are on the extreme spectrum of the legal system, they are usually associated with crisis situations. Viewed from this perspective, more flexibility should be expected in laws dealing with counterrevolutionaries than in other areas of law. A study of the marriage laws, civil law, or ordinary criminal law might reveal that only in periods of crisis or induced crisis (i.e., periods of political movements) is flexibility permitted to the degree observed in counterrevolutionary law. In addition, since 1924-1949 was a period of crisis and revolutionary upheaval in China, limiting the study to this time period reinforces the emphasis on the irregular aspects of the system. Furthermore, the optimal trade-off between flexibility and stability probably

[20] Harry Jones, *op.cit.*, p. 142.
[21] Pfeffer, *op.cit.*, p. 281. Victor Li (*loc.cit.*) makes a similar point.

varies among countries, depending on political legal traditions, stage of economic development, size, etc.

While the above qualifications restrict judgment as to whether the Chinese Communists used excessive flexibility in their specific situation, it is possible to observe that the Chinese Communists have chosen more flexibility than even other Communist states. John Hazard asks: "Is the East Asian Communist position only temporary. . . . Or, should Mao's and Kim's [Ilsong] positions be taken as heralding a permanently espoused hostility toward formality and complexity in the maintenance of social order? If it is the latter, comparatists can note a new element of style. If it is the former, there is only a time differential which, when overcome, will place the entire Marxian socialist legal family, in spite of variations in detail, very close to, if not within, the Romanist tradition of court structure and procedure."[22]

While the future flexibility/stability trade-off, necessary to answer Hazard's question, is unknown, the evidence suggests that during the 1924-1949 period the Chinese Communists were testing to determine the maximum degree of flexibility consistent with the achievement of their other policy objectives.

Implications for the Post-1949 Period

The legal experience of twenty-five years of revolutionary struggle appears to have preconditioned the legal approach adopted by the Chinese Communists in the post-1949 period. The function, procedures, and infra-structure of the legal system were transferred largely intact from the pre-1949 practices. The method of applying justice remained essentially the same, with the criminal progressing through the stages of arrest, preliminary investigation by the police, preliminary investigation by the procuracy, trial, appeal, and execution of sentence. Within this system, the trial continued to perform mainly a review-and-announcement function. Cases continued

[22] John Hazard, *Communists and Their Law* (Chicago: University of Chicago Press, 1969), p. 143.

to be processed by informal and inquisitorial methods rather than by an adversary approach. A confession obtained by intensive interrogation and by the promise of leniency was still considered desirable, although, as in Yenan, the need for corroboration by reliable evidence was stressed.

The two-trial system, experimented with in Kiangsi after 1933, was continued in Yenan and in some post-war liberated areas. Also, a collegiate system of judges, often including assessors, was preserved in preference to a single judge per case. The institution of the procuracy was carried over to the new system but with added functions.[23] Although rejected in theory for a period, political control of the courts also persisted in practice after 1949.[24] In contrast, appeal and automatic review of death sentences appear more meaningful in the later period, for they were not circumvented by the many "special circumstances" clauses of the Kiangsi and Yenan period.

Mass-line techniques remained important, as evidenced by the mass trials (*kung-shen*) held during special campaigns (e.g., the Land Reform, the 1951 Suppression of Counter-revolutionaries Movement, and, more recently, the Cultural Revolution). Also, the dual legal system approach rationalized by the class line continued as special "People's Tribunals" were set up during the Land Reform and the Three-Anti and Five-Anti Movements.

The theories of education, thought reform, and reform through production became even more widely applied in the post-1949 period. Increasingly, labor became viewed as a tool for educating government officials as well as prisoners. Prison-

[23] See three articles by George Ginsburgs and Arthur Stahnke, "The Genesis of the People's Procuratorate in Communist China: 1949-51," "The People's Procuratorate in Communist China: The Period of Maturation: 1951-54," and "The People's Procuratorate in Communist China: The Institution in the Ascendant: 1954-1957," in *The China Quarterly*, October-December 1964, p. 1; October-December 1965, p. 53; and April-June 1968, p. 82.

[24] See Jerome Cohen, "The Chinese Communist Party and Judicial Independence 1949-1959," *Harvard Law Review*, March 1969, pp. 967-1006.

thought reform techniques were also applied to society in general; intellectuals, government cadre, Party members, and military personnel were sent to special revolutionary universities for thought reform.[25]

Consistent with their previous experience, the Communists rejected legal codes and relied on vague terminology and general policies, which allowed flexible interpretation at the discretion of the cadre. Similar to practices at Kiangsi, the police were allowed to by-pass trial procedures and to administer directly a variety of formal and informal sanctions, including supervised labor and rehabilitation through labor. Furthermore, the analogy clause was included in several statutes, e.g., the 1951 "Regulation for the Punishment of Counterrevolutionaries."

The perpetuation of the flexible aspects of the system in the post-1949 period raises the question of the permanence of such a characteristic. In the 1924-1949 period, it can be argued that lack of a well-defined legal framework was a temporary phenomenon necessitated by the unstable environment discussed earlier.

However, other factors suggest that environment is not the sole variable explaining the loosely structured legal system and that rapid change and instability may be permanent aspects of Chinese Communist law. Traditionally, the Chinese turned to family, clan, and village leaders to settle many legal questions, for only the most serious cases were taken before the official judicial officer, the *hsien* magistrate. Law was held in low regard by the Chinese, who viewed it as an inferior method for settling disputes. Secondly, aversion to legal proceedings is also consistent with the Communist mass-line philosophy. As Victor Li points out, "The Communists believe law ought to be simple."[26] Also according to Chinese Communist theory, law has to vary with the circumstances of the revolution:

"The legal system of our people's democracy is a revolu-

[25] For a description of a revolutionary university, see Edward Hunter, *Brain-Washing in Red China* (New York: The Vanguard Press, 1953), pp. 18-57.
[26] Victor Li, *op.cit.*, p. 81.

tionary legal system. . . . This is to say, the legal system follows the permanent revolution in society and undergoes a permanent revolution itself so as to meet the new situation and serve the purpose of permanent revolution . . . , the laws made by our state always combine principle with flexibility. They have only relative stability until the objective situation changes, then they too must change. . . . Some people think that the more detailed the law, the better it is. This is an impractical idea."[27]

Finally, one must question how temporary is the revolutionary situation in light of Mao's theory of "permanent revolution."[28] Only change and instability appear permanent features of Mao's continuing revolution, for he said, "in accordance with materialist dialectic, contradiction and struggle are perpetual; otherwise, there would be no world."[29] Given the continuation of an induced revolutionary environment, a flexible legal system, which is adaptable to the changing environment and political objectives, is a logical response and can be expected to continue in the future.

[27] "Several Problems Relating to the Legal System of the Chinese People's Democracy," *Cheng-fa Yen-chiu* (Political and Judicial Study), April 1959, pp. 3-8. Found in Rickett, *Legal Thought and Institutions of the People's Republic of China: Selected Documents* (University of Pennsylvania Institute for Legal Research, mimeograph, 1963-1964), p. 9.

[28] For a discussion of the theory of the permanent revolution and Mao's "uncertainty principle," see Stuart R. Schram, "Mao Tse-tung and the Theory of the Permanent Revolution, 1958-69," *The China Quarterly*, April-June 1971, pp. 221-244.

[29] John Bryan Starr, "Conceptual Foundations of Mao Tse-tung's Theory of Continuous Revolution," *Asian Survey*, June 1971, p. 621.

Appendices

APPENDIX A: Draft Statute of the Chinese Soviet Republic Governing Punishment of Counterrevolutionaries[1]

Article 1: This statute is applicable to a crime whether committed by a Chinese or a foreigner and whether committed inside or outside of the territory of the Chinese Soviet Republic.

Article 2: Whoever attempts to overthrow the government, which has been established by the constitution of the Chinese Soviet Republic, and the rights and privileges obtained by the Workers' and Peasants' Democratic Revolution, or whoever opposes the Soviet system of the dictatorship of the workers and peasants by attempting to maintain or to restore the rule of the gentry, landlord, and bourgeoisie is considered a counterrevolutionary; no matter what method is used, whether by outside force, by secret organizations, by oral or written propaganda, by espionage, or by bribery.

Article 3: Whoever, with a counterrevolutionary purpose, organizes an armed riot or uses armed troops in collaboration with bandit organizations or local bandits in order to invade the territory of the Chinese Soviet Republic, or whoever uses force to detach a part of the territory of the Chinese Soviet Republic, or even whoever plans to usurp central or local political power for a counterrevolutionary purpose should be sentenced to death. Under less serious circumstances, the punishment may be reduced to a minimum of 5 years in prison. If the courts decide the participant in the crime did not understand the intent of the activities restricted by this article, he is sentenced to a minimum of 3 years in prison.

[1] The Central People's Commissar of Justice drafted and circulated this draft to various level governmental departments and mass groups for their opinions. December 9, 1933. In the *Shih-sou Collection*, No. 008.542, 2837, 0281, reel 6.

Article 4: Collaboration with the KMT warlords to attack the Chinese Soviet Republic, regardless of the method, is punishable according to the provisions of Article 3 of this statute.

Article 5: Those who participate in an organization or who aid an organization which approves of the maintenance of the gentry, landlord, and bourgeoisie or of the restoration of their rule are also punishable according to the provisions of Article 3 of this statute.

Article 6: Those who incite the residents to mass riot or to refuse to pay taxes or not to carry out other obligations or to participate in forming organizations with the aim of carrying out the crimes referred to in Article 3, even though the activities of their organizations have not yet reached the level of armed riot or armed invasion, are punishable according to the provisions of Article 3 of this statute.

Article 7: Those who for a counterrevolutionary purpose organize secret organizations to oppose or sabotage any kind of Soviet organizations, including any kind of business engaged in by the Soviet government, or who utilize any kind of Soviet organization or any kind of business engaged in by the Soviet for a counterrevolutionary purpose, are punishable according to the provisions of Article 3 of this statute.

Article 8: Those who for a counterrevolutionary purpose organize secret organizations to oppose or assassinate persons in places of responsibility within the Soviet government and the assassin, whether he was hired by or belongs to that organization, are sentenced to death. Under less serious circumstances, individuals are sentenced to a minimum of 3 years in prison.

Article 9: Those who for a counterrevolutionary purpose or with expectation of reward carry out any kind of espionage activities or transmit, steal, or collect any kind of secret material, especially important military material, are sentenced to death. Those who disclose the above-mentioned secrets but did not have a counterrevolutionary purpose, did not expect reward, and did not understand the results of their actions, are sentenced to a minimum of 5 years in prison.

Article 10: Those who have had important responsibilities in the reactionary regime and actively have opposed the interests of the workers and peasants and the revolutionary movement are sentenced to death. Under less serious circumstances, individuals are sentenced to a minimum of 5 years in prison.

Article 11: Those who for a counterrevolutionary purpose prepare or preserve any kind of reactionary, deceptive writings in order to make counterrevolutionary propaganda are sentenced to a minimum of 1 year in prison.

Article 12: Those who for a counterrevolutionary purpose manufacture and spread any kind of rumors or incorrect news causing panic in the society, public distrust of the government, or loss of faith in the government are sentenced to a minimum of 6 months in prison. If the rumors have not yet achieved their purpose or have not yet greatly disrupted society, the punishment can be reduced to a maximum of 6 months of hard labor.

Article 13: Those who intentionally use medicine to kill government officials, Red Army soldiers, and other elements of the Workers' and Peasants' Revolution are sentenced to death. Under less serious circumstances, individuals are sentenced to a minimum of 2 years in prison.

Article 14: Those revolutionary traitors who surrender to the counterrevolution and report any kind of secrets of the Chinese Soviet Republic to the counterrevolutionaries are sentenced to death. Under less serious circumstances, individuals can be sentenced to a minimum of 1 year in prison.

Article 15: Those who incite or organize others to surrender to the enemy with their weapons are sentenced to death, no matter whether in times of peace or war. The leaders of those who run away [*t'ao-p'ao*] but do not turn over their weapons to the enemy are sentenced to a minimum of 5 years in prison.

Their followers are sentenced to a minimum of 1 year in prison.

Article 16: Those who for a counterrevolutionary purpose lead or organize desertion [*k'ai-hsiao-ch'ai*] are sentenced to death. Under less serious circumstances, individuals are sentenced to a minimum of 3 years in prison and a maximum of 1 year of hard labor.

Article 17: Those who for a counterrevolutionary purpose intentionally destroy their guns or other military items or who discard them in an unauthorized place or who sell them, resulting in loss of military supplies, are sentenced to death. Under less serious circumstances, individuals are sentenced to a minimum of 1 year in prison.

Article 18: Those who conceal weapons in order to achieve counterrevolutionary aims are sentenced to death.

Article 19: Those who for a counterrevolutionary purpose organize secret organizations to sabotage land and sea transportation, public storage facilities, state-owned enterprises, and any other kind of building are sentenced to death. Under less serious circumstances, individuals are sentenced to a minimum of 6 months in prison.

Article 20: Those who intentionally destroy the Soviet economy by producing or importing counterfeit silver currency of inferior quality, by counterfeiting Soviet paper currency, government bonds, and various kinds of securities, by refusing to use the various kinds of Soviet currency, causing panic in the market, or by inciting residents to make a run on the Soviet banks, causing difficulty for the national economy, are sentenced to death. Under less serious circumstances, individuals are sentenced to a minimum of 1 year in prison.

Article 21: Those who for a counterrevolutionary purpose obstruct or destroy trade with foreign countries so as to inflict loss and damage on national trade or who deliberately close business, causing a decline of commercial activities and destruction to the Soviet economy, are sentenced to death. Under less serious circumstances, individuals are sentenced to a minimum of 1 year in prison.

Article 22: Those who falsely use the name of Soviet organizations or who counterfeit the private or public seals or the documents of any Soviet organization in order to carry out counterrevolutionary activities are sentenced to death. Under less serious circumstances, individuals are sentenced to a minimum of 1 year in prison.

Article 23: Those who abuse the name of the workers and peasants by attacking or falsely accusing a person with responsibility within Soviet organizations or a worker or peasant, who is active in the critical struggle, with the intention of carrying out a counterrevolutionary aim are sentenced to death.

Article 24: Those who have been expelled by the Soviet government and again secretly enter the Soviet territory, attempting to carry out counterrevolutionary tasks, are sentenced to death. Those who have been expelled and sneak back into the Soviet territory, with no intention of conducting counterrevolutionary tasks, are sentenced to a minimum of 1 year in prison.

Article 25: Those who conceal or assist in any kind of criminal behavior regulated in Articles 3 to 24 of this statute are punished the same as for the crime under each article. Those whose action has no direct connection with the various crimes committed or who did not recognize the aim of the crime are sentenced to a minimum of 1 year in prison.

Article 26: Those who plot a criminal activity stipulated in Articles 3 to 25 of this statute but have not yet accomplished their aim (unaccomplished offense [*wei-sui-fei*]) or who act as accomplices in the said criminal activity may have their punishment reduced one degree from that set in the said article.

Article 27: Those whom the court decides have been forced to commit the criminal activities stipulated in Articles 3 to 25 may have their punishment reduced from that set by the said article or may avoid punishment with a special pardon from the Central Executive Committee.

Note: The enlisted men of the KMT who invade the Soviet territory should be dealt with according to this article, since they had no alternative.

Article 28: Those workers and peasants who commit the criminal activities stipulated in Articles 3 to 25 may have their punishment reduced one degree from that set by the said article.

Article 29: Persons 16 years or less who are not yet adults and who have committed the criminal activities stipulated in Articles 3 to 25 may have their punishment reduced one degree from that set in the said article. If a youth is 14 years or less, he should be transferred to an educational organ for reform education.

Article 30: Any counterrevolutionary criminal behavior not included in this statute may be punished according to an article in this statute dealing with similar crimes.

Article 31: Whoever commits a crime listed in this statute, besides the punishment set by the said article, also may have their property confiscated, wholly or in part, and may be deprived of their citizenship rights for a period not to exceed 5 years.

Article 32: The maximum period of imprisonment set by this statute is 10 years.

Article 33: This statute becomes effective as soon as it is promulgated.

APPENDIX B: Statute of the Chinese Soviet Republic Governing Punishment of Counterrevolutionaries[1]

Article 1: Whoever commits one of the crimes listed in this statute will be appropriately punished according to this statute, whether Chinese or foreigners, whether inside or outside of the territory of the Chinese Soviet Republic.

Article 2: Any plot to overthrow or destroy the Soviet government and the rights and privileges obtained by the Workers' and Peasants' Democratic Revolution and any attempt to maintain or to restore the rule of the gentry, landlord, and bourgeoisie, regardless of what method is used, is counterrevolutionary behavior. (Note) That which is deemed by this statute as counterrevolutionary criminal activity toward the Soviet or in the Soviet territory also includes all counterrevolutionary criminal behavior toward the Revolutionary Committees or in the territory under the jurisdiction of the Revolutionary Committees.

Article 3: Whoever organizes counterrevolutionary armed forces and bandit groups to invade the Soviet territory or whoever incites the inhabitants in the Soviet territory to carry out counterrevolutionary riots is sentenced to death.

Article 4: Whoever in conjunction with the imperialists and the Kuomintang warlords uses armed force to attack the Soviet territory or to resist the Soviet Red Army is sentenced to death.

Article 5: Whoever organizes any kind of counterrevolutionary group to oppose or to sabotage the Soviet and to attempt to maintain or restore the rule of the gentry, landlord,

[1] This regulation was promulgated by the Central Executive Committee on April 8, 1934. It is in the *Shih-sou Collection*, No. 008.542, 4424 v. 2, 1146, reel 16.

and bourgeoisie is sentenced to death. Those in less serious circumstances are sentenced to a minimum of 3 years in prison.

Article 6: Whoever organizes or incites residents to refuse to pay taxes or not to carry out other duties or to attempt to endanger the Soviet is sentenced to death. Those in less serious circumstances are sentenced to a minimum of 1 year in prison.

Article 7: Whoever for a counterrevolutionary purpose intentionally disobeys or sabotages the laws and orders of the Soviet or any kind of business engaged in by the Soviet is sentenced to death. Those in less serious circumstances are sentenced to a minimum of 1 year in prison.

Article 8: Whoever for a counterrevolutionary purpose secretly enters Soviet organizations or enterprises managed by the Soviets, attempting to rob or to sabotage the Soviet regime or its enterprises, is sentenced to death. Those in less serious circumstances are sentenced to a minimum of 2 years in prison.

Article 9: Both the instigator and the perpetrator who for a counterrevolutionary purpose assassinate or murder an employee in the Soviet government, Red Army, or revolutionary organization, or any other revolutionary element, no matter what method is used, are sentenced to death.

Article 10: Whoever for a counterrevolutionary purpose or with the expectation of reward does counterrevolutionary work by carrying out any kind of espionage activities or by transmitting, stealing, or collecting any kind of material connected with national or military secrets is sentenced to death. Those who reveal any of the above secrets because of negligence and not realizing the particular result of their action are sentenced to 1 to 5 years in prison.

Article 11: Whoever has had major responsibility on the side of the reactionary regime and has actively carried out activities in opposition to the workers' and peasants' interest and to the revolutionary movement is sentenced to death. But those who have special circumstances may receive lighter punishment.

Article 12: Whoever for a counterrevolutionary purpose uses reactionary writings, illustrations, speeches, and conversation to carry out propaganda toward residents or Red Army soldiers or to manufacture and spread rumors that cause panic in the society and distrust of the Soviet government and the Red Army is sentenced to death. Those in less serious circumstances are sentenced to a minimum of 6 months in prison.

Article 13: Whoever manufactures or preserves any kind of deceptive reactionary writings and illustrations in order to make counterrevolutionary propaganda and agitation is sentenced to from 1 to 5 years in prison.

Article 14: Whoever for a counterrevolutionary purpose makes use of religion and superstition to deceive the residents into sabotaging the Soviet and its laws is sentenced to death. Those in less serious circumstances are sentenced to a minimum of 6 months in prison.

Article 15: Whoever surrenders to the counterrevolution and moreover reports any kind of secrets of the Chinese Soviet Republic to the counterrevolutionaries or whoever aids the counterrevolution by actively opposing the Soviet and the Red Army (revolutionary traitors) is sentenced to death.

Article 16: Whoever surrenders to the enemy, carrying their guns or other military items, and whoever instigates or organizes others to surrender to the enemy is sentenced to death.

Article 17: Whoever for a counterrevolutionary purpose secretly enters a revolutionary armed corps, attempting to seize or to destroy this kind of corps in order to aid the enemy, is sentenced to death.

Article 18: Whoever leads or organizes Red Army soldiers to run away or Red Army soldiers who have run away over 5 times are sentenced to death. Those who have special circumstances may receive lighter punishment.

Article 19: Whoever for a counterrevolutionary purpose intentionally destroys or throws away guns and other military items or whoever secretly sells military items to the enemy is sentenced to death. Those in less serious circumstances are sentenced to a minimum of 1 year in prison.

Article 20: Whoever for a counterrevolutionary purpose intentionally disobeys the orders of a superior commander in order to attempt to sabotage a certain military action or intentionally fires at his own troops or seizes the opportunity to create confusion on the fighting front is sentenced to death.

Article 21: Whoever for a counterrevolutionary purpose murders the revolutionary masses or intentionally destroys or seizes the property of the revolutionary masses or even damages the prestige of the Soviet and Red Army among the masses is sentenced to death. Those in less serious circumstances are sentenced to a minimum of 6 months in prison.

Article 22: Whoever conceals weapons in order to achieve counterrevolutionary aims is sentenced to death.

Article 23: Whoever for a counterrevolutionary purpose organizes secret organizations to sabotage land and sea transportation, public storage facilities, state-owned enterprises, and any other kind of building is sentenced to death. Those in less serious circumstances are sentenced to a minimum of 6 months in prison.

Article 24: Whoever for a counterrevolutionary purpose sets fire to houses or to mountain forests, causing the nation and its residents to suffer great damage, is sentenced to death. Those in less serious circumstances are sentenced to a minimum of 6 months in prison.

Article 25: Whoever for the purpose of sabotaging the economy of the Chinese Soviet Republic produces or imports false Soviet currency, government bonds, or securities, or whoever incites the residents to refuse to use various kinds of Soviet money or lowers the price of Soviet money in order to cause panic in the market, or whoever incites the residents to make a run on the Soviet banks, or whoever conceals large amounts of hard currency or smuggles out large amounts of hard currency, intentionally disturbing the currency system of the Soviet, is sentenced to death. Those in less serious circumstances are sentenced to a minimum of 6 months in prison.

Article 26: Whoever for a counterrevolutionary purpose obstructs or sabotages the trade of the Chinese Soviet Republic, causing great loss to national enterprises, cooperatives, and residents, or whoever intentionally closes enterprises to create economic panic, is sentenced to death. Those in less serious circumstances are sentenced to a minimum of 1 year in prison.

Article 27: Whoever falsely uses the name of the Soviet, Red Army, or revolutionary groups or whoever counterfeits public or private seals and documents of the Soviet, Red Army, or revolutionary groups to carry out counterrevolutionary activities is sentenced to death. Those in less serious circumstances are sentenced to a minimum of 6 months in prison.

Article 28: Whoever for a counterrevolutionary purpose secretly enters a Soviet organization intentionally to encourage any counterrevolutionary element or any criminal element from the landlord or bourgeois classes, or to incite runaways, or to give light punishment for serious crimes, or to make false accusations against revolutionary elements, or to mete out extreme punishments or suppress those who want to accuse and expose the counterrevolutionary elements, is sentenced to death. Those in less serious circumstances are sentenced to a minimum of 2 years in prison.

Article 29: Whoever has been expelled by the Soviet and again secretly enters the Soviet territory in order to carry out counterrevolutionary activities is sentenced to death.

Article 30: Whoever conceals or assists in the crimes stipulated in Articles 3 to 29 of this statute is punished the same as the criminal.

Article 31: After the court has sentenced a criminal to imprisonment, whoever again commits one or more of the crimes listed in Articles 3 to 30 of this statute is punished more severely.

Article 32: Whoever plots a criminal activity stipulated in this statute but has not yet accomplished his aim (unaccomplished offense) or whoever acts as an accomplice [*fu ho*] in the said criminal activity may receive lighter punishment.

Article 33: Whoever commits an offense because he is coerced by others against his will and furthermore has no way of avoiding such coercion, or whoever does not know the end result of the criminal activity, or whoever has no direct connection with the practical application of the crime, may have his punishment reduced or remitted from that stipulated in the said article.

Article 34: Workers and peasants who commit an offense but are not leaders or major offenders may have their punishment reduced from that stipulated in the various articles of this statute compared to elements from the landlords and bourgeoisie who commit the same class of offenses.

Article 35: Whoever has made a contribution toward the Soviet may receive a lighter punishment than that stipulated in the said article of this statute.

Article 36: Whoever violates one of the articles of this statute but reports it himself to the Soviet (elements who voluntarily surrender and confess [*tzu-shou fen-tzu*]) before being discovered or even after discovery, repents, and sincerely reports the contents of his offense and assists organs eradicating counterrevolution in breaking up and arresting other conspirators (elements who reform themselves to become new men [*tzu-hsin fen-tzu*]) shall in the accordance with provisions of the various articles have his punishment reduced.

Article 37: Persons 16 years or less, who are not yet adults, should have the punishment lightened from that stipulated in the said article. If the youth is 14 years or less, he should be transferred to an educational organization for reform education.

Article 38: Any counterrevolutionary criminal behavior not included in this statute shall be punished according to the article in this statute dealing with similar crimes.

Article 39: Whoever commits a crime listed in this statute, in addition to the punishment stipulated by the said article, also may have their property confiscated, wholly or in part, and may be deprived of all or part of their citizenship rights.

Article 40: The maximum period of imprisonment set by this statute is 10 years.

Article 41: This statute becomes effective as soon as it is promulgated.

APPENDIX C: The Shensi-Kansu-Ninghsia
Border Region Statute Protecting
Human and Property Rights[1]

Article 1: The aim of this statute is to protect the human and property rights of the people in the Border Region from illegal encroachment.

Article 2: All the people in the Border Region who resist Japan, regardless of race, class, party, sex, occupation, or religion, have freedom of speech, publication, assembly, association, residence, movement, thought, and belief. Also, they enjoy equal democratic rights.

Article 3: The right of private ownership of all people in the Border Region who resist Japan and their right of freedom to use the property according to the law and to profit from it is protected. (This includes land, houses, rights of creditors, and all other property.)

Article 4: In the areas where land has already been distributed, private ownership rights are guaranteed for all the peasants who received land. In the areas where land has not yet been distributed, the landlords' rights of ownership and the obligations of credit are guaranteed.

Article 5: The two parties of landlord and leasee, creditor and debtor, in accordance with the government's law must reduce rent and interest, and pay rent and interest, respectively. All rent or credit contracts must be made voluntarily by both parties.

[1] This was passed by the Second Session of the Border Region Political Council and was promulgated in February 1942. It is in *Chieh-fang jih-pao* (January 1, 1942, p. 4) and in *K'ang-jih ken-chü-ti cheng-ts'e t'iao-li hui-chi, Shen-Kan-Ning chih-pu,* V. 3, pp. 738-740.

Article 6: The property or residence of a person in the Border Region cannot illegally be taxed, sealed, trespassed against, or searched by any organ, military unit, or group, except for special regulations for the public interest.

Article 7: Besides the judicial organs and the public security organs carrying out their responsibilities according to the law, no organ, military unit, or group can arrest, interrogate, or punish any person. However, a criminal discovered in the act of committing a crime [*hsien hsing fei*] is not included under this article. When the people's interest is damaged, they have the right to accuse in any way the illegal behavior of any official.

Article 8: In arresting people, the judicial organs and public security organs should have sufficient evidence and should proceed according to legally prescribed measures.

Article 9: When arresting a person in the act of committing a crime, any organ, military unit, group, or individual, in addition to the judicial organs or public security organs, must take the suspect and the evidence to the Procurator or the Public Security Bureau within 24 hours for handling according to the law. The Procurator or the Public Security Bureau organ who receives the criminal should conduct an investigation within 24 hours.

Article 10: It is not permissible to insult, to beat, to examine by torture, to force testimony, or to coerce a confession from the arrested criminal. In the trial, evidence rather than testimony should be emphasized.

Article 11: In handling civil and criminal cases, the judicial organs should not allow over 30 days to pass from the day the involved parties are summoned to the time the decision is announced, in order to avoid making the involved parties suffer from an excessive delay of the law suit. However, special circumstances when the trial cannot be carried out immediately should not be restricted under this article.

Article 12: When handling civil cases, the judicial organs should not detain the parties in the law suit, except when a party is resisting summons or not obeying the decision or when there are special circumstances.

Article 13: Except in periods of martial law, non-military personnel who commit crimes will not be tried by military law. When a soldier and a civilian are involved in a criminal case, after an investigation the soldier is sent to the department of military law and the civilian is sent to the judicial organs to be tried according to law. In a civil case, the accusation will be handled by the judicial organs.

Article 14: When people are involved in a law suit, the judicial organs may not collect any kind of fee.

Article 15: The property of an arrested criminal cannot be confiscated until the case is decided. Also it cannot be exchanged or arbitrarily damaged.

Article 16: In those cases involving people residing in the area under their jurisdiction, the *ch'ü* and *hsiang* government can act as conciliators with the consent of both parties involved. If the parties involved do not want to follow the decision of the conciliation, they have the right to take the matter to the judicial organs. The *ch'ü* and *hsiang* government may not deter them or exceed their authority in this matter.

Article 17: The government below the *ch'ü* level, except in matters of disobeying a warning, can merely carry out preliminary investigation and conciliation and absolutely have no right to examine, detain, or execute criminals.

Article 18: People of the Border Region who do not agree with the judicial organ's decision according to law can appeal to the appropriate level.

Article 19: Cases in which any level judicial organ decides on the death penalty must be reported to the Border Region government for inquiry and approval prior to execution, even if no appeal was filed during the prescribed period. However, emergency situations in war times are not restricted under this article.

Article 20: As for those Border Region people who ran away because they opposed the Border Region, if they voluntarily respect the Border Region's laws and return to the Border Region, their past actions will not be brought up and they will receive the protection of the law.

Article 21: The right of interpreting this statute belongs to the Border Region government.

Article 22: This statute has already been passed by the Shensi-Kansu-Ninghsia Border Region People's Political Council and is promulgated and put into effect by the Border Region government.

Draft Statute of the Shensi-Kansu-Ninghsia Border Region Governing Punishment of Traitors During War Times[1]

Article 1: This statute is enacted in order to eliminate traitors completely, to preserve the victory of the War of Resistance, and to strengthen the Border Region.

Article 2: The criminal activities mentioned in this statute are applicable to all persons in the Border Region, no matter who they are.

Article 3: Whoever commits one of the following crimes is considered a traitor:

1) Those who attempt to overthrow the various levels of the national government and plot to establish puppet regimes;

2) Those who destroy the People's Resist-Japan Movement or the mobilization for the War of Resistance;

3) Those who carry out any kind of spying and secret agent work;

4) Those who organize and lead bandit activities and disturbances;

5) Those who signal bombing or shooting targets to the enemy;

6) Those who organize and lead troops to rebel or run away;

7) Those who propagandize and deceive people in order to organize and lead a rebellion;

8) Those who murder leaders of the Party, government, military, and even mass groups or other persons with positions of responsibility;

---

[1] Drafted in 1939. Located in *K'ang-jih ken-chü-ti cheng-ts'e t'iao-li hui-chi, Shen-Kan-Ning chih-pu*, Vol. 3, pp. 778-780.

9) Those who induce or force people to serve the enemy, causing insult, ill-treatment, or danger to the people;

10) Those who run away with their weapons, rebel, and surrender to the enemy;

11) Those who conceal, transport, buy or sell ammunition intentionally to create rebellion;

12) Those who assist in sending food, military equipment, or capital to the enemy;

13) Those who sabotage communications or obstruct transportation and communication;

14) Those who sabotage currency and disturb the banking and financial administration;

15) Those who create or spread rumors;

16) Those who take the opportunity to burn and loot;

17) Those who use articles, illustrations, and books as propaganda or who use religion and superstition to sabotage the War of Resistance.

18) Those who intentionally release traitors, letting them run away or who falsely accuse others as traitors.

Article 4: Those who commit a crime under any of the provisions of Article 3 are sentenced to a prison term or to death according to the seriousness of the situation. Also, the criminal's property can be confiscated or he can be fined.

Article 5: Those who incite, abet, or assist in committing a crime under any of the provisions of Article 3 are considered the same as the criminal himself.

Article 6: Unaccomplished crimes under Article 3 are punishable.

Article 7: Those who commit a crime under any provision of Article 3, if the government considers they were coerced into being an accomplice, can receive a reduced punishment.

Article 8: Those who commit a crime under any provision of Article 3 and voluntarily surrender and confess before being discovered can receive a reduced punishment. The statute governing voluntary surrender and confession [*tzu-shou*] will be enacted separately.

Article 9: Those who commit a crime under any provision of Article 3 and report it before it happens so that the crime can be prevented or the criminal apprehended may receive a reduced or remitted punishment.

Article 10: Those who commit a crime under any provision of Article 3 and are 14 and under, or 80 and over, may have their punishment reduced or remitted.

Article 11: The right to interpret this statute belongs to the Border Region government.

Article 12: The right of amending this statute belongs to the Border Region People's Political Council.

Article 13: After being passed by the Border Region People's Political Council, this statute will be promulgated by the Border Region government and will become effective.

Draft Statute of the Shensi-Kansu-Ninghsia Border Region Concerning Martial Law During War[1]

Article 1: This statute was enacted in order to assist the War of Resistance, to strengthen the rear areas, to stop the activities of traitors and enemy spies, and to maintain peace in the Border Region.

Article 2: Whenever it is necessary to put martial law into effect, the Border Region Committee will order the Border Region garrison commander to proclaim martial law according to the decisions of this statute.

Article 3: The areas under martial law are divided into two kinds:

1) The area under alert [*ching chieh*] which refers to an area that should be under alert because it is affected by the war during wartimes;

2) The area contiguous to the war zone [*chieh chan*], which refers to an area that may be either attacked or defended. When necessary, the area under alert or contiguous to the war zone should be demarcated and notified accordingly.

Article 4: As soon as possible after proclaiming martial law, the Border Region garrison commander should immediately report the circumstances of the martial law and its management to the commander of the war zone and to the Border Region government.

Article 5: As for those criminals who commit the following crimes in the areas near to the war zone, the military judicial organs [*chün-shih ts'ai-p'an chi-kuan*] can try them themselves or transfer them to the courts for trial:

[1] Dated 1939. Located in *K'ang-jih ken-chü-ti cheng-ts'e t'iao-li hui-chi, Shen-Kan-Ning chih-pu*, Vol. 3, pp. 775-776.

1) Those who steal military information and divulge military secrets;

2) Those who carry out activities to sabotage the War of Resistance;

3) Those who incite the troops to rebel;

4) Those who attempt to suppress the Anti-Japanese political regime;

5) Those who destroy transportation that has a connection with military affairs or obstruct important roads;

6) Those who plot sabotage;

7) Those who disrupt the peace of an area.

Article 6: When martial law is proclaimed, the garrison commander has the right to carry out the following things:

1) He may stop assemblies and associations that are destructive to the War of Resistance and may prohibit news, magazines, illustrations, statements, and slogans which are destructive to the War of Resistance;

2) He may open and inspect letters and telegrams, and if they are considered to be impediments to the War of Resistance and to military affairs, they can be detained or confiscated;

3) He may inspect traffic, animal carriers, and travelers, etc.;

4) When necessary, he can search the residence of the people in the area contiguous to the war zone or order the evacuation of the area;

5) During the war, whenever it is unavoidable, he can use or destroy the immovable property of the people, but he should compensate them.

Article 7: When the food and supplies of the people within the area under martial law are used for the military, investigation and recording must be carried out. When necessary, exportation of the goods may be prohibited or goods may be requisitioned. However, an appropriate price must be paid.

Article 8: When the circumstances prompting the martial law end, the ending of martial law should immediately be proclaimed and from that day prior normal conditions should be restored.

Article 9: This statute becomes effective as soon as it is promulgated.

APPENDIX F: Revised Method of Handling Traitors' Property[1]

1. In order to eradicate traitors and to strengthen the power of the War of Resistance, the Shansi-Chahar-Hopei Border Region Administrative Committee (hereafter referred to as "this committee") regulates the confiscation of traitors' property in accordance with the provisions of this statute, in addition to the provisions stipulated in Articles 8-13 of the "Revised Regulations Governing Punishment of Traitors."

2. Those who have conspired with the enemy and have committed crimes stipulated under the categories of Article 2 of the "Revised Regulations Governing Punishment of Traitors" promulgated by the Nationalist Government are considered as traitors and the government may confiscate all or part of their property.

3. Confiscating or sealing a traitor's property should be restricted to his own belongings and not those of his relatives. If the family resides with him, they should be left with living expenses.

4. The government can confiscate all property belonging to the traitor, whether it is movable or immovable.

5. The confiscated movable property belonging to the traitor should be collected by this committee and delivered to the border region banks to be used as reserves or to be distributed as rewards to the guerrilla forces. If there is very heavy property that is not convenient to collect, the *hsien* government may conduct an auction after getting the approval of this committee and then collect the proceeds.

6. All the confiscated immovable property belonging to the traitor will become the public property of the Border Region and will be managed directly by this committee. It should be

[1] Promulgated February 9, 1938 and the revision promulgated January 1, 1939. Found in *K'ang-jih ken-chü-ti cheng-ts'e t'iao-li hui-chi, Chin-Ch'a-Chi chih-pu*, pp. 456-7.

distributed to the poor people to till or to reside on without rent. The method is as follows:

1) After distribution and registration by the government, the right of tilling and residing in those confiscated lands and houses will belong to the poor people to whom they have been distributed. But they cannot sell or mortgage these distributed lands and houses.

2) The families of soldiers in the resistance struggle and poor people have priority rights to a share of those confiscated lands and houses.

3) The local *hsien* government or the *ch'ü* government should decide how much land and how many houses a certain person should have of the confiscated land and houses based on each person as a counting unit. Then they should call a meeting of the people of the village for approval.

4) The *hsien* government should give documentary proof to the people who receive the land or houses and should report it to this committee for recording.

5) In order to protect the public interest, the people who received the distributed land and houses should pay tax to the government according to the original amount due.

6) After receiving the land and houses, if the people are convicted of criminal offenses and punished, the *hsien* government should take away their right of tilling and of residence and should report it to this committee for recording.

7. The mortgage, rent, or loan arrangements on the confiscated traitor's property should be settled by the *hsien* government on behalf of the original owner and reported to this committee for recording.

8. An inventory list for the property confiscated or sealed according to this statute should be made and reported to this committee by the administering organ for recording.

9. Permission of this committee must be granted before carrying out the confiscation or sealing of traitor's property according to this statute, and the administering organ must publicly announce it.

10. This statute becomes effective as soon as it is promulgated.

Editor's Note:

1) The contents of "The Method of Handling Traitors' Property" promulgated in February 1938 is the same or similar to this statute except for Article 2. The original text of Article 2 reads as follows: Article 2: Those who publicly communicate with the enemy to help the enemy and who commit crimes under Articles 1-3 of the "Law Governing Emergency Crimes Endangering the Republic" promulgated by the Nationalist Government on September 4, 1937 are all considered as traitors. . . .

2) The government is again considering revising this statute according to the spirit of Article 17 of the Double Ten Program.

APPENDIX G: Separate Statute of the Shansi-
Chahar-Hopei Border Region
Concerning Voluntary Surrender
and Confession of Traitors[1]
(*Tzu-Shou*)

Article 1: This Border Region has daily increased and been
strengthened, and the enemy puppet organizations one by one
have come to us; thus, in order to further enlarge and strength-
en the United Front, to win the ultimate victory of the War of
Resistance, and especially to provide traitors an opportunity to
reform and become new men (*tzu-hsin*), this statute is enacted
and promulgated.

Article 2: Whoever, because there is no alternative, organized
or participated in the puppet military (the puppet security
forces, puppet Royalist army, puppet Manchurian army, or
puppet police) whether soldiers or officers, is given the opportunity to reform and become a new man, if he individually or
as a member of a group carried out any of the works listed
below:

1) Those puppet troops who, when our troops attack cities
or fortifications, help us from within, causing the city or forti-
fication to be recovered, will be given the name of Resisting
Japan for participating in the work of resisting the Japanese.
Furthermore, this committee will request the Nationalist
Government to reward them.

2) Those officers who lead their soldiers to kill enemy or
puppet officials, to destroy important enemy fortifications and
transportation routes, or to surrender to us carrying arms, all
should be given the name of Resist Japan military men. After
they are trained, they can participate in the work of resisting

[1] Promulgated on November 17, 1938. Found in *K'ang-jih ken-chü-ti
cheng-ts'e t'iao-li hui-chi, Chin-Ch'a-Chi chih-pu*, pp. 458-460.

181

Japan; their troops should not be disbanded or disarmed. Also, this committee will request the Nationalist Government to reward them.

3) Those junior officers who lead the patriotic heroes to kill the diehard puppet military leaders and resolutely come to us, in addition to being properly organized in accordance with the number of their troops, will also be treated according to the first provision of this article.

4) Groups of three or five adults or single persons who return carrying their weapons, in addition to being given the appropriate price according to this committee's method for buying weapons, also will be given appropriate work according to their wishes.

5) Those who have not found an opportunity to rebel against the enemy but constantly provided the various local governments, military units, and mass organizations of this Border Region with secret enemy intelligence or who were passive and sabotaged the enemy's work and can prove it, in addition to being treated well, also will be assigned appropriate work when we recover that area.

Article 3: Those who participated in the puppet regime because there was no alternative but have not killed their Chinese fellow countrymen, regardless of rank, individually or as a group should be given an opportunity to reform and become new men if they carry out any of the works listed below:

1) Those who killed officials of the enemy side or who, after having been obstinate, foolish, and deluded traitors, have resolutely returned and moreover have secretly made rebellion in the enemy territory will be given important work according to their ability. Also, this committee will request the Nationalist Government to reward them.

2) Those who had close relations with any level of this Border Region's government, military units, or mass groups and often supplied enemy information, concealed personnel of this Border Region, exhaustingly protected fellow countrymen in the enemy areas, and have concrete facts to show this,

at the appropriate time will receive good treatment from this Border Region and will be distributed work. Or when our army recovers that territory, besides good treatment, they also will be assigned appropriate work.

3) Those who aided this Border Region in mobilizing money, goods, or manpower or in making government propaganda and have concrete facts to show this will be treated the same as under item 1.

Article 4: As for those who participated in the puppet propaganda team, puppet newspapers, puppet New People Associations, and other traitor organizations, because there was no alternative, regardless of the evilness of their past deception, if they can forsake darkness and surrender to light, correct past crimes, return from the enemy territory, and write a sincere confession, and if their behavior proves they are truly repentant, then they will be assigned appropriate work after they are educated.

Article 5: Those who served the enemy for profit and spied on our military activities, destroyed electric lines, or participated in other plots, and who voluntarily surrender and confess to the local government or troops, bringing secret articles or news reports of the enemy to our side or reporting the details of their traitor accomplices resulting in the accomplices' apprehension, in addition to receiving economic assistance from the local *hsien* government, also will be distributed work according to their ability to work.

Article 6: All those who were utilized by the [Japanese] bandits as the result of a moment's foolishness but did not repent in time [*to tzu-shou*] and who have detected enemy information or seized traitors, and have proof of this work, and who can obtain a guarantee either from five reliable people or from two business firms, shall be given the opportunity to reform and become new men and shall be guaranteed safety of their life and property.

Article 7: This statute becomes effective as soon as it is promulgated.

Appendix H: Method for Temporarily Handling Criminals in Prison in Extraordinary Times[1]

Article 1: Criminals in custody in prisons, except those assigned to serve in the army, and criminals in custody in detention centers should be handled according to this method.

Article 2: Those prisoners who can be paroled according to the law or who can serve outside the prison with guarantees should be released under guarantee. If a guarantee cannot be obtained and martial law has already been proclaimed in the locality, then the prisoners may be released without guarantee.

Article 3: When martial law has already been proclaimed in a locality, the following types of prisoners should be handled according to the stipulations of Article 2:

1) Those with a sentence of imprisonment for five years or less or of detention for a short period;
2) Those whose remaining sentence is less than 3 years;
3) Those over sixty who are really sick.

Article 4: Prisoners besides those listed in the previous two articles will be handled as follows:

1) If the locality has already been designated an area contiguous to the war zone and it is impossible to guard the prison, those who were sentenced to a maximum of 10 years in prison can be temporarily released.

2) As for those who were convicted to life sentences or to more than 10 years in prison, the prisons in the rear area should keep room in reserve for them. When it is necessary, they should be sent to these prisons. However, if the area has already become an area contiguous to the war zone and there

---

[1] No date given. Found in *K'ang-jih ken-chü-ti cheng-ts'e t'iao-li hui-chi, Chin-Ch'a-Chi chih-pu*, pp. 465-466.

is not sufficient time to deliver the prisoners to the rear areas, the method in the previous provision should be applied.

Within 10 days after suspension of martial law in the locality is announced, those who have been released should surrender to the prison or to the police station. Those who exceed the period will be considered as escaped convicts.

Article 5: Those people in detention centers who according to the law may cease to be detained will be handled analogous to the method stipulated in Article 2. Those in serious cases who should be detained will be handled analogous to the first provision of Article 4. Those in very serious cases who could be given capital punishment or life sentences will be handled analogous to the second provision of the same article.

Article 6: Those who are released under guarantee according to the first provision of Article 2 and the first provision of Article 5 should be handled according to common procedure. Those who are freed under the second provision of Article 3, Article 4, and the second provision of Article 5 or who are temporarily released should be approved by the commander of the martial law of that locality. Also a list of names should be made and reported to the Department of Judicial Administration for recording. The names of criminals entrusted to the detention centers by administrative organs should be reported to the original organ or their superior organ.

Article 7: If there are any temporary regulations governing those criminals subject to trial by organs of military justice, then the temporary regulation should be followed.

Article 8: This measure is not applicable to crimes against the security of the state in conjunction with a foreign power [*wai-huan-tsui*]. When it is necessary, those detained in prison who committed the above crime should be sent to the rear areas for imprisonment.

Appendix I: Statute Concerning Voluntary Surrender and Confession (*Tzu-Shou*) of Traitors by the Nationalist Government's Military Affairs Commission[1]

Article 1: Those traitors who voluntarily surrender and confess before being discovered and meet any of the following provisions will have their punishment remitted or suspended:

1) Those who report other cases of traitors resulting in trial and conviction or in valuable evidence being discovered;

2) Those who make credible reports revealing traitors or the plots and plans of spies;

3) Those who secretly report enemy intelligence that is beneficial to our country;

4) Those who surrender to us carrying arms.

Article 2: Those who after having been discovered as committing other crimes, voluntarily confess their traitorous crimes which were undiscovered, should have the punishment for the crime to which they confessed remitted or suspended if they fit into any of the categories of the previous article.

Article 3: Those traitors who after voluntarily surrendering and confessing and having their sentence remitted or its execution suspended, again act as traitors, besides being punished for the previously confessed crime without the originally proposed pardon or reduction, also should have their punishment increased according to the following provisions:

[1] This Statute was promulgated with an introduction by the Shansi-Chahar-Hopei Border Region Administrative Committee on January 15, 1941. It was originally promulgated by the Nationalist Government's Military Affairs Commission in November 1937. It is found in *K'ang-jih ken-chü-ti cheng-ts'e t'iao-li hui-chi, Chin-Ch'a-Chi chih-pu*, pp. 467-471.

186

1) All the person's property is confiscated;

2) His spouse, lineal relatives, members of the family residing with him, and his guarantors are considered as aiding in the crime. But those who report it before the event or who are 80 and over or 18 and under are not so considered.

Article 4: Those who have previously been traitors under this statute and again voluntarily surrender and confess before being discovered, in addition to avoiding the increased punishment of the previous article, should be handled as follows:

1) For those who are ordinary cases of voluntary surrender and confession, it is not appropriate to use the stipulations found in "Lighter Punishment for Those Who Voluntarily Surrender and Confess" of the general principles of criminal law, but the specific circumstances should be considered;

2) Those who voluntarily surrender and confess and meet any of the provisions of Article 1 should have their punishment lightened. Those who voluntarily confess according to the previous provisions after their punishment has been decided can be released under guarantee if they have already served over half of their sentence and can prove they are really repentant. After they are released on guarantee, those who do not again commit a crime during the term of their unfinished sentence will have their unfinished sentence considered as served.

Article 5: Traitors who voluntarily surrender and confess should report to the following organs:

1) Organs or military units that have jurisdiction over military justice;

2) Police organs;

3) Municipal or *hsien* governments and the supervision commissioner's office;

4) Political training departments of the various levels of the unit of independent brigade [*tu-li-lü*] or above. Those illiterate people who voluntarily surrender and confess can make an oral report, but the organ that receives the report should fill out forms in his behalf and ask him to put his fingerprint on it.

Article 6: Those organs or troops mentioned in the first provision of the previous article who do not have the right of trial in cases involving traitors, after they receive the report of the confession, should give their opinions and transport them with the person who voluntarily surrendered and confessed to an organ or troop of that place or nearby which does have the right of trial. However, military units with jurisdiction over military law temporarily may *not* handle the cases of voluntary surrender and confession of Article 1 and Article 4 during periods of fighting.

Article 7: The organ that handles a case of voluntary surrender and confession, after approving the confession, should decide the case according to law. The release of persons who have voluntarily surrendered and confessed and have already had their cases decided should be handled according to the following:

1) The spouse or lineal relatives of the person who voluntarily surrendered and confessed should be summoned and two people should be sought to guarantee and to be jointly responsible for his supervision.

2) Those who have traveled far away from their relatives or who cannot find guarantors should be taken to the municipal or *hsien* government of their original registration or to the supervision commissioner's office to be handled according to the above provisions.

3) Those who because of special circumstances cannot be taken to the district of their original registration should be taken to the municipal or *hsien* government of a nearby place or to the supervision commissioner's office to be received and supervised temporarily. Those who are 80 and over or 18 and under cannot act as guarantors.

Article 8: Until the war has ended, the spouse, lineal relatives and the guarantors of persons who have voluntarily surrendered and confessed should closely supervise the criminal's words and actions and are given the following special rights:

1) To prohibit the person who has voluntarily surrendered and confessed from discussions of national affairs;

2) To forbid the person who has voluntarily surrendered and confessed from having contacts with suspicious persons;

3) To inspect the letter sent or received by the person who has voluntarily surrendered and confessed;

4) To interfere with the movements or distant travel of the person who has voluntarily surrendered and confessed;

5) To keep books or newspapers that should not be read away from the person who has voluntarily surrendered and confessed.

If the spouse, lineal relatives, or guarantors discover that the person who has voluntarily surrendered and confessed is guilty of illegal behavior or even that there are other suspicious circumstances, they should immediately report it to the municipal or *hsien* government or to the supervision commissioner's office or to the organ that originally handled the voluntary surrender and confession.

Article 9: After receiving a report, those organs listed in the second part of the previous article should temporarily detain and examine the person who voluntarily surrendered and confessed until he is truly repentant and can again be turned over to the original guarantors for supervision.

Article 10: The spouse, lineal relatives, and guarantors or the organ that received and handled the case should provide means for indoctrinating and reforming the person who has voluntarily surrendered and confessed.

Article 11: The organ that handles a voluntary surrender and confession should submit the detailed facts and the written judgment to its highest governing body and to the highest organ of military affairs of the central government for recording. [*Chung-yang tsui-kao chün-shih chi-kuan*].

Article 12: Having recognized their mistakes, persons who voluntarily surrender and confess have the ability to assist in investigating traitors or may be retained for service when necessary. They will be given living expenses, but they cannot be ordered to handle matters related to the national military defense or political affairs.

Article 13: Those persons who voluntarily surrendered and confessed and who are detained for service or to aid in a traitor's case will fall under the stipulations of provision 1 of Article 1 and provision 3 of Article 2. Those whose achievements are considered especially good will be reported to the highest military organ of the central government for reward.

Article 14: This regulation becomes effective as soon as it is promulgated.

Editor's Note: When actually carrying it out, still rely on the previous "Separate Statute."[2]

[2] Refers to the "Separate Statute of the Shansi-Chahar-Hopei Border Region Concerning Voluntary Surrender and Confession of Traitors," promulgated November 17, 1938. See Appendix G.

APPENDIX J: Revised Laws Governing Emergency Crimes Endangering the Republic[1]

Article 1: Those who for the purpose of endangering the Republic commit one of the following acts is sentenced to death:

1) Those who privately communicate with enemy countries to plot to disturb the public order and peace;

2) Those who in league with traitors plot to disturb the public order and peace;

3) Those who for an enemy country or for a traitor procure or transport militarily useful goods;

4) Those who disclose or deliver government or military secrets to enemy countries or traitors;

5) Those who destroy transportation or military establishments;

6) Those who incite soldiers to disobey discipline, to abandon their jobs or to be in league with enemy nations or traitors;

7) Those who incite others to communicate privately with enemy nations or to be in league with traitors or to disturb the public order and peace;

8) Those who make rumors to confuse the masses and to reduce their confidence in the military or to disturb the public order and peace;

9) Those who use articles, illustrations, or speeches as propaganda for an enemy nation or traitors.

Those who were incited to commit the previous crimes and voluntarily surrender and confess may have their sentence lightened or may be exempt from punishment.

[1] The original text was promulgated on September 4, 1937. The Border Region Administrative Committee copied it and issued it February 10, 1938. Found in *K'ang-jih ken-chü-ti cheng-ts'e t'iao-li hui-chi, Chin-Ch'a-Chi chih-pu*, pp. 471-473.

Article 2: Those who know others who privately communicate with enemy countries or act as traitors but conceal this and do not report the information are sentenced for a minimum of 5 years in prison. Those who commit the above crime and voluntarily surrender and confess will have their punishment lightened or will be exempt from punishment.

Article 3: Those who organize groups or associations for the purpose of endangering the Republic are sentenced to a minimum of 5 and a maximum of 15 years in prison.

Article 4: In periods of war against a foreign country, those who take articles, illustrations, or speeches and use them as propaganda for the enemy country, even if they did not intentionally endanger the Republic, are sentenced to a maximum of 3 years in prison.

Article 5: In periods of war against a foreign country, those who transmit untrue news sufficient to disturb the public order and peace or to shake people's confidence are sentenced to a maximum of 1 year in prison or detention.

Article 6: In periods of war against a foreign country, those who send letters to people of the enemy country without the government's permission are sentenced to a maximum of 1 year in prison or detention.

Article 7: Those who commit crimes under this law will be tried by the highest organ or military justice of that area.

Article 8: Crimes judged under this law should be reported with the facts of the case by the highest organ of military justice of that area to their superior organ of military justice for approval prior to implementation.

Article 9: When the military or police organs arrest a person suspected of the behavior in this law, they should notify the governing organ immediately.

Article 10: Crimes not covered under this law should be handled according to the stipulations of criminal law.

Article 11: This law goes into effect as soon as it is promulgated.

Appendix K: Revised Statute Concerning Punishment of Traitors[1]

Article 1: Cases of traitors are handled according to this statute.

Article 2: To cooperate with an enemy country and to do one of the following types of behavior is to be a traitor and is punished by the death sentence or life imprisonment:

1) Those who plot to resist their own country;
2) Those who plot to disturb the public order and peace;
3) Those who recruit troops or other personnel for military service;
4) Those who supply and sell or procure and transport militarily useful goods or who manufacture the materials for weapons and ammunition;
5) Those who supply and sell or procure and transport grains, rice, wheat, flour, and other items that can be substituted for grains;
6) Those who supply currency or capital;
7) Those who disclose, transmit, spy, or steal news, documents, illustrations, or goods concerning the military, political or economic situation;
8) Those who act as guide or do other service connected with the military;
9) Those who obstruct public officials from carrying out their duties;
10) Those who disturb the currency;
11) Those who sabotage transportation, communication, or military fortifications or blockades;
12) Those who put poison in food and drink;
13) Those who incite military men, government officials, or the people to go over to the enemy;

[1] Promulgated October 15, 1938. Found in *K'ang-jih ken-chü-ti cheng-ts'e t'iao-li hui-chi, Chin-Ch'a-Chi chih-pu*, pp. 473-475.

14) Those who are incited by those in the previous category and follow them to incite others.

Article 3: Those who harbor or abet the criminals of the previous article are considered jointly as the main criminal.

Article 4: Those who know of crimes under Article 2 but conceal them and do not report them are sentenced to life in prison or to a minimum of 7 years in prison.

Article 5: Those who falsely accuse others of any crime under this statute should be punished according to that article.

Article 6: Those who attempt to commit a crime under this statute will be punished.

Article 7: Those who prepare or conspire to commit the crimes under Articles 2 and 3 are sentenced to a minimum of 7 years in prison. Those under Articles 4 and 5 are sentenced to a minimum of 1 year and a maximum of 7 years in prison.

Article 8: Things which are used to violate articles under this statute or which are supplied to criminals to be used in the crime or which are used in preparation for the crime should be confiscated, no matter whether or not they belong to the criminal.

Article 9: All the property of those whose crimes are under Article 2 should be confiscated. Confiscation of all the property of those who are wanted but not yet arrested for the crimes in the previous provision should be announced separately.

Article 10: When all the property is sealed or confiscated according to this statute, the family should be left with living expenses.

Article 11: The handling of the property sealed or confiscated according to this statute is entrusted to the administrative organ of that governing territory. The organ that carries out the previous provisions should immediately make a list of the property and report it to the highest organ of military affairs of the central government.

Article 12: The property confiscated according to Article 8 should be turned over to or reported to a nearby military post or to the administrative organ of that place to take control and to report it to the highest organ of military affairs of the central government.

Article 13: The property that is sealed or confiscated according to this statute should be publicly announced by the administering organ.

Article 14: Those who have committed crimes under this statute are tried by an organ or military unit having the right of trial by military law. Jurisdictional conflicts should be reported to and settled by the highest organ of military affairs of the central government.

Article 15: Within 5 days after the decision is announced in cases decided according to this statute, a summary of the original copy of the decision should be prepared. The defense of the accused, together with the evidence, should be sent to the central highest organ of military affairs for decision. However, when there is a need for immediate settlement, the facts of the case, the law that has been applied, and the reasons necessitating an immediate settlement may be stated clearly and communicated by telegraph in a request for a decision. The military commander in the war zone near to the area where the cases of the previous provision occurred should be authorized to handle these cases.

Article 16: In cases submitted according to the previous article, the highest organ of military affairs of the central government may summon the criminal to trial or may send personnel to the locale to conduct the trial or may transfer the case to other organs.

Article 17: The provisions of criminal procedure of general criminal law are applicable if not in conflict with this statute.

Article 18: Those who have committed the crimes of this

statute and who voluntarily surrender and confess before being discovered are handled according to the "Statute Concerning Voluntary Surrender and Confession of Traitors."

Article 19: This statute becomes effective as soon as it is promulgated.

Appendix L: Temporary Statute of Shantung Province for Punishing War Criminals and Traitors[1]

Article 1: We specially made this statute in order to protect the thorough victory of the national war and to strengthen the work of world peace and to provide deserved punishment to war criminals and traitors.

Article 2: Whoever has done the following activities is sentenced to death or to a minimum of 10 years in prison and is disfranchised for life: (The method for handling his property will be decided separately.)

1) Those who were loyal to Japanese militarism from beginning to end of the war and have committed very evil crimes so as to be hated by the people;

2) Those who were commanding officers or principal conspirators in the liaison department of the secret agent organizations and in the military police of the Japanese military department;

3) Those who after Japan announced her surrender organized to oppose the surrender and to resist resolutely or to massacre people;

4) Those who in the confusion of the war took the opportunity to burn, kill, and create internal disorder;

5) Those commanding officers or primary conspirators of puppet troops, puppet regimes, and puppet organizations who actively sabotaged the business of national liberation;

6) Those who massacred or ill-treated prisoners of war;

[1] This was Section B of the Shantung Provincial Government's Proclamation Order #1 signed by Li Yü and dated August 15, 1945. It is found in "A Collection of All Kinds of Statutes, Programs and Methods Promulgated by the Shantung Provincial Government and the Shantung Military Region," which was compiled by the Shantung Ch'ü Administrative Office on August 29, 1945.

7) Those primary conspirators or instigators who organized feudalistic societies and superstitious groups to perform effective labor for the enemy and actively to sabotage the work of national liberation;

8) Those who sabotaged our sides' military, political, economic, cultural, and communication facilities causing loss and damage;

9) Those who conclusively organized the sabotage of our front line or rear area causing loss and damage;

10) Those who organized rebellion and surrender to the enemy or who rebelled and surrendered to the enemy and actively sabotaged the business of national liberation;

11) Those who made grief and slaughtered people;

12) Those who stole national military or political secrets and the main conspirators and instigators who sabotaged the struggle to resist Japan;

13) Those primary conspirators and instigators who seized able-bodied men and summoned them to labor for the enemy;

14) Those primary conspirators and instigators who plundered military weapons, goods, money, and grain for the enemy and the puppets;

15) Those war criminals and traitors who out of fear ran away and then were apprehended.

Article 3: Those who have the following behavior are sentenced to a minimum of 1 year but less than 10 years in prison and are disfranchised for a like period:

1) Accessory criminals [*ts'ung fan*] to the previous provisions 3, 7, 8, 9, and 10;

2) Unaccomplished crimes [*wei-sui-fan*] under the previous provisions 2, 3, 4, 5, 6, 7, 8, 9, 10, 11, 12, 13, and 14;

3) Traitors in addition to those mentioned under the various articles above, who communicate with the enemy or aid the enemy in sabotaging the War of Resistance.

Article 4: Those who concealed, hid, or abetted criminals listed in Article 2 are sentenced to 3 to 10 years in prison.

Those who concealed, hid, or abetted criminals listed under Article 3 are sentenced to less than 3 years in prison.

Article 5: Any person has the right to report, investigate, and arrest any criminal listed under the previous articles for trial.

Article 6: The right of interpreting and revising this statute belongs to the Shantung Provincial People's Political Council.

Article 7: This statute becomes effective as soon as it is promulgated.

Glossary

A-B t'uan   A-B League
A - B 團

an-chüan   records of a case
案 卷

Borodin, Michael
鮑 羅 庭

ch'a-feng   seal
查 封

Chahar
察 哈 爾

Ch'a-t'ien yün-tung   Land Investigation Drive
查 田 運 動

chan-cheng tsui-fan   war criminals
戰 爭 罪 犯

Chan-fan shen-li wei-yuan-hui Committee for Handling War
戰 犯 審 理 委 員 會   Criminals

Chan-fan tiao-ch'a wei-yuan-hui Commission of Inquiry Concerning
戰 犯 調 查 委 員 會   War Criminals

Chang Chen
張 眞

chang-ch'eng   regulations
章 程

Ch'ang cheng   Long March
長 征

ch'ang-ch'i k'u-kung   long term hard labor
長 期 苦 工

Chang Hsüeh-liang
張 學 良

Chang Kuo-t'ao
張 國 燾

Chang Kwei-chao
張 貴 昭

GLOSSARY

Ch'ang-wei
常 委
Standing Committee

Chang Wen-t'ien
張 聞 天

chen-ch'a
偵 查
to investigate

Ch'en Ch'eng
陳 誠

chen-tieh
偵 諜
spy

Ch'en Tu-hsiu
陳 獨 秀

chen-ya
鎮 壓
suppress

cheng-chih chih-tao-yuan
政 治 指 導 員
Political Commissar

cheng-chih-pu
政 治 部
political department

cheng-chü
證 據
evidence

cheng-fa
徵 發
to levy

Cheng-feng yün-tung
整 風 運 動
Cheng-feng Movement

cheng-jen
証 人
witness

Cheng-wu hui-i
政 務 會 議
Political Affairs Conference

Chi
冀
Hopei

Ch'i Li
齊 禮

chi-nien k'u-kung
幾 年 苦 工
long term hard labor

ch'i-t'u 企圖	to attempt, to try or to plan
chi-ya 羈押	confine to custody
chia-shih 假釋	parole
Chiang-hsi 江西	Kiangsi
Chiang-hsi sheng hsing-wei 江西省行委	Kiangsi Provincial Action Committee
Chiang Kai-shek 蔣介石	
ch'iang-pao 牆報	wall posters
ch'iang-p'o lao-tung 強迫勞動	hard labor
ch'iang-p'o ming-ling 強迫命令	oppressive commandism
Chiang-su 江蘇	Kiangsu
chiao-k'uan 繳款	to hand in money
Ch'iao-tung Chang-i p'ing-yuan 膠東昌濰平原	Chang-i Plain
chiao-yu p'i-p'ing 教育批評	education and criticism
chieh-chang 接戰	area contiguous to the war zone
chieh-shih ch'u 揚示處	proclamation stand
chieh-yen 戒嚴	martial law
chien-ch'a 檢查	to examine, to inspect, to investigate

GLOSSARY

Chien-ch'a kuan 檢 查 官	Procurator
Chien-ch'a-pu 檢 查 部	Procuracy
Chien-ch'a yuan 檢 察 院	Procuracy
Chien-ch'a wei-yuan-hui 檢 察 委 員 會	Procuratorial Committee
Chien-ch'a wei-yuan-hui 監 察 委 員 會	Control Commission
chien-shih 監 視	to hold in confinement or imprisonment
chien-chü 檢 舉	to accuse
chien-chü-hui 檢 舉 會	Accusation Meeting
chien-hsi 奸 細	spy
chien-hsing 減 刑	reduced sentence
ch'ien-ju 潛 入	to infiltrate
chien-shih 監 視	surveillance
chien-so 監 所	prison
chien-tieh 間 諜	espionage
Chien-tsu yün-tung 減 租 運 動	Reduce Rents and Interest Movement
chien-wai chih-hsing 監 外 執 行	serve one's sentence outside of prison
chien-wei 奸 僞	traitors and puppets

206

Ch'ien-wei
前委
Front Committee

chih-hsing
執行
execute, execution

chih-hsing-shu
執行書
written order for execution
(of sentence)

Chih-hsing wei-yuan-hui
執行委員會
Executive Committee

ch'ih-se k'ung-pu
赤色恐怖
red terror

chih-shih
指示
directive

Ch'ih-wei-chün (tui)
赤衛軍(隊)
Red Guards

Chin
晉
Shansi

Chin-Ch'a-Chi pien-ch'ü
晉察冀邊區
Shansi-Chahar-Hopei Border Region

Chin-Chi-Yü chün-ch'ü
晉察豫軍區
Shansi-Hopei-Honan Military
Region

chin-pi
禁閉
confine

Chin-Sui pien-ch'ü
晉綏邊區
Shansi-Suiyuan Border Area

Chin-kung lu-hsien
進攻路線
Forward and Offensive Line

ching-chieh
警戒
area under alert

ching-chieh
警戒
warning

ch'ing-hsing
輕刑
punish lightly

Ching-kang-shan
井崗山
Ching-kang Mountains

GLOSSARY

ching-kao
警告
warning

Ch'ing-li wei-yuan-hui
清理委員會
Clearance Committee

ch'ing-nien t'uan
青年團
Youth League

chiu-shen
就番
on-the-spot trial

cho-na
捉拿
arrest

Chou En-lai
周恩來

Chou Hsing
周興

ch'ü
區

ch'ü-chang
區長
head of ch'ü government

ch'u-chüeh
處決
execute (usually capital punishment)

Ch'u-chien wei-yuan-hui
鋤奸委員會
Weed Out Traitors Committee

Ch'ü Ch'iu-pai
瞿秋白

ch'ü-chu
驅除
banishment

chu-fan
主犯
principal offender

chu-hsi
主席
chairman

chu-hsi-t'uan
主席團
presidium

chu-kuan
主管
commanding officer

chu-mou
主謀

ringleader

chu-shih
主使

instigator

Ch'ü-hsiao chu-i
取消主義

Liquidationist

chü-i
拘役

detention for a short period

ch'u-li
處理

handle a case

chü-liu
拘留

detain

chü-p'iao
拘票

detention warrant

chu-shen-kuan
主番官

chief judge

Chu Te
朱德

Chu Ying
朱嬰

Chuan-chih
專置

Special Commissioner

chüan-k'uan
捐款

donate

Ch'üan-kuo hu-chi
  hui-tsung-hui
全國互濟會總會

National Mutual Aid
Association

Ch'üan-kuo su-wei-ai
  ch'u-yü tai-piao hui-i
全國蘇維埃區域代
  表會議

National Conference of Delegates
from the Soviet Areas

Ch'üan-kuo tai-piao ta-hui
全國代表大會

National Congress

GLOSSARY

chuan-p'iao
傳票

summons to trial

chueh-ting
決定

to decide a case

ch'ün-chung kung-shen-hui
群眾公審會

mass public trial

ch'ün-chung lu-hsien
群眾路線

mass line

chün-shih fa-t'ing
軍事法庭

court martial tribunal

chün-shih fa-yuan
軍事法院

a military court

chün-shih ts'ai-p'an-pu
軍事裁判部

judicial department for
military affairs

Chung-hua su-wei-ai kung-ho-kuo
中華蘇維埃共和國

Chinese Soviet Republic

Chung-kung liu-tz'u ta-hui
中共六次大會

Sixth National Congress of
the CCP

Chung-kuo ko-ming chün-shih
    wei-yuan-hui
中國革命軍事委員會

Chinese Revolutionary Military
Council

Chung-kuo kung-ch'an tang
中國共產黨

Chinese Communist Party

Chung-kung
中共

Chinese Communist Party

Chung-kuo kung-nung-ping hui-i
    (su-wei-ai) ti-i-tz'u
    ch'üan-kuo tai-piao
    ta-hui
中國工農兵會議(蘇維
    埃)第一次全國代表
    大會

First National Congress of the
Chinese Workers', Peasants',
and Soldiers' Council (Soviet)

Chung-ts'ai wei-yuan-hui
仲裁委員會

Arbitration Committee

Chung-yang cheng-chih chü   Central Politburo
中 央 政 治 局

Chung-yang chih-hsing wei-yuan-hui   Central Executive Committee
中 央 執 行 委 員 會

Chung-yang chü   Central Bureau of the CCP
中 央 局

chung-yang tsui-kao chün-shih   the highest organ of military
   chi-kuan   affairs of the central government
中 央 最 高 軍 事 機 關

Chung-yang wei-yuan-hui   Central Committee
中 央 委 員 會

erh-liu-tzu   loafer
二 流 子

fa-kuan   judge
法 官

fa-k'uan   fine
罰 款

fa-kuei   laws and regulations
法 規

fa-lu kuan-nien   legalistic viewpoint
法 律 觀 念

fa-t'ing   people's tribunal
法 庭

fa-yuan chang   president of a court
法 院 長

fa-yuan fu-yuan chang   vice president of a court
法 院 副 院 長

Fan-chien ch'ing-suan   Anti-Traitors Settlement
反 奸 清 算   Movement

Fan-chien su-k'u   Anti-Traitors Accusation
反 奸 訴 苦   Movement

fan-jen   offender
犯 人

GLOSSARY

Fan-jih t'ung-i chan-hsien   Anti-Japanese United Front
    kang-ling   Program
反 日 統 一 戰 線 綱 領

fan ko-ming   counterrevolutionary
反 革 命

fan-kung fen-tzu   anti-Communist elements
反 共 份 子

Fan-shen
翻 身

fan-shui   run away, change sides
反 水

fan tsui   crime
犯 罪

fan-tsui che   criminal
犯 罪 者

fan-tsui fen-tzu   criminal
犯 罪 分 子

fan-tung fen-tzu   reactionary elements
反 動 分 子

Fang-chien yün-tung   Guard Against Traitors Movement
防 奸 運 動

Fang Chih-min
方 志 敏

fang-tsung   to abet
放 縱

fen-chü   branch bureau of the PSB
分 局

fen-ch'ü   a sub-district
分 區

fen-t'ing   branch court
分 庭

Feng Yü-hsiang
馮 御 香

Fu-ch'ou k'ung-su
復仇控訴   Revenge and Complaint Movement

Fu-chien
福建

fu-ho   accomplice
附和

fu-nung   rich peasants
富農

fu-pu chang   vice director of judicial
副部長   departments

Fu-t'ien
富田

Hai-feng
海豐

Hai-hsiang fu-ch'ou-tui   Committees to Return to the
還鄉復仇隊   Villages

Hainan
海南

Hai-yen
海燕

han-chien   treason, traitor
漢奸

hao-shen   gentry
豪紳

Hatano, Kenichi
波多野幹一

Ho-nan   Honan
河南

Ho-pei   Hopei
河北

Ho Lung
賀龍

Hou-pu chung-yang wei-yuan   Alternative Member of the
候補中央委員   Central Committee

GLOSSARY

Hsi-an
西安
Sian

hsia-fang, hsia-hsiang
下放下鄉
to the village campaign

Hsiang
鄉

Hsiang-o-hsi chung-yang fen-chü
湘鄂西中央分局
Hunan-West Hupei Central Sub-bureau

Hsiang-o-kan pien t'e-ch'ü
湘鄂贛邊特區
Hunan-Hupei-Kiangsi Special Border Area

Hsiang-o pien t'e-ch'ü
湘鄂邊特區
Hunan-Hupei Special Border Area

Hsiang Ying
項英

hsiao-tzu-ch'an chieh-chi
小資產階級
petit bourgeoisie

hsieh-chu
協助
assists

hsieh-p'o
脅迫
coerced

hsieh-ts'ung
脅從
coerced accomplice

hsien
縣

hsien-chang
縣長
<u>hsien</u> magistrate

hsien-ch'eng
縣城
capital city of a <u>hsien</u>

hsien-hsing-fei
現行罪
in the act of committing a crime

hsien-kuan
縣官
<u>hsien</u> magistrate

Hsin-min-chu chu-i
新民主主義
New Democracy

Hsin-min-hui 新民會	New People's Association
Hsing-cheng tu-ch'a 　chuan-yuan kung-shu 行政督察專員公署	Supervision Commissioner's Office
Hsing-cheng wei-yuan-hui 行政委員會	Administrative Committee
hsing-fa 刑法	criminal law
Hsing-kuo 興國	
Hsing-tung wei-yuan-hui 行動委員會	Action Committee
hsüan-p'an ta-hui 宣判大會	mass trial to announce the decision
hsün-chieh 訓誡	a reprimand, a warning
hsün-hui fa-t'ing 巡廻法庭	circuit tribunal
hsün-ling 訓令	instructions
hsün-shih yuan 巡視員	circuit judge
hsün-wen 訓問	to question, to interrogate
Hu-nan 湖南	
Hua-pei 華北	North China
huan-ch'i 緩期	suspended sentence
huan-hsing 緩刑	suspended sentence

GLOSSARY

Huang-p'o
黃坡

hui-kuo-shu
悔過書   statement of repentence,
                              confession

hui-ts'un chih-hsing   return to the village to serve
囘村執行   a sentence

hui-ts'un fu-i   return to the village to
囘村服役   perform service

i-chi chieh-chi   class deviates
異己階級

i-chi fen-tzu   class deviates
異己分子

jao-luan chih-an   disturb the public order
擾亂治安

Jen-min wei-yuan-hui   Council of People's Commissars
人民委員會

Jih-k'ou   Japanese bandits
日寇

jou-hsing   corporal punishment
肉刑

Jui-ch'ang
瑞昌

Jui-chin
瑞金

Kai-tzu p'ai   Reorganizationalist
改組派

k'ai-hsiao-ch'ai   desertion
開小差

Kan   Kiangsi
贛

kan-hua chiao-yu   reform education
感化教育

Kan-min-wan pien-ch'ü   Kiangsi-Fukien-Anhwei Border
贛閩皖邊區   Region

kan-pu
幹部
cadre

k'an-shou-so
看守所
detention center

Kan-su
甘肅

Kao Kang
高崗

kao-mao tzu
高帽子
tall paper hats

Kao-teng fa-yuan
高等法院
High Court

Kao-teng fa-yuan chien-yu
高等法院監獄
High Court Prison

Ko Lao Hui
哥老會
Elder Brother Society

ko-ming p'an-t'u
革命叛徒
deserters of the revolution

kou-chieh
勾結
in league with

k'ou-su
口訴
oral testimony

ku-i
故意
intentionally

k'u-i
苦役
hard labor

k'u-kung
苦工
hard labor

k'u-kung-tui
苦工隊
hard labor groups

kuan-chih
管制
control

kuan-ta cheng-ts'e
寬大政策
lenient policy

GLOSSARY

Kuang-chou 廣州	Canton
Kuang-tung 廣東	Kwangtung
Kuei-tui yün-tung 歸隊運動	Return to the Troops Movement
Kung-an-chü 公安局	Public Security Bureau
kung-jen chieh-chi 工人階級	working class
kung-k'ai shen-p'an 公開審判	trial open for public attendance, public trial
k'ung-kao-chü 控告局	accusation boxes
k'ung-kao-jen 控告人	complainant
Kung-nung chien-ch'a wei-yuan-hui 工農檢查委員會	Workers' and Peasants' Inspection Committee
Kung-nung hung-chün 工農紅軍	Workers' and Peasants' Red Army
Kung-nung ko-ming wei-yuan-hui 工農革命委員會	Workers' and Peasants' Revolutionary Committee
Kung-nung-ping tai-piao hui-i 工農兵代表會議	Workers', Peasants' and Soldiers' Council
K'uo-ta hung-chün yün-tung 擴大紅軍運動	Enlarging the Red Army Movement
K'uo-ta te szu-chung ch'üan-hui 擴大的四中全會	Enlarged Fourth Plenum
kung-shen 公審	mass trial
kung-su 公訴	to prosecute

Kuo-chia cheng-chih pao-wei-chü   State Political Security Bureau
國 家 政 治 保 衞 局

Kuo-min-tang   Kuomintang or Nationalist Party
國 民 黨

lao-i   labor service
勞 役

lao-i-tui   labor groups
勞 役 隊

lao-tung kai-tsao   reform through labor
勞 動 改 造

lao-tung kan-hua-yuan   labor reformatories
勞 動 感 化 院

Li Li-san
李 立 三

Li Po-fang
李 伯 芳

Li Wei-han
李 維 漢

Liang Po-t'ai
梁 伯 台

lieh-shen   evil gentry
劣 紳

lin-shih-te lao-i-tui   temporary labor groups
臨 時 的 勞 役 隊

Liu Po-ch'eng
劉 伯 承

Liu Ti
劉 敵

Lo-an
樂 安

Lo Fu   alias for Chang Wen-t'ien
洛 甫

GLOSSARY

Lo Jui-ching
羅 瑞 卿

Lo Mai   alias for Li Wei-han
羅 邁

Lo Ming
羅 明

Lu   Shantung
魯

Lu Pi-min
魯 佛 民

Lu Ti-ping
魯 滌 平

Machiaho, Hsiangtan
湘 潭, 馬 家 河

Ma Hsi-wu
馬 錫 五

mang-tung chu-i   blind-actionism
盲 動 主 義

Mao Tse-tung
毛 澤 東

mi-shu   secretary of a judicial department
秘 書

mien-ch'u   exempted from punishment, punish-
免 除   ment remitted

mien-hsing   exempted from punishment, punish-
免 刑   ment remitted

Min   Fukien
閩

Min-che-kan pien-ch'ü   Fukien-Chekiang-Kiangsi Border
閩 浙 贛 邊 區   Region

min-fa   civil law
民 法

min-tsu tzu-ch'an chieh-chi   national bourgeoisie
民 族 資 產 階 級

min-t'uan 民 團	private troops of landlords
Min-yüeh-kan pien t'e-ch'ü 閩 粵 贛 邊 特 區	Fukien-Kwangtung-Kiangsi Special Border Area
ming-ling chu-i 命 令 主 義	commandism
mo-shou 沒 收	confiscation
mu-fan-tui 模 範 隊	model troops
Nan-ch'ang 南 昌	
Nan-ching 南 京	Nanking
Ning-hsia 寧 夏	
Ning Hsien 凝 先	
Ning-wu 寧 武	
Nung-hui 農 會	Peasant Associations
nung-min chieh-chi 農 民 階 級	peasant class
Nung-min chiu-hui 農 民 救 會	Peasant Associations
Nung-min hsieh-hui 農 民 協 會	Peasant Associations
Nung-min-pu 農 民 部	KMT Peasant Bureau
Nung-min tzu-wei chün 農 民 自 衞 軍	Peasant Self-Defense Army
Nung-min yün-tung chiang-hsi-so 農 民 運 動 講 習 所	Peasant Movement Training Institute

GLOSSARY

O 鄂	Hupei
o-pa 惡霸	local despots
O-yü-wan su-ch'ü 鄂豫皖蘇區	Oyuwan Soviet Area, Hupei-Honan-Anhwei Soviet
Pa-lu chün 八路軍	Eighth Route Army
pai-hua 白話	simplified modern language
pai-sha 白沙	pei-sa
pai-se k'ung-pu 白色恐怖	white terror
p'an-chüeh 判決	to judge a case
p'an-chüeh-shu 判決書	written decision
p'an-ch'u 判處	to sentence
p'an-hsing 判刑	to sentence
p'an-kuo 叛國	treason
p'an-ting 判定	to decide a case
p'an-tsui 判罪	to convict, conviction
p'an wu-tsui 判無罪	to acquit
Pao-an 保安	Political Security Bureau

pao-chang 保障	to guarantee
pao-cheng 保証	to guarantee
pao-cheng jen 保証人	guarantor
pao-jen 保人	guarantor
pao-pi 包庇	to harbor, to protect
pei-an 備案	recording a case
pei-kao jen 被告人	defendant
Pei-p'ing 北平	Peping or Peking
p'ei-shen-yuan 陪審員	assessor
P'eng P'ai 彭湃	
P'eng Te-huai 彭德懷	
p'o-huai 破壞	to destroy or to sabotage
Po-sheng 博生	
pu-chang 部長	director of a judicial department
pu-huo 捕獲	to arrest
pu-kao 佈告	announcement
pu-ya 捕押	to arrest

GLOSSARY

P'u-yang
濮陽

san-chi san-shen-chih 三級三審制	three level trial system
San-kuang cheng-ts'e 三光政策	Three All Policy--Kill All, Burn All, Loot All
Shan-hsi 山西	Shansi
shan-huo 煽惑	to incite
Shan-t'ou 汕頭	Swatow
Shan-tung 山東	
shan-tung 煽動	to incite
Shang-hai 上海	
shang-su 上訴	appeal
She-hui min-chu-tang 社會民主黨	Social Democratic Party
shen-ch'a 審查	examination, period of observation
shen-ch'a wei-yuan-hui 審查委員會	Supervisory Committee
Shen-hsi 陝西	Shensi
shen-hsün 審訊	to question, to interrogate
Shen-Kan-Ning pien-ch'ü 陝甘寧邊區	Shensi-Kansu-Ninghsia Border Region
shen-p'an 審判	to adjudicate

Shen-p'an wei-yuan-hui
審判委員會
Trial Committee

shen-p'an-yuan
審判員
judge

shen-su
申訴
petition for review

sheng
省
province

Sheng-ch'an yün-tung
生產運動
Production Movement

shih-ch'ü
市區
municipal

shih-fang
釋放
release

Shih-ta cheng-kang
十大政綱
Ten Great Political Programs

Shou-chi liang-shih yün-tung
收集糧食運動
Collecting Supplies Movement

shou-yao
首要
principal or main criminal

sou-ch'a-p'iao
搜查票
search warrant

su-ch'ing
肅清
liquidate

Su-ch'ü chung-yang-chü
蘇區中央局
Central Bureau of the Soviet Area

su-fan
肅反
liquidate or suppress counterrevolutionaries

Su-fan-hui
肅反會
Committee for the Suppression of Counterrevolutionaries

Su-wei-ai
蘇維埃
Soviet

GLOSSARY

Sui-te fen-ch'ü
綏德分區

Sun Yat-sen
孫中山

szu-fa 司法	to administer justice
szu-fa ch'u 司法處	justice bureaus
Szu-fa hsing-cheng-pu 司法行政部	Department of Judicial Administration
Szu-fa jen-min wei-huan-hui 司法人民委員會	People's Commissar of Justice
Szu-fa-pu 司法部	Ministry of Justice
szu-hsiang kai-tsao 思想改造	thought reform
szu-hsing 死刑	death penalty
Ta-tao-hui 大刀會	Big Sword Society

T'ai-hang Ch'ü
太行區

tai-piao kung-shen-hui 代表公審會	mass trial by representatives
tai-pu 逮捕	to arrest
tai-pu cheng 逮捕証	arrest warrant
t'an-pai shu 坦白書	statement of confession
T'an-pai tzu-hsin ta-hui 坦白自新大會	Honestly Reform into New Man Meeting

Tan Ping-shan
譚平山

tao-fei 刀匪	bandits connected with the Big Sword Society
t'ao-p'ao 逃跑	run away
t'ao-p'ao chu-i 逃跑主義	escapism
t'e-p'ai yuan 特派員	special agents of the PSB
t'e-pieh fa-t'ing 特別法庭	special tribunals
t'e-wu 特務	spy or intelligence agent, usually used for KMT spies as opposed to foreigners
Teng-fa 鄧發	
Teng Yen-ta 鄧演達	
ti-chu 地主	landlords
ti-fang fa-yuan 地方法院	local courts
Ti-san tang 第三黨	The Third Party
tiao-ch'a 調查	to investigate
Tiao-ch'a wei-yuan-hui 調查委員會	Commission of Inquiry Concerning War Criminals
T'iao-chieh wei-yuan-hui 調解委員會	Mediation Committees
t'iao-li 條例	statute
T'ien-chin 天津	Tientsin

GLOSSARY

tou-cheng
門爭
struggle

tou-cheng-hui
門爭會
struggle meetings

ts'ai-chüeh
裁決
to decide a case

ts'ai-chüeh shu
裁決書
written decision

ts'ai-p'an
裁判
judge (v)

ts'ai-p'an-pu
裁判部
judicial departments

ts'ai-p'an wei-yuan-hui
裁判委員會
judicial committee

ts'ai-p'an yuan
裁判員
judge

Ts'an-i-hui
參議會
People's Political Council

ts'ang-ni
藏匿
to conceal, to hide

ts'ao-an
草案
draft of an act

tsao-yao
造謠
to spread rumors

tso-i
左翼
left wing

tso-p'ai
左派
left wing

tsui-fan
罪犯
criminal

tsui-kao fa-yuan
最高法院
Supreme Court

Tsung-ch'ien-wei
總前委
General Front Committee

ts'ung-fan
從犯

accomplice

Tsung-hsing-wei
總行委

General Action Committee

tsung-jung
縱容

to abet

tso-t'an-hui
座談會

discussion meeting

t'u-chi-tui
突擊隊

Sudden Attack Patrols

t'u-fei
士匪

bandits

t'u-hao
士豪

village bosses

t'u-hsing
徒刑

imprisonment

tu-li-shih
獨立市

independent brigade

t'uan-fei
團匪

bandit groups

Tuan Hsi-p'eng
段錫朋

Tuan Liang-pi
段良弼

t'ui-fan
推翻

overthrow

t'ung-chih
統治

to rule

T'ung-chih shen-p'an-hui
同志審判會

Comrades' Adjudication Committee

T'ung-i chan-hsien
統一戰線

United Front Policy

t'ung-kao
通告

circular

GLOSSARY

Tung-ku
東固

t'ung-mou ti-kuo   to cooperate with an enemy
通謀敵國   country

Tung-yün-hui   Mobilization Committee
動運會

tzu-ch'an chieh-chi   bourgeoisie
資產階級

tzu-hsin   to reform and become a new man
自新

Tzu-hsin hsueh-i-so   Reformed Persons' Trade School
自新學藝所

Tzu-hsin-t'uan   New Men Groups
自新團

tzu-pen chia   capitalists
資本家

tzu-shou   to surrender and confess
自首   voluntarily prior to discovery

wai-huan-tsui   a crime against the security of
外患罪   the state in conjuncture with a
                   foreign power

Wan   Anhwei
皖

Wan-t'ai, Ho-tung
萬泰, 河東

Wang Chien-min
王健民

Wang Ching-wei
汪精衛

Wang-p'ai   Wang Ching-wei clique
汪派

wei   puppet
僞

wei-chiao
圍剿

encirclement campaign

wei-sui-fan
未遂犯

unaccomplished offenses

wen-shu
文書

clerk of a judicial department

wo-ts'ang
窩藏

to conceal

wu-ch'an chieh-chi
無產階級

proletariat

wu-ch'i t'u-hsing
無期徒刑

life imprisonment

wu-tsui
無罪

innocent

Wu-tung
武東

Yang Ch'i
楊琪

Yang Hu-ch'eng
楊虎城

Yen Hsi-shan
閻錫山

Yenan
廷安

yin-mou
陰謀

to conspire, to plot

yin-ts'ang
隱藏

to conceal

Yü
豫

Honan

yu-chi chu-i
游擊主義

guerrillaism

yu-ch'i t'u-hsing
有期徒刑

imprisonment for a fixed term

GLOSSARY

yu-ch'ing
右傾
right wing

yu-p'ai
右派
right wing

yu-p'i
誘逼
to induce or force

yü-shen
預審
preliminary investigation either
by the PSB or by the Procuracy

Yü-tu
雩都

Yüeh
粵
Kwangtung

Yün-chi
雲溪

yung-chiu te lao-i-tui
永久的勞役隊
permanent labor groups

Bibliography

Bibliography

References

Annual Legal Bibliography. Cambridge, Mass.: Harvard University Press.

Berton, Peter, and Wu, Eugene. Edited by Howard Koch, Jr. *Contemporary China: A Research Guide*. Stanford: Hoover Institute, 1967.

Bibliography of Asian Studies. Annual volume of the *Journal of Asian Studies* (formerly the *Far Eastern Quarterly*).

Bilancia, Philip R. *Dictionary of Chinese Communist Legal and Administrative Terms*. Manuscript Edition, University of Washington School of Law, 1967.

Black, Henry Campbell. *Black's Law Dictionary*. St. Paul, Minn.: West Publishing Co., 1968.

Boorman, Howard (ed.). *Biographical Dictionary of Republican China*. New York: Columbia University Press, 1967.

———. *Men and Politics in Modern China*. New York: Columbia University Press, 1960.

Brainwashing: A Guide to the Literature. A Report from the Society for the Investigation of Human Ecology, December 1960.

Fairbank, John K., and Liu, Kwang-ching. *Modern China: A Bibliographical Guide to Chinese Works 1898-1937*. Cambridge, Mass.: Harvard University Press, 1950.

Fenn, Courtenay H. *The Five Thousand Dictionary*. Shanghai: Mission Book Co., 1926.

Hsia, Tao-tai. *Selected Legal Sources of Mainland China*. Washington, D.C.: Library of Congress, 1967.

Hsüeh, Chün-tu. *The Chinese Communist Movement 1921-37*. Stanford: Hoover Institute, 1960.

———. *The Chinese Communist Movement 1937-49*. Stanford: Hoover Institute, 1962.

Index to Legal Periodicals. New York: H. W. Wilson Co.

Klein, Donald W., and Clark, Anne B. *Biographical Dictionary of Chinese Communism 1921-1965*. Cambridge, Mass.: Harvard University Press, 1971.

Kuo-yü tz'u-tien. Shanghai: 1943.

Kyriak, T. E. *China: A Bibliography and Guide to Contents of a*

Collection of United States Joint Publications Research Service Translations in the Social Sciences Emanating from Communist China. Annapolis, Maryland: Research Microfilms.

Library Catalogs of the Hoover Institute on War, Revolution and Peace, Stanford University Catalogue of the Chinese Collection. Boston: G. K. Hall & Co., 1969.

Lin, Fu-shun. *Chinese Law Past and Present.* New York: East Asian Institute, 1966.

Mathews, R. H. *Mathews' Chinese-English Dictionary.* Cambridge, Mass.: Harvard University Press, 1966.

Mersky, Roy M., and Jacobstein, J. Myron (eds.). *Index to Periodical Articles Related to Law.* Dobbs Ferry, New York: Glanville Publishers.

Oksenberg, Michel. *A Bibliography of Secondary English Language Literature on Contemporary Chinese Politics.* New York: East Asian Institute, 1970.

Perleberg, Max. *Who's Who in Modern China.* Hong Kong: Ye Olde Printerie, 1954.

Preliminary Union List of Materials on Chinese Law. Cambridge, Mass.: Harvard Law School Studies in Chinese Law No. 6, 1967.

Sorich, Richard. *Contemporary China.* New York: East Asian Institute, 1962.

Who's Who in Communist China. Hong Kong: Union Research Institute, 1969.

Wilbur, C. Martin, and How, Julie Lien-ying. *Documents on Communism, Nationalism and Soviet Advisers in China, 1918-1927: Papers Seized in the 1927 Peking Raid.* New York: Columbia University Press, 1956.

Wu, Eugene. *Leaders of 20th Century China: Annotated Bibliography of Selected Chinese Biographical Works in the Hoover Library.* Stanford: Stanford University Press, 1956.

English Language Sources

Books

Bao-Rue-Wang and Chelminski, Rudolph. *Prisoner of Mao.* New York: Coward, McCann and Georghegan, Inc., 1973.

Barnett, A. Doak (ed.). *Chinese Communist Politics in Action.* Seattle: University of Washington Press, 1969.

Belden, Jack. *China Shakes the World*. New York: Harpers, 1949.

Berman, H. J. *Justice in the USSR*. New York: Vintage Books, 1963.

———. *Materials for Comparison of Soviet and American Law*. Cambridge, Mass.: Harvard Law School, 1958.

———. *Soviet Criminal Law and Procedures: The R.S.F.S.R. Codes*. Cambridge, Mass.: Harvard University Press, 1966.

Blaustein, Albert P. *Fundamental Legal Documents of Communist China*. South Hackensack, New Jersey: Fred B. Rothman & Co., 1962.

Bodde, Derk, and Morris, Clarence. *Law in Imperial China: Exemplified by 190 Ch'ing Dynasty Cases (translated from Hsing-an hui-lan) with Historical, Social, and Judicial Commentaries*. Cambridge, Mass.: Harvard University Press, 1967.

Bonnichon, Father Andre. *Law in Communist China*. Hague: International Commission of Jurists, 1956.

Brandt, Conrad; Schwartz, Benjamin; and Fairbank, John K. *A Documentary History of Chinese Communism*. New York: Atheneum Press, 1966.

Ch'ü T'ung-tsu. *Law and Society in Traditional China*. Paris, 1961.

———. *Local Government in China under the Ch'ing*. Cambridge, Mass.: Harvard University Press, 1962.

Chugunov, Vladimir E. *Ugolovnoye Sudoproizvodstvo Kitayskoy Narodnoy Respubliki* [Criminal Court Procedures in the People's Republic of China] Moscow: 1959. Translated in Joint Publications Research Service No. 4595 (May 8, 1961).

Chung-hua jen-min kung-ho-kuo hsing-fa tsung-tse chiang-i [Lectures on the General Principles of Criminal Law in the People's Republic of China] Peking: Legal Press, 1958. Translated in Joint Publications Research Service No. 13331 (March 30, 1962).

Cohen, Jerome (ed). *Contemporary Chinese Law*, Cambridge, Mass.: Harvard University Press, 1970.

———. *The Criminal Process in the People's Republic of China 1949-1963: An Introduction*. Cambridge, Mass.: Harvard University Press, 1968.

Davies, S. J. *In Spite of Dungeons*. London: Hodder and Stoughton, 1954.

Escarra, Jean. *Chinese Law: Conception and Evolution, Legislative and Judicial Institutions, Science and Teaching*. Trans. Gertrude R. Browne (for Works Progress Administration W.P. 2799, University of Washington, Seattle; Peking, 1936), Cambridge, Mass.: Harvard Law School, 1961.

Fairbank, John K.; Reischauer, Edwin O.; and Craig, Albert. *East Asia: The Modern Transformation*. Boston: Houghton Mifflin Co., 1965.

Ford, Robert. *Wind Between the Worlds*. New York: David Mc-Kay Co., Inc., 1957.

Gelder, Stuart (ed.). *The Chinese Communists*. London: V. Gollanez, 1946.

Hazard, John. *Communists and Their Law*. Chicago: The University of Chicago Press, 1969.

Hinton, William. *Fanshen: A Documentary of Revolution in a Chinese Village*. New York: Vintage Books, 1968.

Ho Kan-chih. *A History of the Modern Revolution*. Peking: Foreign Language Press, 1960.

Ho, Ping-ti, and Tsou, Tang (eds.). *China in Crisis: China's Heritage and the Communist Political System*. Chicago: The University of Chicago Press, 1968.

Hsiao, K. C. *Rural China: Imperial Control in the Nineteenth Century*. Seattle: University of Washington Press, 1960.

Hsiao, Tso-liang. *Power Relations within the Chinese Communist Movement 1930-34: A Study of Documents*. Seattle: University of Washington Press, 1961.

Hsu, Yung Ying. *A Survey of Shensi-Kansu-Ninghsia Border Region*. New York: Institute of Pacific Relations, 1945.

Hunter, Edward. *Brain-washing in Red China*. New York: The Vanguard Press, 1953.

Kim, Ilpyong. *The Politics of Chinese Communism: Kiangsi Under the Soviets*. Berkeley: University of California Press, 1973.

Kun, Bela. *Fundamental Laws of the Chinese Soviet Republic*. International Publishers, 1934.

Kuo, Warren. *Analytical History of Chinese Communist Party*. Taipei: Institute of International Relations Republic of China, 1966.

Leng, Shao-chuan. *Justice in Communist China*. Dobbs Ferry, New York: Oceana Publications, Inc., 1967.

Lifton, Robert J. *Thought Reform and the Psychology of Totalism: A Study of Brainwashing*. New York: Norton, 1961.

Mao Tse-tung. *Selected Works of Mao Tse-tung*. Peking: Foreign Language Press, 1965.

Pye, Lucian W. *The Spirit of Chinese Politics*. Cambridge, Mass.: M.I.T. Press, 1968.

Rickett, Allyn and Adele. *Prisoners of Liberation*. New York: Cameron Associates, 1957.

Rigney, Harold W. *Four Years in a Red Hell*. Chicago: Henry Regnery Co., 1956.

Rue, John. *Mao Tse-tung in Opposition 1927-35*. Stanford: Stanford University Press, 1966.

Schein, Edgar H. *Coercive Persuasion: A Social-Psychological Analysis of American Prisoners by the Chinese Communist*. New York: Norton, 1961.

Schwartz, Benjamin. *Chinese Communism and the Rise of Mao*. New York: Harper & Row, 1967.

Selden, Mark. *The Yenan Way in Revolutionary China*. Cambridge, Mass.: Harvard University Press, 1971.

Seybolt, Peter. *Revolutionary Education in China, Documents and Commentary*. White Plains, New York: International Arts and Sciences Press, 1973.

Shewmaker, Kenneth E. *American Chinese Communists, 1927-45: A Persuading Encounter*. Ithaca: Cornell University Press, 1971.

Smedley, Agnes. *Battle Hymn of China*. New York: Alfred A. Knopf, 1943.

Snow, Edgar. *Random Notes on Red China 1936-45*. Cambridge, Mass.: Harvard University Press, 1957.

———. *Red Star Over China*. New York: Modern Library, 1944.

Solomon, Richard H. *Mao's Revolution and the Chinese Political Culture*. Berkeley: University of California Press, 1971.

Tennien, Father Mark. *No Secret is Safe*. New York: Farrar, Straus and Young, 1952.

Treadgold, Donald W. (ed.). *Soviet and Chinese Communism: Similarities and Differences*. Seattle: University of Washington Press, 1967.

Tsou, Tang. *America's Failure in China*. Chicago: University of Chicago Press, 1963.

Van der Sprenkle, Sybille. *Legal Institutions in Manchu China, A Sociological Analysis*. London: Athlone Press, 1962.

Van Slyke, Lyman P. (ed.). *The Chinese Communist Movement:*

BIBLIOGRAPHY

A Report of the United States War Department, July 1945.
Stanford: Stanford University Press, 1968.
Van Slyke, Lyman P. *Enemies and Friends: The United Front in Chinese Communist History.* Stanford: Stanford University Press, 1967.
Wales, Nym. *Red Dust.* Stanford: Stanford University Press, 1952.
White Book on Forced Labour and Concentration Camps in the People's Republic of China. Commission Internationale Contre Le Regione Concentrationnaire, 1954.
Yakhontoff, Victor A. *The Chinese Soviets.* New York: Coward-McCann, Inc., 1934.

Articles

Buxbaum, David C. "Preliminary Trends in the Development of the Legal Institutions of Communist China and the Nature of Criminal Law," *International and Comparative Law Quarterly,* Vol. 11, pp. 1-30.
Chen, Chin-jen. "Book Review on T'ang Leang-li's *Suppressing Communist Banditry in China," The Chinese Social and Political Science Review,* Vol. xix (April 1935), pp. 140-145.
Cohen, Jerome. "The Chinese Communist Party and Judicial Independence 1949-1959," *Harvard Law Review,* Vol. 82 (March 1969), pp. 967-1006.
———. "Chinese Mediation on the Eve of Modernization," *California Law Review* (August 1966), pp. 1201-1226.
Eto, Shinkichi. "Hai-lu-feng—The First Chinese Soviet Government," *The China Quarterly,* Part 1 (October-December, 1961); Part 2 (January-March 1962), pp. 149-181.
Finklestine, David. "The Language of Communist China's Criminal Law," *Journal of Asian Studies,* Vol. 27 (May 1968), pp. 503-521.
Ginsburgs, George, and Stahnke, Arthur. "The Genesis of the People's Procuratorate in Communist China: 1949-1951," *The China Quarterly,* No. 20 (October-December 1964), pp. 1-37.
———. "The People's Procuratorate in Communist China: The Period of Maturation: 1951-1954," *The China Quarterly,* No. 24 (October-December 1965), pp. 53-91.
———. "The People's Procuratorate in Communist China: The Institution in the Ascendant: 1954-1957," *The China Quarterly,* No. 34 (April-June 1968), pp. 82-132.

Halpern, A. M. "Contemporary China As a Problem for Political Science," *World Politics* (April 1963), pp. 361-376.

Hofheinz, Roy. "The Ecology of Chinese Communist Success: Rural Influence Patterns, 1923-45," in A. Doak Barnett, *Chinese Communist Politics in Action*, pp. 3-77.

Johnson, Chalmers. "Chinese Communist Leadership and Mass Response: The Yenan Period and the Socialist Education Campaign Period," in Ping-ti Ho and Tang Tsou (eds.). *China in Crisis*, Vol. 1, Book 1, pp. 397-437.

Jones, Harry. "The Creative Power and Function of Law in the Historical Perspective," *Vanderbilt Law Review,* Vol. 17 (December 1963), pp. 135-146.

Kim, Ilpyong J. "Mass Mobilization Policies and Techniques Developed in the Period of the Chinese Soviet Republic," in A. Doak Barnett (ed.), *Chinese Communist Politics in Action*, pp. 78-98.

Li, Victor. "The Role of Law in Communist China," *The China Quarterly* (October-December 1970), pp. 66-111.

Lin, Fu-shun. "Communist China's Emerging Fundamentals of Criminal Law," *The American Journal of Comparative Law*, Vol. XIII (Winter 1964), pp. 80-93.

Lipson, Leon. "Law: The Function of Extra-Judicial Mechanisms," in Donald W. Treadgold (ed.), *Soviet and Chinese Communism: Similarities and Differences*, pp. 144-167.

Lubman, Stanley. "Form and Function in the Chinese Criminal Process," *Columbia Law Review*, Vol. 69 (April 1969), pp. 535-575.

―――. "Mao and Mediation: Politics and Dispute Resolution in Communist China," *California Law Review* (1967), p. 1284.

Massell, Gregory. "Law as an Instrument of Revolutionary Change in a Traditional Milieu: The Case of Soviet Central Asia," *Law and Society Review*, Vol. 2 (February 1968), pp. 179-229.

McAleavy, Henry. "The People's Courts in Communist China," *The American Journal of Comparative Law*, Vol. 11 (1962), pp. 52-65.

McColl, Robert. "The Oyüwan Soviet Area, 1927-32," *Journal of Asian Studies*, Vol. 27 (November 1967), pp. 41-60.

Peng, Ming-min. "Political Offences in Taiwan: Laws and Problems," *The China Quarterly*, No. 47 (July-September 1971), pp. 471-493.

Pfeffer, Richard. "Crime and Punishment: China and the United States," *World Politics*, Vol. xxi (1968), pp. 163-173.

Pye, Lucian. "Law and the Dilemma of Stability and Change in the Modernization Process," *Vanderbilt Law Review* (December 1963), pp. 15-27.

Rickett, W. Allyn. "Voluntary Surrender and Confession in Chinese Law: The Problem of Continuity," *Journal of Asian Studies*, Vol. 30 (August 1971), pp. 797-814.

Schram, Stuart. "Mao Tse-tung and the Theory of the Permanent Revolution, 1958-69," *The China Quarterly*, No. 46 (April-June 1971), pp. 221-244.

Schwartz, Benjamin. "On Attitudes Toward Law in China," in Milton Katz (ed.), *Government Under Law and the Individual*. Washington: American Council of Learned Societies, 1957.

Selden, Mark. "The Yenan Legacy: The Mass Line," in A. Doak Barnett (ed.), *Chinese Communist Politics in Action*, pp. 99-151.

Stahnke, Arthur. "The Background and Evolution of Party Policy on the Drafting of Legal Codes in Communist China," *The American Journal of Comparative Law*, Vol. 15 (1966-1967), pp. 506-525.

Starr, John Bryan. "Conceptual Foundations of Mao Tse-tung's Theory of Continuous Revolution," *Asian Survey*, Vol. xi (June 1971), pp. 610-628.

Suleski, Ronald. "The Fu-t'ien Incident, December 1930," *Michigan Papers in Chinese Studies*, No. 4 (1969).

Tao, Lung-sheng. "The Criminal Law of Communist China," *Cornell Law Quarterly*, No. 52 (Fall 1966), pp. 43-68.

Tsou, Tang. "Revolution, Reintegration, and Crisis in Communist China," in Ping-ti Ho and Tang Tsou (ed.), *China in Crisis*, Vol. 1, Book 1, pp. 277-347.

Vogel, Ezra F. "Voluntarism and Social Control," in Donald W. Treadgold (ed.), *Soviet and Chinese Communism: Similarities and Differences*, pp. 168-184.

Wu, Tien-wei. "The Kiangsi Soviet Period: A Bibliographical Review on the Ch'en Ch'eng Collection," *Journal of Asian Studies* (February 1970), pp. 395-412.

Unpublished Materials

Gundersheim, Arthur. "Terror and Political Control in Communist China." Unpublished paper for the Center for Social Organization Studies, University of Chicago, August, 1966.

Hofheinz, Roy Mark. "The Peasant Movement and the Rural Revolution: Chinese Communist in the Countryside (1923-7)." Unpublished Ph.D. dissertation, Harvard University, 1966.

Rickett, W. Allyn. "Legal Thought and Institutions of the People's Republic of China: Selected Documents." University of Pennsylvania Institute of Legal Research, 1963-1964. (Mimeographed.)

Seybolt, Peter. "Yenan Education and the Chinese Revolution 1937-1945." Unpublished Ph.D. dissertation, Harvard University, 1969.

Waller, Derek John. "The First and Second National Congresses of the Chinese Soviet Republic 1931 and 1934." Unpublished Ph.D. dissertation, University of London, 1968.

Foreign-Language Sources

Books and Articles

Ch'i Li. *Shen-Kan-Ning pien-ch'ü shih-lu* (A True Account of the Shensi-Kansu-Ninghsia Border Region). Liberation Press, 1939.

Ch'ih-fei fan-tung wen-chien hui-pien (A Collection of Red Bandit Reactionary Documents). Taipeh, 1960.

"Chiang-hsi sheng su-wei-ai ts'ai-p'an pu p'an-chüeh shu #1" (Kiangsi Soviet Judicial Department Written Decision No. 1). Vol. 5, 1673.

"Chung-chü chih-hsing wei-yuan-hui ti-liu-hao hsün-ling" (Central Executive Committee's Instruction No. 6). December 16, 1931, Vol. 5, 1608-1612.

"Chung-hua su-wei-ai kung-ho-kuo kuo-chia cheng-chih pao-wei-chü tsu-chih kang-yao" (Organic Program of the State Political Security Bureau of the Chinese Soviet Republic). Vol. 5, 1616-1621.

"Chung-hua su-wei-ai kung-ho-kuo ti-fang su-wei-ai tsan-hsing tsu-chih fa" (Temporary Organic Law of the Local Soviets). 1933, Vol. 3, 725-793.

"Jui-chin hsien su ts'ai-p'an pu p'an-chüeh shu #19" (Juichin Hsien Judicial Department Written Decision No. 19). May 26, 1932, Vol. 5, 1617.

Chung-hua jen-min kung-ho-kuo fa-kuei hsüan-chi (Selected Laws and Regulations of the People's Republic of China). Peking: 1957.

Hatano, Kenichi (ed.). *Chugoku kyosanto shi* (History of the Chinese Communist Party). Tokyo: Jiji Press, 1961.

Hsien-hsing fa-ling hui-chi (Compendium of Current Laws). Compiled by the Administrative Committee of Shansi-Chahar-Hopei Border Region, 1945.

Hua-pei jen-min cheng-fu fa-ling hui-pien (Compendium of Laws of the North China People's Government). Peking: Secretariat of the North China People's Government, 1949.

K'ang-jih ken-chü-ti cheng-ts'e t'iao-li hui-chi, Chin-Ch'a-Chi chih-pu (Compendium of Policy Statements and Statutes of the Anti-Japanese Border Regions, Shansi-Chahar-Hopei Section). Shansi-Chahar-Hopei Border Region Government, June 20, 1941.

"Chin-Ch'a-Chi pien-ch'ü cheng-fu ch'eng-li san-chou nien kao pien-ch'ü t'ung-pao shu" (A Report to the Compatriots of the Border Region on the Accomplishments of the Shansi-Chahar-Hopei Border Region Government in Three Years). January 18, 1941, 7-12.

"Chin-Ch'a-Chi pien-ch'ü han-chien tzu-shou tan-hsing t'iao-li" (Separate Statute of the Shansi-Chahar-Hopei Border Region Concerning Voluntary Surrender and Confession of Traitors). 458-460.

"Chin-Ch'a-Chi pien-ch'ü kung-an chü tsan-hsing t'iao-li" (Temporary Statute of the Public Security Bureau of the Shansi-Chahar-Hopei Region). April 10, 1941, 454-456.

"Fei-ch'ang shih-chi chien-so jen-fan lin-shih ch'u-chih pan-fa" (Method for Temporarily Handling Criminals in Prison in Extraordinary Times). 465-466.

"Han-chien tzu-shou t'iao-li" (Statute Concerning Voluntary Surrender and Confession of Traitors). Nationalist Government's Military Affairs Commission, 467-471.

"Hsiu-cheng ch'eng-chih han-chien t'iao-li" (Revised Statute Concerning Punishment of Traitors). 473-475.

"Hsiu-cheng ch'u-li han-chien ts'ai-ch'ang pan-fa" (Revised Method of Handling Traitor's Property). 456-457.

"Hsiu-chen wei-hai min-kuo chin-chi chih tsui-fa" (Revised Laws Governing Emergency Crimes Endangering the Republic). 471-473.

K'ang-jih ken-chü-ti cheng-ts'e t'iao-li hui-chi, Shen-Kan-Ning chih-pu (Compendium of Policy Statements and Statutes of the Anti-Japanese Border Regions, Shensi-Kansu-Ninghsia Section). Shensi-Kansu-Ninghsia Border Region Government, July 18, 1942.

"Pien-ch'ü cheng-fu i-nien kung-tsou ts'ung-chieh" (Summary of One Year's Work of the Border Region Government). January 6, 1944, Supplement, 25-57.

"Shen-Kan-Ning pien-ch'ü cheng-fu chih-shih hsin (chih-tzu ti-szu-shih-pa hao)" (Shensi-Kansu-Ninghsia Border Region Government Directive No. 48). February 18, 1944, Supplement, 271-273.

"Shen-Kan-Ning pien-ch'ü chu-chien wei-yuan-hui tsu-chih t'iao-li ts'ao-an" (Draft Organic Regulation for the Shensi-Kansu-Ninghsia Border Region Weed-out Traitors Committee). Vol. 3, 746-750.

"Shen-Kan-Ning pien-ch'ü hsien szu-fa-ch'u tsu-chih t'iao-li ts'ao-an" (Draft Organic Regulation of the Shensi-Kansu-Ninghsia Border Region's *Hsien* Justice Bureaus). March 1943, Supplement, 99-100.

"Shen-Kan-Ning pien-ch'ü kang-chan shih-chi ch'eng-chih han-chien t'iao-li (ts'ao-li)" (Draft Statute of the Shensi-Kansu-Ninghsia Border Region Governing Punishment of Traitors During War Times). Vol. 3, 778-780.

"Shen-Kan-Ning pien-ch'ü kao-teng fa-yuan fen-t'ing tsu-chih t'iao-li ts'ao-an" (Draft Organic Regulation on Branch Courts of the Shensi-Kansu-Ninghsia Border Region High Court). March 1943, Supplement, 96-98.

"Shen-Kan-Ning pien-ch'ü kao-teng fa-yuan tsu-chih t'iao-li" (Organic Regulations of the High Court of the Shensi-Kansu-Ninghsia Border Region). Vol. 1, 43-49.

"Shen-Kan-Ning pien-ch'ü kao-teng fa-yuan tui ko-hsien szu-fa kung-tsou te chih-shih" (Directive from the Shensi-Kansu-Ninghsia Border Region High Court Concerning Each *Hsien*'s Judicial Work). May 10, 1941, Vol. 3, 750-753.

"Shen-Kan-Ning pien-ch'ü pao-chang jen-ch'üan ts-ai-ch'üan

t'iao-li" (The Shensi-Kansu-Ninghsia Border Region Statute Protecting Human and Property Rights). Vol. 3, 738-740.

"Shen-Kan-Ning pien-ch'ü shih-cheng kang-ling" (Program of Administration of the Shensi-Kansu-Ninghsia Border Region). May 1, 1941, Vol. 1, 4-8.

Kuang-tung nung-min yün-tung pao-kao (A Report on the Kwang-tung Peasant Movement). October 1926.

Kung-fei fan-tung wen-chien hui-pien (A Collection of Bandit Reactionary Documents). June 1948.

Ma Hsi-wu. "The People's Judicial Work in Shensi-Kansu-Ninghsia Border Region During the State of the New Democratic Revolution," *Cheng-fa yen-chiu* (Studies in Political Science and Law), Peking, No. 1 (1955), 8.

Shan-tung sheng cheng-fu chi Shan-tung chün-ch'ü kung-pu chih ko-chung t'iao-li kang-yao pan-fa hui-pien (Collected Statutes, Regulations and Outlines Issued by the Shantung Provincial Government and the Shantung Military Region). Shantung *Ch'ü* Administrative Office, August 29, 1945.

Shih-sou tzu-liao-shih kung-fei tzu-liao. Stanford: Hoover Institute, 1960.

"Chiang-hsi sheng su-wei-ai cheng-fu wu-chih-shih liu-ko yueh kung-tso pao-kao kang-yao" (Summary Report of Six Months' Work, May through October, of the Kiangsi Provincial Government). November 2, 1932, No. 008.61026, 3119, 0269, reel 10.

"Chiang-hsi sheng ts'ai-p'an pu pan-yueh k'an" (Kiangsi Provincial Judicial Department's Semi-Monthly). No. 008.-54105, 1732, 0658, reel 6.

"Ch'ih-fei chung-yang chü t'ung-kao #10" (Red Bandit Central Committee Circular No. 10). October 30, 1931, No. 008.2129, 4074, 0255, reel 20.

"Ch'ih-fei wen-chien hui-pien" (A Collection of Red Bandit Documents). No. 008.2129, 4074, 0255, reels 20 and 21.

"Chung-hua su-wei-ai kung-ho-kuo ch'eng-chih fan ko-ming t'iao-li" (Statute of the Chinese Soviet Republic Governing Punishment of Counterrevolutionaries). Central Executive Committee of the Chinese Soviet Republic, April 8, 1934, No. 008.542, 4424, v. 2, 1146, reel 16.

"Chung-hua su-wei-ai kung-ho-kuo ch'eng-chih fan ko-ming t'iao-li (ts'ao-an)" (Draft Statute of the Chinese Soviet Republic Governing Punishment of Counterrevolutionaries).

Central People's Commissar of Justice, December 9, 1933, No. 008.542, 2837, 0281, reel 6.

"Chung-hua su-wei-ai kung-ho-kuo chung-yang chih-hsing wei-yuan-hui ming-ling #25 kuan-yu hung-chün chung t'ao-p'ao wen-t'i" (Order No. 25 of the Central Executive Committee of the Chinese Soviet Republic Concerning the Problem of Deserters from the Red Army). December 15, 1933, No. 008.452, 4424, v. 2, 1146, reel 16.

"Chung-hua su-wei-ai kung-ho-kuo chung-yang su-wei-ai tsu-chih fa" (Organic Law of the Central Soviet of the Chinese Soviet Republic). February 17, 1934, No. 008.61029, 5044, reel 16.

"Chung-hua su-wei-ai kung-ho-kuo szu-fa ch'eng-hsü" (Judicial Procedures of the Chinese Soviet Republic). Central Executive Committee, April 8, 1934, No. 008.542, 4424, v. 2, 1146, reel 16.

"Chung-kuo kung-nung hung-chün ti-i fang-mien chün-tsung szu-ling-pu pao-kao ch'u-chüeh Huang Mei-chuang" (Announcement from the Headquarters of the First Army of the Workers' and Peasants' Red Army of China: Execute Huang Mei-chuang). June 1931, No. 008.1052, 2125, v. 1, reel 16.

"Chung-kuo kung-nung hung-chün ti-san chün-t'uan cheng-chih pu shih ch'eng-chih hao-shen ti-chu" (Directive of the Chinese Workers' and Peasants' Red Army Third Army Corps' Political Department on Punishing Gentry and Landlords). No. 008.638, 0067, 0152, reel 10.

"Chung-yang cheng-fu kuan-yu t'u-ti tou-cheng chung i-hsieh wen-t'i te chüeh-ting" (The Central Government's Decisions Concerning Some Questions in the Land Struggle). Council of the People's Commissars, October 10, 1933, No. 008.743, 4047, 1166, reel 17.

"Chung-yang chü kuan-yu su-fan kung-tsou chien-yüeh chüeh-i" (A Review Decision by the Central Committee Concerning the Work of Eradicating the Counterrevolution). December 14, 1932, No. 008.237, 5071, c. 1, 0291.

"Chung-yang chü t'ung-kao ti-er-hao tui Fu-t'ien shih-pien te chüeh-i" (Circular Note No. 2 of the Central Bureau—Resoultion on the Fu-t'ien Incident). January 16, 1931, No. 008.2107, 5044, reel 14.

"Chung-yang Wan-t'ai Ho-tung wei-yuan-hui t'ung-kao (ti-er hao) chia-chin su-fan kung-tsou cheng-chiu er-ch'i ko-ming chang-cheng" (Wan-t'ai Ho-tung Branch Central Committee Circular No. 2: Intensify the Work of Eradicating the Counterrevolutionaries and Attaining Full Victory in the Second Revolutionary War). No. 008.237, 4675, 0293, reel 14.

"Fan-tung wen-chien hui-pien" (A Collection of Reactionary Documents). No. 008.2129, 7120, v. 1, reel 19.

"Fei-chün wei fan-tui t'ao-p'ao tou-cheng wen-t'i hsün-ling" (Instructions on Questions Concerning the Struggle to Oppose Runaways from the Army). June 21, 1933, No. 008. 2129, 4074, reel 21.

"Hsing-kuo hsien su ts'ai-p'an pu chao-chi ko-ch'ü ts'ai-p'an pu shu-chi hsün-lien shih-hsi i-hou te kung-tsou chi-hua" (Work Plans Following the Classes of All *Ch'ü* Judicial Secretaries Called by the Hsing-kuo Hsien Judicial Department). December 31, 1933, No. 008.548, 7767, 0761, reel 6.

"Hsing-kuo hsien su-wei-ai cheng-fu t'ung-kao kuan-yu san-shih t'zu ch'ang-wu-hui chüeh-i shih-chien" (Hsing-kuo Hsien Soviet Government Circular Concerning the Discussions, Facts and Decisions of the 30th Meeting of the Standing Committee). No. 008.631, 3039, 0889, reel 10.

"Kuan-yu su-ch'ü su-fan kung-tso chüeh-i an" (Draft Decisions Concerning the Work of Eradicating Counterrevolutionaries in the Soviet Areas). Central Bureau of the Kiangsi Soviet, January 7, 1932, No. 008.237, 4475, c. 2, 0292, reel 14.

"Su-fan wen-t'i" (The Question of Eliminating Counterrevolutionaries). December 12, 1931, No. 008.237, 5077-2, 0290, reel 14.

"Su-fan wen-t'i t'i-kang" (Presentation of the Leading Points on the Question of Eliminating Counterrevolutionaries). August 1933, No. 008.237, 5077, 0289, reel 14.

"Su-wei-ai ch'ang-shih ch'ing-shou ta-kang (hsü)" (Summary Transmitting General Knowledge about the Soviet [Supplement]). May 11, 1934, No. 008.45, 6072, v. 2, 0408, reel 5.

"Szu-fa jen-min wei-yuan-hui tui ts'ai-p'an chi-k'uan te kung-tso chih-shih #14" (The People's Commissariat of Justice Directive No. 14 Concerning the Work of Judicial Organs). June 1, 1933, No. 008.548, 3449, 0759, reel 6.

T'ai-hang ch'ü i-chiu-ssu-liu nien chung-yao wen-chien hui-chi (Collection of the Most Important Documents of the T'ai-hang Ch'ü in 1946).

T'ai-hang ch'ü szu-fa kung-tso kai-k'uang (Report on the General Situation in Judicial Work in T'ai-hang Ch'ü). T'ai-hang Administrative Office, May 1946.

Wang Chien-min. *Chung-kuo kung-ch'ang-tang shih-kao* (History of the Chinese Communist Party). Taipei: Arthur, 1965.

Yang Ch'i. "A Preliminary Discussion of the Development of the People's Criminal Law during the New Democratic Stage," *Fa-hsüeh* (Jurisprudence) Shanghai, No. 3 (1957), 40-44.

Newspapers and Periodicals

Cheng-fa yen-chiu (Studies in Political Science and Law).

Chieh-fang jih-pao (Liberation Daily). Yenan.

Ch'ing-nien shih-hua (True Words of Youth). *Shih-sou Collection*, No. 008.2105, 3002, 1152, reel 18 and No. 008.2105, 5083, 1143, reel 18.

Fa-hsüeh (Jurisprudence).

Hsin-hua jih-pao (New China Daily).

Hung-se Chung-hua (Red China). *Shih-sou Collection*, No. 008.-1052, 2125, reel 16 and No. 008.1052, 2125, 1937, reel 17.

Hung-te Chiang-hsi (Red Kiangsi). *Shih-sou Collection*, No. 008.-1052, 2123-2, 0817, reel 1.

Jen-min jih-pao (People's Daily).

Sheng-wei t'ung-hsün (Bulletin of the Provincial Committee). *Shih-sou Collection*, No. 008.2105, 9023, 1156, reel 17.

Szu-fa hui-k'an (Justice Magazine). *Shih-sou Collection*, No. 008.-54105, 1732, 0658, reel 6.

Tou-cheng (Struggle). *Shih-sou Collection*, No. 008.2105, 7720, 1133, reel 18.

Index

Studies in East Asian Law
Harvard University

1. *Law in Imperial China Exemplified by 190 Ch'ing Dynasty Cases* (*translated from the* Hsing-an hui-lan) *with Historical, Social, and Juridical Commentaries.* By Derk Bodde and Clarence Morris. Cambridge, Mass.: Harvard University Press, 1967.
2. *The Criminal Process in the People's Republic of China, 1949–1963: An Introduction.* By Jerome Alan Cohen. Cambridge, Mass.: Harvard University Press, 1968.
3. *Agreements of the People's Republic of China, 1949–1967: A Calendar.* By Douglas M. Johnston and Hungdah Chiu. Cambridge, Mass.: Harvard University Press, 1968.
4. *Contemporary Chinese Law: Research Problems and Perspectives.* Edited by Jerome Alan Cohen. Cambridge, Mass.: Harvard University Press, 1970.
5. *The People's Republic of China and the Law of Treaties.* By Hungdah Chiu. Cambridge, Mass.: Harvard University Press, 1972.
6. *China's Practice of International Law: Some Case Studies.* Edited by Jerome Alan Cohen. Cambridge, Mass.: Harvard University Press, 1972.
7. *The Internal Organization of Ch'ing Bureaucracy—Legal, Normative, and Communication Aspects.* By Thomas A. Metzger. Cambridge, Mass.: Harvard University Press, 1973.
8. *People's China and International Law: a Documentary Study.* By Jerome Alan Cohen and Hungdah Chiu. Princeton, N.J.: Princeton University Press, 1974.

Library of Congress Cataloging in Publication Data

Griffin, Patricia E   1944-
  The Chinese communist treatment of counter-revolutionaries, 1924-1949.

  Bibliography: p.
  Includes index.
    1. Political crimes and offenses—Kiangsi, China
(Province)   2. Political crimes and offenses—Yenan,
China.   3. Punishment—Kiangsi, China (Province)
4. Punishment—Yenan, China.   I. Title.
Law   345′.51′023   75-30193
ISBN 0-691-09232-X

LIBRARY